THE ORDER OF SOUNDS

THE ORDER OF SOUNDS
A Sonorous Archipelago

FRANÇOIS J. BONNET

Translated by
ROBIN MACKAY

URBANOMIC

Published in 2016 by
URBANOMIC MEDIA LTD,
THE OLD LEMONADE FACTORY,
WINDSOR QUARRY,
FALMOUTH TR11 3EX,
UNITED KINGDOM

Originally published in French as *Les mots et les sons. Un archipel sonore.*
© Éditions de l'eclat, 2012.

ROYAUME-UNI

This book is supported by the Institut Français
as part of the Burgess Programme.

BRITISH LIBRARY CATALOGUING-IN-PUBLICATION DATA

A full catalogue record of this book is available
from the British Library

ISBN 978-0-9930458-7-5

Type by Norm, Zurich
Printed and bound in the UK by
TJ International, Padstow

www.urbanomic.com

CONTENTS

Preface: The Otographer *Peter Szendy*   vii

Introduction   1

1. The Grip of Sound   **5**

    The Trace of Sound   7

    Imprints   31

    Area and Metamorphoses   50

    The Grip of Sound   66

2. Apprehending Sound   **69**

    Perceive, Hear, Listen   71

    The Nature of Sound: Phenomenon vs. Event   81

    The Range of Sound   87

    Perception-Continent   97

3. Form and *Voice* of Sound   **99**

    The Sound Object   101

    There Is No Reduced Listening   111

    Autonomous Sound   117

    Beliefs and Perception   130

4. Desiring-Listening and Fetishism of Listening   **133**

    Desiring-Listening   135

    Listening and Fetishism   149

    Beyond Sound   162

    Music and Crystallization   184

    Fiction-Listening   192

5. Authoritarian Listening   **195**

    Discourse and the Anchoring of Sound   197

    Listening, Instrument of Authority and Power   204

    Modelizations   226

    Territorial Logics and Metaphors: The Archipelago   242

    Insularity and Authority   259

6. Phonophanies   261
   Extraterritorialities   263
   'Oblique Strategies' I:
     The Shifting Sands of the Given-to-be-Heard   277
   'Oblique Strategies' II: Explosion of the Sign-Sound   303
   Sonorous Resistance   318
   Phonophany vs. Apophenia   326
Epilogue   329

   Bibliography   335
   Index of Names   349

PREFACE:
THE OTOGRAPHER

PETER SZENDY

In the *Cahiers* of 1936–7, Paul Valéry jotted down a potential subject for a short story:

> Tale—for children or others—
> Keen-ear; True-ear—One can hear the grass grow. The other recognizes in a sound an infinity of *interrelations*—
> Music tears him apart, for in the most perfect performance, in sounds that others find the purest, he perceives a dreadful number that are not.
> The same tale is possible for sight. The pilot; the expert in shades of colour; the foreteller spotting, like a fencer, the slightest sign on the opponent's face.
> Or for touch, or taste.
> It involves taking the different types of acuteness of any one sense, and the results, to the level of the fantastic.[i]

For the heightened sense of sight, Valéry indicates professions or activities that specifically call for visual hyperaesthesia: the pilot, the fencer.... Whereas for Keen-ear and True-ear he gives no such examples, but only speaks in general of a hyperbolic auditory sensibility capable of detecting even the sound of grass growing.

Yet there are many professions that require an acute ear. For example the personnel known in French military jargon as '*oreilles d'or* [golden ears]', charged with listening out for and identifying the sounds of submarines for strategic purposes. Or doctors, whose auscultation of patients involves an attention to detail which may be appreciated by reading some remarkable pages in which Laënnec, inventor of the technique of mediate

---

i.   P. Valéry, *Cahiers/Notebooks* 2, tr. P. Gifford, S. Miles, R. Pickering and B. Stimpson (Frankfurt am Main: Peter Lang, 2000), 436.

auscultation by means of the stethoscope, describes what the instrument is capable of picking up. Or spies, as innumerable novels and films have given us to imagine.

In establishing himself as an otographer,[ii] François J. Bonnet does not privilege any particular one of these 'sonorous professions'. When he writes on the ear—and one sometimes has the impression that he is writing from the eardrum itself—when he thinks hearing, neither does he insist on any ontological figure in particular. What he follows, what he tracks, is the latent Fine-ear behind all the various forms and guises he may take on; Fine-ear *before* he adopts any particular visage.

In short, it is a logic of listening—or perhaps we should say a graphism of listening—that Bonnet seeks in sound. Not in the ear, but within the very structure of sound itself.

Certainly, in the following pages we also meet numerous characters who listen, each more remarkable than the last. Of course we have the 'Magician of Menlo Park', Thomas Alva Edison, in his guise as a character in Villiers de L'Isle Adam's *The Future Eve*. And Nikola Tesla, the Serbian inventor who, in his writings on radio, claims to make the earth itself into a cosmic transceiver for interplanetary communications. We encounter practitioners of auditory espionage and surveillance who decipher the sound of fingertips on keyboards. And finally those anonymous ears, those masses of ordinary ears damaged by the military use of sound—in particular the acoustic cannons that bring noise onto the battlefield, instrumentalizing it for the purposes of warfare.

---

ii.   In *Sur écoute. Esthétique de l'espionnage* (Paris: Minuit, 2007), I proposed the term 'otography' for the writing of listening, from one ear to another. In so doing I was inspired by a literary character—not Fine-ear but Earwicker, whom Joyce, in *Finnegans Wake*, characterizes as a 'paradigmatic ear.'

In short, whether it concerns the sonic weapons envisaged by William Burroughs in *Electronic Revolution*, or the voices of the dead captured by Konstantin Raudive, each of Bonnet's otographies, each of his cartographies of the territories of listening, invites us to plunge into remarkable and unrecognized territories.

But I would say that what the 'sonorous archipelago' entitled *The Order of Sounds* aims to outline is a true thinking of listening, a thinking announced already in what we might call the graphical structure of sound—that is, its trace-being. This is what all the chronicles, all the regional explorations of the indefatigable otographer, on the road with his journals and logbooks, work toward.

From those who lent an ear to the voices of the dead, for example, Bonnet unhesitatingly draws the idea that hallucination—which he therefore takes very seriously, and avoids reducing 'to the manifestation of pathologies, whether hysterical or schizophrenic'—is no more or less 'a *mode of hearing* that functions on the basis of traces' than any other. The same fundamental intuition returns later on when he speaks of *fiction-listening*. Or again when he describes and analyzes *fetishism in hearing*, reinterrogating a notion which, since Adorno, has fairly dwindled into cliché: but here it is a matter of a fetishism that is anything but pathological (he states this as clearly as can be: 'this cannot be a question of assimilating the act of listening to a fetishistic pathology'); that is to say, what Bonnet indicates is a fetishism that is in fact *constitutive of listening* in so far as listening perhaps *essentially* involves an overvaluation of the sonorous. Here we find some admirable pages which ought to prompt a renewed reflection on *value*, the value of listening and value in listening.

There is no doubt that what lies at the heart of Bonnet's archipelago is the distinction between the audible and the sonorous, a distinction which itself rests upon a thinking of the trace. This is stated from the very outset, immediately following the Introduction: 'Even before materializing or becoming a signal, the sonorous—sound—in order to be, must *leave a trace*.' From this primary distinction there unfolds a ramified or reticulated series of motifs which radiate across the archipelago. For 'to leave a trace', as the otographer tells us, to be a trace, is already for a sound to be 'somewhat more than a sound'.

INTRODUCTION

To bring a seashell to one's ear is to give oneself to hear a whole ocean. The coloured sound ebbs and flows in interminable waves immured in the confined nacreous space. And yet what we perceive is an outside, an open space. The ear carries the listener far afield. The *impression* of the sea attests to the tangibility of a sound imprisoned within a shell. It is indeed *the* sound of *the* sea that we hear in the seashell. But the sound to which this listening exposes us is not an oceanic sound. On the contrary, it reveals territories scattered across the ocean, territories in the form of an archipelago.

The seashell is not the seashore. It is not the site of the experience of an authentic sea, even if the experience of listening to the sea through it *is* authentic. Neither is it the site of mystery—quite the contrary. The sound of the sea is all the seashell has to offer us. Why would we even trouble ourselves, were we not sure of hearing the sea as we cupped it to our ear? The experience of the seashore, on the other hand, may offer something unheard-of.

Throughout the world, on certain shores, unexplained sounds have been heard, probably linked to atmospheric events. These sounds, called 'mistpouffers' in Europe, 'uminari' in Japan, resist any straightforward description. Often compared to thunderclaps or to the sound of cannon fire, they are sometimes likened to the rumbling of a chariot, or a rockfall. In any case, these 'sonorous exhalations', audible for kilometres around, impact on the ear as if they are going to 'break through the eardrum', seizing the auditor and engendering '*a distress both physical and moral*,' both intriguing and disquieting.[1]

---

1. Cf. E. Van Den Broeck, 'Un phénomène mystérieux de la physique du globe', *Ciel & Terre* 17 (1897).

The sound of the sea captive in the seashell does not disquiet us. On the contrary, it reassures us, comforts us. It speaks of permanence and tranquillity, whereas the mysterious sound by the shore reveals nothing. In fact, such a sound indicates no origin, and leads nowhere; it is a sound that has no place, or one that simply has not taken place. The inexplicable sound occupies space and dissipates *without leaving a trace*—apart, perhaps, from the disquiet we feel precisely when we observe that there is no trace.

In and around Naples, there is a belief that the origin of folk songs can be attributed to Virgil. A collection written by his own hand supposedly fell to the bottom of the sea; it is by means of a seashell held to the ear that the poet's songs were discovered.

Through the seashell is revealed the twofold character of a listening in which a function of language is always superimposed upon the function of the sensible. The sound of the sea and Virgil's poems both have the same sensible vector, and the same destination: Sound, and hearing.

Depending on the vicissitudes of such a listening, the ear is disquieted, is reassured, weaves intimate relations with the unknown, or forges knowledge through language. The ear is a delicate thing. It is under the influence.

1

THE GRIP
OF SOUND

THE TRACE OF SOUND

Even before materializing or becoming a signal, the sonorous—sound—in order to be, must *leave a trace*. Like a parasite, in order to exist it first of all needs a host. This necessary support is not so much the air, or any other medium that is informed by sound and testifies to it through the trail it leaves behind as it propagates. The trace is not necessarily a material, physical host; it precedes the pertinence of any such distinction. It is that which testifies to a passage, that which harbours and reveals a past presence by continuing to manifest it. Sound disappears the very moment it appears, or more exactly *in the moment of its appearing*, and so the trace is the primordial means by which it can be integrated into a regime of permanence—one that must, moreover, be distinguished from the regime of representation: sound recording (and its associated process of playback, which is nothing other than the re-presentation of sound held in memory) can only reproduce, infinitely if so required, the cycle of the appearing and disappearing of sound; that is to say, it can only reveal, over and over again, its irreducible fugacity. In any case, it does not fix sound—all it can do is to reactualize it on demand, which is something entirely different. Without itself being *presence*, the trace draws sound toward a regime of permanence that is located upstream of any process of 'conservation'. It is the manifestation of sound, the 'both suprasensible and sensible' halo surrounding it, affirming and activating its existence. It anticipates the possibility of a place for sound, a stable *space*, albeit a precarious one.

A means or a medium, the trace is first and foremost our fragile link with *the certain place* where the sonorous *was* and the *certain place* whence it may be *brought forth* once again.

The trace is therefore an auxiliary of sound which takes its place and is indispensable for its existence—or at least for its existence to last, to be perpetuated. Moreover, there is no perceived sound that does not leave a trace. For sound is not simply that which we hear; as soon as it exists, as soon as it leaves a trace, it is already somewhat more than that. It has functions to perform, expectations to meet, *things to say*. In fact, the utilitarian reinvestment of the sonorous is always already in play as soon as its tracing comes into effect.

The trace of sound, neither purely sensible nor solely signi-fying, is where the sonorous opens onto the *audible world*, the great matrix of interfacing between sounds and listeners. The sonorous and the audible are not opposed to each other even though, at the extremes, we may find a savage sonorous up against a domesticated audible. The sonorous *sounds*, whereas the audible *gives itself to be heard*. Thus every audible is, a priori, sonorous, but the sonorous is not always audible. The passage from the sonorous world[2] to the audible world unfolds across a veritable genealogy of the sensible which goes back to the origins that brought forth the first myths of the sonorous, myths which introduce it into the audible world.

Mythologies of the Sonorous

The identity of sound has not always been with us. It is in fact the result of a disentangling of sound from its 'carriers'. For a long time, sound, air, and the soul cohabited in such promiscuity that they were sometimes fused in one and the same concept. Living, breathing, perceiving, and movement

---

2. The reader is referred to a curious text by Victor Segalen, *Dans un monde sonore* [1907], which describes a room in which the sonorous does not yet seem to have been domesticated.

were all made possible through the action of one unique fluid,
the *pneuma*. The Greek term *pneuma* (literally 'breath') is
ambiguous. It is found in Greek treatises of medicine from
antiquity, and subsequently in Plato. Aristotle even makes
it the vehicle of the soul (*pneuma symphyton*).[3] It was also
central to Stoic doctrine before Christian gnosis, inspired by
ancient myths and drawing on Genesis,[4] began to consider it
as spirit itself.

The *pneuma*, qua vital principle, is a fluid that encompasses
speech, breath, and soul. Here, therefore, sound is a substance,
albeit an impalpable one. It is not yet a wave transported
through the air. The air does play a fundamental role in the
theory of the *pneuma*, though: it moves along with sound. Or
rather, breath-sound moves and enters back into the body of
the hearer, as Plato tells us in the *Timaeus*:

> We may in general assume sound to be a blow which passes
> through the ears, and is transmitted by means of the air, the
> brain, and the blood, to the soul, and that hearing is the vibration
> of this blow which begins in the head and ends in the region of
> the liver.[5]

In Plato, the movement of air is not inductive in character:
it is not the result of an energetic reaction transmitted from
one place to another, prefiguring the wave theory. Instead it
is propulsive, the result of the displacement of a substance

---

3.   See Aristotle's texts *On the Movement of Animals*, chapter X, and *On the Soul*.

4.   Genesis 2:7: 'And the Lord God formed man of the dust of the ground, and breathed into his nostrils the breath of life; and man became a living soul.'

5.   Plato, *Timaeus*, 67a (tr. B. Jowett).

propelled from the sounding body into the body (and soul) of the hearer, whose auditory canals were already irrigated by it. In Plato, sound is still pneumatic in nature; it moves within its own element.

According to Garnault, 'the Greeks, like the Egyptians, knew nothing of the eardrum, which would have been considered an absolutely unintelligible and pathological obstacle to the absorption of *pneuma* and of sound-images'.[6] In fact it seems that the auditory membrane was indeed known to the disciples of Pythagoras (in particular Alcmaeon of Croton, who discovered it by dissecting goats). However, knowing that such a membrane exists does not necessarily imply that one understands its function, and its existence does not immediately imply an explanation of hearing by way of vibratory phenomena. This is the mistake made by numerous analysts and translators of Greek antiquity who blithely use the word 'eardrum' (which was not introduced until the sixteenth century, by Italian anatomist Gabriele Fallopio),[7] thus suggesting a functional knowledge of a membrane unknown to Democritus and Epicurus, and disregarded by Plato.

Aristotle, though, does mention an auditory membrane. According to his theory, a sound is only produced at the moment when moving air strikes a smooth surface and is set resonating. Sound is not a property of the air, which, as it dissipates, produces no sound. It is the result of a 'shock', a compression. Moving air arrives at the ear, thereby setting in motion the

6.   P. Garnault, 'Les théories paléo-égyptiennes de la circulation, de la respiration, de la phonation et de l'audition, dans leur rapports avec la théorie du pneuma', *Bulletins de la Société d'anthropologie de Paris* 2:1 (1901), 50.

7.   See J.-M.-G. Itard, *Traité des maladies de l'oreille et de l'audition* (Paris: Méquignon-Marvis Libraire, 1821), 7.

immobile air trapped inside the auditory canal, which then resonates.[8] We might think that, in developing this mediated approach to hearing (in which air, when subjected to shock, does indeed become the carrier of sound), Aristotle distanced himself from a pneumatic conception of sound, tending instead toward a 'proto-wave theory'. However, although his account of the organ of hearing includes the presence of an air proper to it (and which, according to him, allows one to hear even under water) and although it replaces the conception of an immediate transmission of sound, a fluid circulation and irrigation, with a mediated transmission in which external and internal air interface with each other, he nonetheless reaffirms the substantial imperative of *pneuma*, the *animated* character of air:

> The organ of hearing is physically united with air, and because it is in air, the air inside is moved concurrently with the air outside. Hence animals do not hear with all parts of their bodies, nor do all parts admit of the entrance of air; for even the part which can be moved and can sound has not air everywhere in it.[9]

The fact that in Aristotle we find an intuition of a complex relation between event (shock), air, and sound, must not lead us to hasty conclusions, or tempt us to interpret his observations in terms of the precepts of a classical acoustics that only appeared almost twenty centuries later. For although he does not entirely identify sound with air, it does remain linked to an absolute displacement of air (as opposed to a relative

---

8.   'But the air proper to hearing is "built into", or firmly set in, the ears with a certain stillness' (Thomas Aquinas, *Commentary on Aristotle's Treatise on the Soul* [1267–1268]).

9.   Aristotle, *On the Soul*, Book II, part 8 (tr. J. A. Smith).

movement around a point of origin, which is the principle of vibration). Moreover, for Aristotle it is impossible to conceive of air moving in two ways at once (vibrating as it moves), particularly in the case of speech:

> This is confirmed by our inability to speak when we are breathing either out or in—we can do so only by holding our breath; we make the movements with the breath so checked.[10]

Aristotle envisages the movements of air linked to respiration and those dedicated to speaking as being uniform; and since they are of the same nature, they are mutually exclusive. Air set in motion can thus serve either for breathing or for speech, but never both at the same time. As far as the generation of sound is concerned, then, Aristotle's remains a 'substantialist' approach to sonorous phenomena. It is still largely permeated by pneumatic theories according to which sound is conceivable only as the setting in motion of matter.[11] Thus Cleomedes, in the first century BC, maintained that 'if *pneuma* were not cohesive through and through, it would be impossible for us to see or hear'.[12]

If at this point sound already harbours a certain mystery, it does not yet owe this to the inscrutability of its vibratory nature. It owes it to its strange interaction with breath, things, and bodies. This is why breath and voice occupy a privileged place in the

---

10.   Ibid.

11.   Indeed, certain observers will go so far as to consider Aristotle's contribution in the matter of hearing as nonexistent: 'Aristotle, who did so much for the progress of the natural sciences, added nothing to the knowledge of the Greeks in relation to the ear.' (Itard, *Traité des maladies de l'oreille*, 2).

12.   Cleomedes, *De motu circulari corporum caelestium*, 8, 21–2.

sacred space inhabited by sound. For breath and voice are immediately and intimately bound to those endowed with them, and are directly linked to origin myths.[13] The *Word*, as *pneuma*—that is to say, as the breath of life and as its primordial principle—is the primary element in the animation of things and beings. Meaning that every thing, in order to exist, must first be named; and as it receives its name, it is irrigated by the creative breath.

To be endowed with voice is to contain within oneself the proof of being animate; it is to possess an apportionment of creative breath. along with the power to manifest it. It is no doubt the sensation of hearing one's own voice immediately, the inextricably intimate hyper-presence of the sonorous, that is the primary foundation of this sacred supplement connatural to sound. It is also what prompts Roland Barthes to say that song, the art of the voice, bears within it a movement that is linked to the presence of myth.[14] Sound apprehends itself originally through voice, then—not even yet as language, but simply as breath, merging with this substance in an unarticulated and primordial complex which Jacques Derrida calls *neume*, 'pure vocalization, form of an inarticulate song without speech, whose name means breath, which is inspired in us by God and may address only Him'.[15] Sound has always been *charged* with something more, and it is this charge that forms

---

13.   'The Antique gods, Thot, Jehovah, etc., make things come forth through their creative breath and through their voice, because breath or the voice represent the souls or essential parts of created objects.' (Garnault, 'Les théories paléo-égyptiennes', 48).

14.   'The breath is the pneuma, the soul swelling or breaking, and any exclusive art of breathing is likely to be a secretly mystical art.' R. Barthes, 'The Grain of the Voice', in *Image–Music–Text*, tr. S. Heath (London: Fontana, 1977).

15.   J. Derrida, *Of Grammatology*, tr. G. C. Spivak (Baltimore, MY: Johns Hopkins University Press, 1997), 249.

a trace where it is supposed to 'have been'. A trace as the index of a locality of sound, a trace that marks it out, exceeds it, and completes it.

Voice is the first way in which a bond of intimacy is woven between sound and the one who experiences it (the first staking out of the path that leads from the sonorous towards the audible, the first step in the domestication of the sonorous); but it is also expressive power, the power of evocation. Vocal rituals are the clearest manifestation of this. For sound, whether produced vocally or instrumentally, fulfils a catalytic function, accompanying the ritual, enabling it to unfold.

Whether in the form of prayer, music, tumult, or mimetic expression (the imitation of animal cries or natural noises), in ritual sound is turned to as a sensible vector of communication with the gods, the spirits, or even the forces of nature. Incidentally, in the West church bells facilitate this same kind of communication.[16]

Thus, when sound participates in myth, it never announces itself by way of its pure phenomenality. Instead it is integrated into a 'regime of audibility' that calls for corresponding regimes of listening. A regime of audibility is above all else a *way of using sound* (whether pertaining to the generation of sound, its transmission, or its reception) which depends directly upon the manner in which sound leaves a trace. Whereas in the pneumatic tradition sound is substantialized in and by breath, in many cultures it is actualized and defined through its sacred

---

16.   'In addition to summoning the congregation to the church, bells had a meteorological, and even a cosmic, function. Their reverberations drove storms away, dispelled clouds and hail, and even destroyed evil spells.' C. Lévi-Strauss, *From Honey to Ashes: Introduction to a Science of Mythology: 2*, tr. J. and D. Weightman (London: Cape, 1973), 404.

character or its 'magical' properties, and leaves its trace in their supposed effects.

Sound can also take on a sacred character. For the sacred, as well as suffusing things, beings, places, and moments, can imbue phenomena (eclipses, storms, screams, noises, etc.). So sound itself is sometimes charged with a sacred quality, by way of various divergent yet ultimately common processes. It can take on this sacred character through a kind of contamination: by being freighted with the presence of the spirit or god, the sound in question becomes sacred, conveying the presence of the sacred and manifesting it. This is the case, for example, in certain South American myths where the sound of the bull-roarer is said to be the voice of a legendary lake-monster,[17] or where the rustling of leaves in the trees testifies to the presence of *mana*, magical and vital energy.[18] Sound become sacred through contamination is elevated into a sonorous emanation whose very existence is supernatural or magical.

Equally, sound can become sacred by acquiring a specific function within a certain context. It then becomes an auxiliary of ritual, helping to place the individual or the collective in relation to the divine, that with which the sacred communicates (the divine is not sacred; the sacred is that which touches the divine, that which stands in some relation to it).

The sacred function of sound, resulting from its use in a certain context (rituals, masses, festivals) can also 'contaminate'

---

17.   Ibid., 414–15.

18.   '[*Mana*] is represented as a material body. It may be heard and seen, leaving objects where it has dwelt. *Mana* makes a noise in the leaves....' The sound of leaves thus becomes sacred, in so far as it reveals the magical presence of *mana* ('It is really mana which gives things and people value, not only magical religious values, but social value as well.') M. Mauss, *A General Theory of Magic* [1903], tr. R. Brain (London and New York: Routledge, 2001), 135, 134.

sound itself by conferring upon it a permanent sacred connotation (as is the case, to some extent, with the sound of bells). But most often it is use that confers or revokes such a sacred character. For example, this is the case with sounds produced by the 'instruments of darkness',[19] rudimentary instruments (screech rattles, clapper boards, etc.) which are used at Easter time when church bells fall silent. The sounds generated by the instruments of darkness, which in other circumstances would simply be a racket, during this well-defined period and under prescribed conditions of usage are charged with a religious aura which sacralizes them.

Sacred sound is therefore sound that harbours a sacred presence or function, manifests it, and is superimposed upon it. So the sacred modifies the sound *formally*, in so far as it leaves a trace in it—that is to say, it conditions its existence by assigning it a 'place' (precisely that place where the sacred appears) and a regime of audibility—a *way of being heard*.

Sometimes, sound can possess supposedly magical properties whose effects pertain to fields as disparate as medicine, religious incantation, and curses. This magical sound is distinct from sacred sound, in that it applies a principle so as to obtain a certain effect. Sacred sound, whose cause and impact alike belong to the mysteries, attains its status by way of its 'resonance'. It is placed alongside the listener, leaving a trace through that which inhabits him. Magical sound, on the other hand, is active. It exists neither for itself nor for what it evokes, but strives for a certain result. It is on the side of the producer (the magician, the shaman, the sorcerer), and does not even

---

19.   Cf. Lévi-Strauss, 'The Instruments of Darkness', in *From Honey to Ashes*, 359–422.

have to be listened to in order to act, since the supernatural forces it brings to bear exceed the field of listening.

Indeed, music and songs of healing, magical songs par excellence, are very rarely addressed to the patient as auditor, but more often to the source of the illness, as is the case in tarantism, for example:

> [I]t is because the melody 'conforms' to the music emitted by the spider that it has the virtue of relieving the sick person. We in fact know that there are various kinds of tarantulas, and that the tarantulee is only supposed to react to the sound of the tarantella specific to the tarantula that has bitten her.[20]

Magical sound functions through coupling, often in an analogical manner—what principle is more important in magic than that of analogy, or more exactly homology? It obeys a function and an order that are superimposed on its phenomenality. Whereas the sacred invests sound with its own aura, magic is more like an activating property, drawing its efficacy from the formal modalities of sound, displacing it from its status as mere event. In his study on shamanism, Mircea Eliade establishes an additional distinction between 'the magic of noise' and 'the magic of music'. According to Eliade the magic of noise is a magic for the expulsion of demons, resulting from the production of a racket that serves to drive them away, whereas musical magic, the 'voice of the spirits' of the drum, is a magic provoked by the drum which brings on shamanic ecstasy.[21]

---

20.   G. Rouget, *Music and Trance: A Theory of the Relations between Music and Possession* (Chicago: University of Chicago Press, 1985), 163.

21.   M. Eliade, *Shamanism: Archaic Techniques of Ecstasy*, tr. W. R. Trask (Princeton, NJ: Princeton University Press, 2004), 174–5.

The twofold magical function of the shaman's drum can be explained by the variety of sounds it produces, which can be either tumultuous (magic of noise) or rhythmic, that is to say *organized* (magic of music). Thus magical power is correlated with sonorous form. In the same way, the power of the tarantella is expressed through its repetitive and hypnotic character, which puts the patient into a hysterical trance associated with the dispossession of evil—that is to say, it leads to healing. The magical coding that is borne by formed sound seems to be the true essence of this power rooted in sound. What unites magic and the sonorous is therefore a mechanism of mutual conveyance: sound as the vehicle of magic, magic as the qualitative trace of sound.

The magical sound par excellence is incantation. Its magical power resides in the very form of the song, but equally in the code that it delivers, a code which, since it can very well be absolutely unintelligible to the singer, must be distinguished from normal language. Incantation either falls short of language, or is a beyond of language; in any case, it is not entirely *of* language. The way in which the code is formed, its tonality, is just as important as the syllables themselves and their concatenation. Here the magical effect flows uniquely from the conjunction of the code and the sonority in which it is clothed.

Phantom Sounds

If the sonorous has always been associated with rites, and has always been disposed to harbour magic or mystery, this is doubtless in virtue of its unique bond with the voice, a bond which constitutes the primordial complex of language. There are other reasons, though: in particular, the absolutely fugitive character of sonorous phenomena. Everyone has at some time had the experience of not being able to determine the provenance of a sound. This impossibility of defining an origin, an impossibility resulting from the fleeting nature of the phenomenon, its dispersion into the distance and its inexplicable character, have always been the source of myths and beliefs.

Faced with such *phantom sounds*, hearing becomes disquieted and, in the very moment of perception, convokes some system of beliefs in the hope of making good the unknown origin of the sound. Hence the legend of the thunder-bird,[22] or the myth of the sirens whose accursed song brings ruin upon anyone who trusts in it. Phantom sounds, in so far as they are no longer fully audible, often become accursed sounds. This is precisely the case with Maurice Blanchot's siren-song:

> The Sirens: it seems they did indeed sing, but in an unfulfilling way, one that only gave a sign of where the real sources and real happiness of song opened. [...] It was an inhuman song—a natural noise no doubt (are there any other kinds?), but on the fringes of nature, foreign in every possible way to man, very low, and awakening in him that extreme delight in falling that he cannot satisfy in the normal conditions of life.[23]

Accursed sounds play tricks on listening, in the sense that they do not hold together, and refuse to participate in bringing about comprehension through listening. On the contrary, they disperse, they agglomerate, resulting in an inaudibility (in that 'unfulfilling way') that can only be overcome by bringing to bear an apparatus of belief, exorcising them of the curse that

---

22.   In numerous Native American tribes, it was thought that the thunder came from the beating of the wings of the thunder-bird, a gigantic, divine bird.

23.   M. Blanchot, *The Book to Come*, tr. C. Mandell (Stanford, CA: Stanford University Press, 2003), 3.

is their foreignness. Disquieted when faced with these sounds that are 'natural [...] but on the fringes of nature', our hearing must generate some ad hoc belief capable of bringing them into the domain of the audible.

Moreover, this disposition, this mythical mechanism, is not purely the preserve of the past or of 'primitives': even in post-industrial societies where the spirit of rationalism has long since solidly established its reign, there remain certain niches of belief wherein sound retains its supernatural aura. In the 1960s, one of them, part of a lineage of traditions that link sound to death and the voice to spirits, gave rise to the research carried out by Konstantin Raudive, following preliminary work by a certain Friedrich Jürgenson who, aside from his activity as a painter and portraitist of Pope Pius XII, had, with the help of a simple tape recorder initially acquired to record his singing performances, captured 'the voices of the dead'. From that point on, this research programme was known by the generic appellation 'electronic voice phenomenon'.

Raudive established three different techniques for recording the voices of deceased persons (whom he always invited to speak in advance). The first, and simplest, consists in simply letting the tape recorder run for a few minutes in complete silence. In the second variant, the sound recorded is no longer the ambience of the room in which the experiment takes place, but a radio signal meticulously selected from among the empty frequencies of the radio band. The final technique, designed so as to obviate the need for ambient sounds or the overloaded radio band, consists in recording the signal from a diode.

From these experiments resulted the appearance of extremely ephemeral sounds, 'voices' possessed of very peculiar characteristics:

1. The voice-entities speak very rapidly, in a mixture of languages, sometimes as many as five or six in one sentence.

2. They speak in a definite rhythm, which seems to be forced upon them by the means of communication they employ.

3. The rhythmic mode of speech imposes a shortened, telegram-style phrase or sentence.

4. Presumably arising from these restrictions, grammatical rules are frequently abandoned and neologisms abound.[24]

In these experiments Raudive sought to identify, in the ambient sound or in the background sound of radio waves, almost indistinct voices with a specific syntax and rhythm, veritable reverse incantations. Raudive does not deny the fact that such undertakings require an apprenticeship:

At first, most people had difficulties, depended often only on feeling and guessing, and heard only vague noises; after a period of practice, however, the noises emerged as definite sound-shapes and meaningful sentences. Audibility of the voices, therefore, depends on practice, ability of the ear to distinguish, and the extent of undivided attention given whilst listening.[25]

According to Raudive, the ability to hear the dead is developed through the acquisition of a certain skill, an acclimatization to inaudible sounds. A placing of oneself into the appropriate condition, a *conditioning*, is thus necessary in order for a listener to *make out for himself* these inaudible sounds and to

---

24. K. Raudive, *Breakthrough: An Amazing Experiment in Electronic Communication with the Dead* (Gerrards Cross: Colin Smythe, 1971), 32–3.

25. Ibid., 19.

identify in them a composite discourse spoken with a strange scansion and amalgamating many languages.

In Raudive's experiment, it is not the audible that contains the voice of the dead, but the inaudible sonorous. When the tape is replayed at the end of the seance, sounds *that no one heard* during the recording appear, emerging from the electromagnetic background noise. What is given to be heard is thus only the *trace* of a sound. Here, the metaphorical trace of the recorded sound and the trace of sound itself are one and the same, for the sound whose trace testifies to a presence was never heard by anyone.

What is given to be heard, then, must bear characteristic traces, which will be identified and validated effectively *as* sound (rather than as background noise or parasitical noise). In this process, in order to become audible the sonorous must bear the trace of the dead, a trace that is nothing but a formal signature.

At the limit, the trace can even do without sound qua event, and can stand in for this event. This is the case in phenomena of hallucination, where only the trace of sound is manifested, and presents itself to the hallucinating ear as a pure audible that no sound has *physically* generated.[26] This perceptual paradox (How can one hear a sound that has not been produced?) is the limit case of what we might group together under the term 'perceptual distortions', which give onto either the domain of psychopathology (the schizophrenic who hears voices) or that of 'modified states of consciousness', whether provoked by the absorption of toxins (as described by Aldous Huxley or Henri Michaux) or by ecstatic processes.

---

26.   We said above that every audible was a priori sonorous. Hallucination is perhaps the only exception, but it is indeed an exception.

We should therefore not imagine that sound hallucination is
limited to the domain of messages 'whispered into the ear' of
a hallucinating person (whether saint or madman). It must not
be systematically reduced to the manifestation of pathologies,
whether hysterical or schizophrenic, or indeed to the manifestation of delirious ecstasy or access to the mystical. It is a
mode of hearing that functions on the basis of traces. Thus
it is with the rumour of the sea in the hollow of the seashell
cupped against an ear which perceives waves rushing land-
ward on a distant shore. The seashell, of course, contains no
ocean. Yet it is *the sea* that we hear, that we hallucinate, or
rather the *reminiscence* of the sea, as conserved by this relic
of the seabed, captured and detained like a past impression.

Echos

Nonetheless, we should not think that the trace is always a
matter of an immaterial *charge*, the direct corollary of religious
and cultural phenomena. It can just as well be intimately associated with the sonorous phenomenon itself, or more exactly
with an epiphenomenon resulting from the actual production of sound. The trace, that supplement to the sonorous
that introduces it into the audible, is neither entirely ideal nor
entirely material. Although in configurations of listening linked
to belief systems it is usually composed in large part of the
presence of those spirits that inhabit and 'possess' the sound,
at the same time it operates an implicit formal conjunction
with that sound. Moreover, this conjunction is not a matter
of a simple causal relation. It can also obtain in registers of
listening that are not necessarily concerned with religiosity
or active mysticism, but at most with a larval superstition—
cases where the sound does not have a dedicated function

in relation to some specific belief, but where instead a belief is primed by the sound itself.

Certain natural phenomena give rise to situations in which sound takes on a halo of mystery which popular beliefs identify as a manifestation of the divine. Indeed, Lucretius (whose theory of sound is still corpuscular) explains how religions emerge as a response to natural phenomena that cannot be explained (thunder, earthquakes) and whose origins are attributed to higher forces. He gives the example of the echo:

> Again, one word,
> Sent from the crier's mouth, may rouse all ears
> Among the populace. And thus one voice
> Scatters asunder into many voices,
> Since it divides itself for separate ears [...]

> But whatso part of voices fails to hit
> The ears themselves perishes, borne beyond,
> Idly diffused among the winds. A part,
> Beating on solid porticoes, tossed back
> Returns a sound; and sometimes mocks the ear
> With a mere phantom of a word. [...]

> I have seen
> Spots that gave back even voices six or seven
> For one thrown forth—for so the very hills,
> Dashing them back against the hills, kept on
> With their reverberations. And these spots
> The neighbouring country-side doth feign to be
> Haunts of the goat-foot satyrs and the nymphs;
> And tells ye there be fauns, by whose night noise
> And antic revels yonder they declare

The voiceless silences are broken oft,

And tones of strings are made and wailings sweet

Which the pipe, beat by players' finger-tips,

Pours out; [...]

Other prodigies

And wonders of this ilk they love to tell,

Lest they be thought to dwell in lonely spots

And even by gods deserted. This is why

They boast of marvels in their story-tellings;

Or by some other reason are led on—

Greedy, as all mankind hath ever been,

To prattle fables into ears.[27]

For Lucretius, the echo, produced by the repercussions of a multiplied sound, plays a part in establishing a supernatural sonorous environment, ultimately providing alterity where there is only identity. The echo affirms the presence of a sound by revealing the milieu within which it is deployed, as the points from which it is reflected delimit its zone of influence. The sensation of space when one cries out in the mountains is precisely established by the sonorous trail the cry leaves behind as it is re-presented to us. The echo is the trace of a sound that gives itself to be heard again *from afar*.

The myth of Echo begins with Juno cursing the nymph, causing her to lose sovereignty over her voice so that she can no longer do anything but 'repeat the last of what is spoken and return the words she hears.'[28] Echo becomes infatuated with Narcissus, but is cursed with an inability to express her devotion to him,

---

27.   Lucretius, *De rerum natura*, book IV v. 4.563–4.594 (tr. W. E. Leonard).

28.   Ovid, *The Metamorphoses*, book III, v (tr. A.S. Kline).

and can only repeat the last syllables of his sentences. At first intrigued by hearing his own words spoken back to him, Narcissus, whose eyes find grace only in his own reflection, refuses the nymph's advances:

> Scorned, she wanders in the woods and hides her face in shame among the leaves, and from that time on lives in lonely caves. But still her love endures, increased by the sadness of rejection. Her sleepless thoughts waste her sad form, and her body's strength vanishes into the air. Only her bones and the sound of her voice are left. Her voice remains, her bones, they say, were changed to shapes of stone. She hides in the woods, no longer to be seen on the hills, but to be heard by everyone. It is sound that lives in her.[29]

Echo is the mythical metaphorization of a phenomenon, its explanation in terms of the divine. And as the incarnation of an invisible phenomenon, her body is bound to dissipate. The Narcissus episode is but the natural consequence of what was instigated by Juno—that is to say, the process of Echo's depersonalization owing to her inability to express herself *by herself*. The logical conclusion of such a curse is a becoming-trace and the disappearance into inorganicity of everything in her that was not a mirror of the other.

Stripped of the power to be for herself, Echo will now manifest herself only through the other, will be engulfed, will hide away and become stone. No doubt it was the experience of echoes that suggested the transformation of the nymph into stone. And no doubt it must have been the empirical association of the phenomenon with rock faces that prompted the mythical

---

29.   Ibid., book III, v.

story's mineralization of Echo, that 'transubstantiation' of the sound of her voice into an eternal prisoner of the rocks. Once incarnate, the voice of Echo now becomes incarcerated.

In re-exhibiting its own voice, the echo relays its own existence back to itself. Such is the strangeness of hearing oneself speak at one remove, mediated by the distance. The existence of the sound relayed by the echo is confirmed by the fact that the echo phenomenon can only exist on condition of an initial presence. The echo is the trace of the sonorous, revealing the milieu within which it is deployed and affirming sound through the sense impressions it brings about within that milieu.

This observation is not exclusive to the echo, though; it applies to all phenomena of resonance. Resonance and reverberation have always fascinated listeners, taking on a character as sacred as the inexplicable noises of the forces of nature. Caves were doubtless the first theatres within which the perception of resonance came into dialogue with religious belief. Indeed, the young discipline of acoustic archaeology studies the links between cave art and the echoes of caves.[30]

But if 'reverberation [...] invokes the sacred',[31] the sacred also calls for reverberation. The example of acoustic vases,

---

30.   'Steven J. Waller, a pioneer of acoustic architecture, suggested that the paleolithic art found in the caves of Lascaux and Font-de-Gaume was influenced by the acoustic character of the chambers in which it was created. Pictures of bulls, bison, and deer were more likely to be found in chambers with strong echos, spaces whose acoustics created percussive sounds similar to the hoofbeats of a stampeding herd.' B. Blesser, L.-R. Salter (eds.), *Spaces Speak, Are You Listening? Experiencing Aural Architecture* (Cambridge, MA: MIT Press, 2007), 27.

31.   D. Toop, *Ocean of Sound: Aether Talk, Ambient Sound and Imaginary Worlds* (London: Serpent's Tail, 1995), 244.

found in numerous churches throughout Europe, and whose use goes back to antiquity, is most enlightening on this point. The vases placed in churches were specifically designed to correct their acoustics, while those of antique theatres served to amplify the actors' voices.[32] But whatever the precise function of these vases, they testify to an 'acoustic consciousness' which is certainly empirically based, but which constituted an architectural proto-acoustics that had succeeded in mastering techniques and methods for the creation of specific acoustical effects. Indeed, a whole chapter of Athanasius Kircher's *Musurgia Universalis* (1650) is dedicated to a discussion of these problems ('Magia Phonocamptica').

There is also a term, today fallen into disuse, which was associated with such studies: echometry. It designates the 'science and art of making echoes; of the making of buildings whose disposition—above all their vaults—favours echoes'.[33] Although the origins of this science of echoes are lost in the distant epoch of antiquity, it has regularly been supplemented with new theoretical contributions through the ages, formalizing its employment.

The elaborate architecture of temples is certainly not secretly driven by acoustics alone. The combined effects of archetypal religious construction (monumental buildings elevated toward the sky, comprising large spaces, high ceilings, the choice of hard, solid materials to ensure a long-lasting edifice, etc.) produced an archetypal acoustics that itself

---

32. On the study of acoustic vases, the reader is referred to R. Floriot, *Contribution à l'étude des vases acoustiques du Moyen Âge* (Paris: Gap, 1965).

33. Definition from the so-called *Trévoux Dictionnaire Universel François et Latin* (the dictionary, itself a synthesis of sixteenth-century dictionaries, was compiled between 1704 and 1771).

eventually became a phenomenon to be studied and utilized.
But the resulting theoretical formalization, echometry, was foreshadowed by religious and doctrinal considerations that authorized the consideration of acoustics at the level of dogma, as we can see in the sermons of Bernard of Clairvaux, for instance:

> The hearing succeeded where the sight failed. Appearances deceived the eye, but truth poured Itself into the ear. [...] What wonder if the ear catches the truth, since faith comes from what is heard, and what is heard comes by the word of God, and the word of God is truth? [...] Only the hearing that catches the word possesses the truth.[34]

What we see taking shape in Bernard of Clairvaux is a theological legitimation of things that had been come upon intuitively and empirically. According to his doctrine, which privileges hearing over the visual, church architecture explicitly took the sonorous component into account.[35] And even if *the explicit bias toward the ear* disappears along with Bernard of Clairvaux, phonocamptic art[36] carries on and continues to be developed, irrevocably attaching a sacred character to resonance, a veritable acoustic cloud. The sonorous trail that is reverberation, amplifying sound, sublimating it, and even

---

34. *Commentary on the Song of Songs,* sermon XXVIII, 'The Blackness and Beauty of the Bridegroom and the Bride. Prerogative of the Ear over the Eye in the Matter of Faith' (tr. D. Wright).

35. Cf. H. Larcher, *L'Acoustique cistercienne et l'unité sonore* [1968] (Paris: Labergerie, 1971). Larcher shows very clearly how Bernard's precepts influenced the architecture of Cistercian abbeys, in particular that of Le Thoronet.

36. The term 'phonocamptic' designates everything relating to the reflection of sounds.

derealizing it, forms a supernatural trace, holding sound in suspense *a little longer* than it would otherwise last, rendering it at once tangible and ethereal, affirming the materiality of sound's existence at the same time as its fantastic irreality.

Echo and reverberation re-present sound, confirm it, even as they modulate it more or less perceptibly, establishing a relation of both foreignness and homogeneity between phonic centre and phonocamptic points, between sound and its surrounding doubles, which are anyway never really distinct from one other.

But resonance is not solely physical. On the contrary, we should recognize that there is a correspondence between the phenomenal resonance of sound, the acoustic cloud, and figurative, speculative resonance, which in fact is always inherent to the perceptual apparatus. Resonance designates both the physical trace of sound, the relic of a sound that has disappeared and yet persists, and the memorial trace, the reminiscence that is convoked to *embody* memories. Perhaps above all, then, sound is traced in the memory of he or she to whom it is given to hear. For it is doubtless the first trace, the memory trace, that dams up sound into a semblance of permanence, retaining for a few moments more a sound that has already evaporated.

The memory of a sound thus implies a re-sonance, a re-presentation of sound, or more exactly a re-exhibiting of its trace, its phantom. And it is indeed owing to such an analogy between physical resonance and 'mental' resonance that we call such memory *echoic memory*.

Such reminiscences, whether they are echoes or memories of the sonorous, are therefore possible only through the more or less successful redoubling of the sound and of its trace. What is given by memory, when a sound is retroactively re-exhibited, is not of the order of the sonorous, but that of the audible. What is given is not sound, but its trace.

The trace, once more, must be understood beyond any nature-culture division or physical-ideal separation. What characterizes it, beyond any distinction pertaining to its address or mode of production, is its twofold destiny, in the sense that it is at once a supplement perennializing the sonorous and rendering it audible, and an infinitely precarious entity which cannot *be* for itself. A trace is always the trace of something, and is always threatened with disappearance.[37]

IMPRINTS

Infra-Thin

The substantialization of sound as breath; sound as the avatar of the spirit of gods or of the dead; the bestowing upon it of a sacred, magical character; the superimposition of reverberative clouds, of phenomenal haloes in so many reflecting mirrors reaffirming the existence of that which they reflect while rendering it ungraspable; reminiscences and memorializations: these are just some of the different ways in which sound is traced.

The trace is a residue, a supplement to that which has sounded, a sort of phenomenal hysteresis. A sound, in order to be audible, must leave a trace. A sound that no one hears, that no one perceives, or that no one manages to grasp, is not entirely a sound. Whereas a perceived sound, a sound that leaves a trace, is already somewhat more than a sound.

Although not entirely captured by the concept, the trace can be compared to Marcel Duchamp's 'infra-thin': 'the warmth

---

37.   'An unerasable trace is not a trace, it is a full presence […].' J. Derrida, *Writing and Difference*, tr. A. Bass (Chicago: University of Chicago Press, 1993), 289.

of a seat (which has just been left)', says Duchamp, 'is an infra-thin'.[38] The infra-thin can therefore be understood as being the qualitative category proper to the trace, testifying at once to its materiality and its precariousness:

> Velvet trousers— / their whistling sound (in walking) by / brushing of the 2 legs is an / infra-thin separation signalled / by sound. (it is *not?* an infra-thin sound).[39]

The infra-thin is an absent presence, a residue of presence that marks and actualizes the difference, as miniscule as it may be, between what has been and what persists, at the point where the trace draws out presence to the point of disappearance. The notion of the infra-thin is positioned *dialectically*[40] between contact and the *attenuation* of contact, between the present and the evaporated. This is why the sound of the trousers is not itself infra-thin, but *signals* the infra-thin (this in fact raises a question for Duchamp: further on, he describes this phenomenon as yielding an auditory infra-thin, although this still does not persuade him to consider the sound itself as an infra-thin sound).

More precisely speaking, the infra-thin of a sound is situated at the divergence between sound and what remains of it, that is to say its trace. The infra-thin is what persists of the sonorous when we take away the audible, constituting, in short, an *imperceptible*. The trace stands in an intimate relation to

---

38. Note 4, M. Duchamp, *Notes* [1980] (Paris: Champs-Flammarion, 1999), 19–37 ('Notes on the infra-thin').

39. Ibid., note 9v.

40. See note 35rv: 'All "identicals" as identical as they may be (and the more identical they are), are compared with that infra-thin separative difference'. (ibid).

that from which it emanates. The infra-thin is equally close to both of the terms that constitute its universe of appearance, contact and separation. It is fundamentally differential, as Duchamp remarks:

> The difference (dimensional) between two mass-produced objects [from the same mold] is an infra-thin when the maximum (?) precision is obtained.[41]

The infra-thin is difference at the threshold of identity. In this respect it can be contrasted with the notion of the *imprint*, which reveals itself in the *consummation/consumption* of the gap between presence and absence. As Georges Didi-Huberman writes:

> The imprint may well touch us through the adherence from which it proceeds, but this contact ends up, almost fatally, being thought in the element of separation, of loss, of absence. In order for an imprint of steps to be *produced* as a process, the foot must sink into the sand, the walker must *be there*, in the very place of the mark to be left. But in order for the imprint to *appear* as a result, the foot must also be lifted again, separated from the sand and moved away toward other imprints to be produced elsewhere; at which point, of course, the walker *is no longer there*.[42]

Whereas the trace must sooner or later disappear along with that which produced it, the imprint survives, testifying to

---

41. Ibid.

42. *L'Empreinte*, ed. G. Didi-Huberman (Paris: Editions du Centre Pompidou, 1997), 181.

this presence *without being able to reproduce it*. The trace of sound can be equated with the original phenomenon. The imprint cannot, since it cannot be of the same nature. It is fundamentally other, and maintains a far more complex relation to its original than that obtaining in the trace. For 'there is probably, in every imprint, a mystery of reference. [...] To resemble via contact is often to rule out recognition'.[43] Indeed, this characteristic of the imprint is revealed within certain disciplines—in cryptography, for example, where a 'hashing function' produces an imprint in the form of a 'message digest' which contains all of the information necessary to reconstitute the original phrase, but does not resemble it directly. The imprint, then, is always the result of a *coding*, and must always be decoded in order to reveal its origin.

The imprint is indeed the 'moulding', the testimony via contact, of a past presence. In order to exist, therefore, a sonorous imprint must have been in contact with a sound that has since vanished, and must harbour within itself the energetic characteristics of that sound. In order to do so, it must freeze time. The sonorous imprint thus necessarily belongs to an environment or medium other than the sonorous, but one that is confronted by the presence of the sound and is modulated, modelled, by it. Strictly speaking, then, there can be no sonorous imprint, but only imprints of sound— when applied to the imprint, the term 'sonorous' does not relate directly to it, but only to the object of which it is an imprint.

This means that trace and imprint cannot communicate, even though they participate in one and the same process of rendering the sonorous audible. The trace is beyond the

---

43.   Ibid, 151 [in French the result of a hashing function is an 'empreinte'—trans.]

nature-culture distinction, capable of designating indifferently either an echo or a sound-memory. It accompanies sound, and outstrips it, like a path it takes so as to be able to give itself to be heard; whereas the imprint is strictly material, and draws off sound toward materiality by making it tangible. One functions via supplementarity, the other via materialization.

Transduction

What the imprint freezes is therefore not sound, since sound itself is only *a succession, through time, of changes in the state of its medium of propagation*, but rather the energy that it expresses.

One of the first significant experiments in sonorous imprinting goes back to around 1807, with the discovery of Ernst Florens Friedrich Chladni. Sprinkling sand onto a copper disc (or a glass plate, according to some sources) which was then set vibrating with the aid of a violin bow rubbed against its edge, Chladni saw the sand organize itself immediately into geometrical patterns. By varying the size of the disc or plate and the points at which the bow was applied, he found that various different forms could be obtained. These 'Chladni figures' are doubtless the first methodically produced sonorous imprints. They are not a direct imprint of sound, but an imprint of the energetic configuration of sound deployed in a given medium (the copper disc or glass plate).

Another example of the transduction of sound would turn out to be far more fertile than Chladni's somewhat cryptic figures: phono-graphic transduction. The first attempts at the direct writing[44] of sound would have to be attributed to

---

44. By 'direct' writing we mean a writing that is not representative, that is not of the order of notation, but is established through direct contact, and which is therefore, above all, a plot.

acoustician and polymath Thomas Young (1773–1829). Such procedures were later the subject of extensive experiments by Edouard-Léon Scott de Martinville (who invented the phonautograph in 1857),[45] and subsequently by Alexander Graham Bell and Clarence Blake, in their own version of the phonautograph, where the apparatus of transduction proposed by Scott de Martinville is replaced by nothing less than an actual human ear: Bell and Blake connected an excised ear to their apparatus by attaching the chain of ossicles to a stylus that transcribed their vibrations onto a plate of smoke-blackened glass.

The transduction of sound by way of a graphic imprint inaugurates a regime of permanence for sound which, prior to this point, had only been approached symbolically or phonocamptically. Although the imprinting of sound does not yet enable its reproduction, it will henceforth permit *the close observation* of sound, albeit in a form entirely other than the sonorous (namely, a scriptural or graphic form); and as sound becomes an object of knowledge, this opens up new possibilities for theorization.[46]

Sound, conducted through the new modality of the imprint, acquires another way of leaving a trace—by being made into a scientific object. Such a tracing inscribes sound abstractly in a concrete materiality that is not its own, granting it a semblance of locality. Having been rendered audible, sound will now, little by little, become *comprehensible*.

---

45.   A machine which, with the help of a pencil, 'transcribed' the sonic vibration received by a sheet of parchment onto a sheet of smoke-blackened paper. This machine, then, was capable of imprinting, but not reproducing, sound. However, a phonautogram dating from 1860 was rediscovered in 2008 and has been analyzed, reread, and resynthesized with the aid of digital technology, thus revealing an important fact: the imprint is always a potential for reproduction.

46.   Cf. J. Sterne, *The Audible Past* (Durham, NC: Duke University Press, 2003).

The transduction of sound operates in two directions: it deploys sound, transmits it across potentially unlimited distances, sending it across oceans, freeing it from a certain locality inherent to the power of the emitting source itself,[47] while at the same time freezing it in this new materiality, a sort of retarius net from which it cannot escape.

Transduction implies an *alternative state resulting from contact* with sound: for example, the phonautograph generates a graphical state, electrical transduction involves a dynamic electrical state (the most well-known application of which is the telephone) which can in turn bring about an electrochemical state (as in semiconductor memory technology); the tape recorder produces a magnetic state, etc. The imprint resulting from transduction, in particular the graphic imprint, must therefore not be considered as a symbolic representation of sound, but rather as a re-exhibiting of sonorous energy in different forms, with the energy becoming prisoner of its new materiality. When the imprint first allowed sound to be fixed and erected into an object of knowledge, the possibility of regenerating sound from the imprint was only a distant promise, one that many of the inventors of phono-mechanical and then phono-graphic transduction did not even imagine. So transduction does not 'presuppose' the reproduction of that which makes an imprint; yet it does *predispose* itself to such reproduction.

Reproduction

The imprint always brings reproduction with it as a potential. When this promise, this omen, is actualized, when the

---

47. Until the advent of transduction, the cry of a raven had not been heard more than a few kilometres away. It could now be heard anywhere, providing it was transduced and transmitted.

reproduction of sound finally becomes technically realizable, a question will then immediately creep in, without always being clearly or consciously formulated: an uncertainty as to how this new entity, reproduced sound, stands in relation to its original.

This problematic will crop up from the very beginnings of sound reproduction, under the auspices of the notion of *fidelity*. On the pretext of the impossibility of detecting the difference between original and reproduction,[48] the marketing proselytism that accompanied the commercial debut of phonographic machines generated a confusion that would be obstinate and long-lived: the confusion between the concept of reproduction and that of *restitution*. Restitution, the 'act of returning something which one has improperly taken possession of', supposes a return to an original (albeit phantasmatic) situation, along with a liberation via reinvocation of that which is returned and which had in some way been 'imprisoned'. But sound reproduction does not reinstate sound: it produces a copy, by virtue of the energetic information it has secured. This confusion, whose effects are still felt today, was criticized from the time of the very first techniques of reproduction. While some argued in its favour, emphasizing the sensible similarity between original and copy, others emphasized the gap—irreducible and persistent, even if infra-thin: a gap that could never be closed.

This perennial confusion which is still with us today ultimately concerns the distance between what is heard and what is *given to be heard*, between the sensible phenomenon and its

---

48. In *The Audible Past*, Sterne gives the example of a press release for Victor Records which, comparing the recording with the true tenor Enrico Caruso, concludes: 'Both are Caruso'.

original, contextual mode of appearing.[49] Hence the development of procedures of reproduction led to the reinterrogation of the notion of authenticity.

In Walter Benjamin, the concept of aura is central to the question of the survival of the traditional, unique, authentic work of art faced with the development of *technically* reproducible artworks and with the new behaviours linked to the reception of these unprecedented types of works. For Benjamin, the advent of technically reproducible works implied the potential destruction of the aura. To the question: 'But what is aura, actually?', Benjamin responds: 'A strange weave of space and time: the unique appearance or semblance of distance, no matter how close it may be.'[50] To define the aura in this way 'represents nothing but the formulation of the cult value of the work of art in categories of space and time perception. Distance is the opposite of closeness. The essentially distant object is the unapproachable one'.[51]

Aura functions primarily to evoke a faraway, an unattainable. This unattainable is also the site of the infra-thin, that minute gap in manufacturing procedures that makes each copy an original, and which Didi-Huberman says we 'must inhabit' in order to be able to approach its origin. This auratic distance is not a spatial distance, however: 'The closeness which one

49.   Strictly speaking, the sound of a bell is a sound produced by a bell in the moment of hearing it. The sound of a bell diffused by a phonograph is *before anything else* the sound of a phonograph copying the energetic characteristics of the sound of a recorded bell. The striking character of the illusion produced by the apparatus in no way changes the fact of this separation.

50.   W. Benjamin, 'Little History of Photography', in *Selected Writings, Volume 2 1927–1934*, tr. R. Livingstone et al (Cambridge, MA and London: Belknap Press of Harvard University Press, 1999), 507–30: 518.

51.   Ibid., 243.

may gain from its subject matter does not impair the distance which it retains in its appearance.'[52]

Thus the authenticity of a sensible experience lies in the unique conjunction of an object and a context. The experience of the aura is a unique experience and, by this token alone, an experience *of* the unique. And sound reproduction brings about a clear break in the apprehension of sound, or in the possibilities of the experiences that it offers, in so far as it calls for a new mode of listening in which the aura is distorted by sonorous replicas.

The revolutionary import of the phonographic procedure is such that certain thinkers and writers even went so far as to rewrite history *backwards* from the moment of its discovery. This is what Villiers de l'Isle-Adam does in *The Future Eve*, whose principal protagonist is none other than Thomas Alva Edison, the 'Magician of Menlo Park'.

The story (whose subterranean strategy consists in continually reversing the relation between facticity and reality) opens with Edison's dreams and conjectures about one of his inventions: the phonograph. Edison voices his regret that it did not appear sooner in the history of humanity, and was not able to record the speech of emperors and messiahs, or the mythical sounds disseminated throughout the course of history:

> Even among the *noises* of the past, how many mysterious sounds were known to our predecessors, which for lack of a convenient machine to record them have now fallen forever into the abyss? ... Who nowadays could form, for example, a proper notion of the sound of the trumpets of Jericho? Of the bellow of

---

52. Ibid.

Phalaris' bull?[53] Of the laughter of the augurs? Or the morning melody of Memnon? And all the rest?

Dead voices, lost sounds, forgotten noises, vibrations lockstepping into the abyss, and now too distant ever to be recaptured! ... What sort of arrows would be able to transfix such birds?[54]

Continuing his reflections, he adds a further nuance to this train of thought:

If the phonograph never had the chance to record the authentic, original sound of those famous words, well, that's too bad; but to worry about missing those enigmatic or mysterious sounds that I was thinking about just now, that would be ridiculous.

For they are not what has disappeared, but rather the awe-inspiring character with which they were invested in the hearing of the ancients—and which all by itself served to animate their basic insignificance. So that neither then nor nowadays could I possible record exactly sounds whose significance and whose reality depends on the auditor. [...]

So that, in the last analysis, one can say that *only the walls of the city of Jericho heard the trumpets of Joshua, since only they were fitted to do so.* Neither the army of Israel, nor the besieged Canaanites recognized anything unusual in the sound: which comes down to saying that *nobody ever heard it.*[55]

---

53.   This is how Kierkegaard describes the bronze bull of the tyrant Phalaris: '[the] poor wretches in Phalaris's bronze bull, who were slowly tortured over a slow fire; their screams could not reach the tyrant's ears to terrify him; to him they sounded like sweet music.' S. Kierkegaard, 'Diapsalmata', in *Either/Or, Part 1*, tr. H.V. Vong and E.H. Hong (Princeton, NJ: Princeton University Press, 1987), 19.

54.   A. de Villiers de l'Isle-Adam, *Tomorrow's Eve*, tr. R. M. Adams (Chicago: University of Illinois Press, 2001), 10.

55.   Ibid., 15.

Here Villiers delivers a sophisticated reflection on the question of reproduction and its influence upon the constitution of sound itself. Edison's statements first of all establish a separation in principle between speech and 'mysterious sounds': whereas the reproduction of speech seems worthwhile, that of the mysterious sounds is ultimately seen as 'ridiculous'. For the phonography of speech reproduces not only the phonatory phenomenon, but also a meaning borne by a language whose sonorous rendition augments, or at least modulates, its intelligibility. And for Edison it is this meaning, conveyed and modulated by the orator's mode of expression, that is worthy of being recorded. It is the trace of language borne by sound that merits reproduction.

Inversely, the mysterious sounds do not 'speak' for themselves and do not bear any directly intelligible message. Their awe-inspiring character is itself non-reproducible, in so far as it depends upon a context of hearing *and upon the auditors who participate in this context*. Deprived of 'the hearing of the ancients', the 'mysterious sounds' lose their substance and their singularity, and are themselves lost.

In this way, through his character's divagations and mental simulations, and the conclusions at which he arrives, Villiers sets out the idea that a sound, in so far as it is audible, is constituted not only by the phenomenon that produces it, but also by the ears to which it is addressed. He gives the example of the trumpets of Jericho, meant only, *qua trumpets of Jericho*, for the walls of the city, which alone can 'receive' their sound. The reproduction of such a sound would be fatally *inaudible*, for its address, its intention, its reception and its *reason* (the walls themselves) are not reproducible.

What Villiers teaches us is that not every sound is reproducible; and that if we reproduce a sound that is not meant to be reproduced, it loses, along with its address, its destination,

and its origin, an element that is constitutive of it and which
binds it to its auditor. Benjamin says that 'to experience the
aura of a phenomenon means to invest it with the faculty to
open its gaze'.[56] This 'faculty to open its gaze' is a metaphor for
the address of the phenomenon. If a sound is only authentic
when it is directly linked to its context of appearing, that is
to say to its recipient, then inversely, a reproduced sound can
accede to authenticity only on condition that one considers it
for itself, and not as a phantom of the original sound.

Reproduction imprisons sound and never lets it go. It sends
out only doubles, sonorous doppelgangers. Through the intermediation of the phonograph, as actual and artificial source of
the phenomenon, the original source of the reproduced sound
may be suggested, but remains inaccessible. Sound is so to
speak 'naturalized', 'goes native' in the reproductive apparatus. The original source is *simulated* by a standard generator,
the phonograph.

This machine ushers in a new era in the history of techniques of sonorous simulacra. Unlike the first attempts at
automatic sonorous illusionism,[57] which sought to copy the
emitting organs of the sound source to be simulated, the
phonographic enterprise is born of a new direction in research
which aims to understand the mechanisms of *reception*. Sonorous reproduction will now develop on the basis of the ear, and

---

56. W. Benjamin, 'On some Motifs in Baudelaire', in *Illuminations*, tr. H. Zohn
(New York: Schocken Books, 2007), 152–96.

57. We could cite the example of Tipu's Tiger, an automaton that represents
a tiger seizing an English colonist in his mouth and imitates the roar of the tiger;
or that of Wolfgang von Kempelen's speaking automaton (dating from 1769)
which could apparently speak whole sentences in different languages.

no longer the voice; and will be constructed by way of what Jonathan Sterne calls the 'tympanic function':

> The ear—in its tympanic character—became a diagram of sound's reproducibility. The ear, as a mechanism, became a way of organizing a whole set of sounds and sonic functions; it was an informal principle by which the mechanics of sound reproduction were arranged.[58]

If the reproduction of sound is therefore distinct from the automaton that simulates natural sounds in a *trompe l'oreille* fashion, it remains no less a function of illusion. When we reread an imprint, a phonogram, we do not reproduce sound, but a double which has, *to the nearest infra-thin*, the same physical characteristics as the original sound—characteristics which are inscribed, in inverted form, in the imprint as in a matrix. But the imprint cannot reinstate what it never received—namely, the sound's *reason for having been sounded* (its situation of appearing). In a certain sense, in the reproduction of sound *the imprint prevails over that which enacted it, it prevails over the action that made the imprint*.

Furthermore, in the wake of transduction, sound reproduction perpetuates and amplifies the tendency toward the objectivation of sound. Reproduced, siphoned-off sound can now be extracted from one temporality (that intrinsic to the unicity of a phenomenon) while remaining the captive of another (that intrinsic to the unicity of the event). Thanks to reproduction, we can hear a sound more than once, illusorily.[59]

---

58. Sterne, *The Audible Past*, 83.

59. Once again, *to the nearest infra-thin*, for it is never the same sound that we hear. And yet the fidelity to the original sound has such force that we find it easy to equate the sonic avatars with the original.

A sound that is three seconds long, for example, will only last, as such, for three seconds, and will inevitably disappear and fade to nothing, until the next time it is 'played', at which time it will then have become an *other* sound. So it is incorrect to say that the phonograph fixes sounds; what it fixes is their imprints. Now, the imprint is always ambivalent. It may allow us to re-present a sound, to create a simulacra of presence, but at the same time it reveals that which is no longer present: 'The imprint makes of absence something like a power of form.'[60] This ambivalence is intrinsic to the phonograph. It is always poised between that which seems to be once more, and that which definitively is no longer, between that which seems ceaselessly to live again and that which is forever lost.

Transmission

There is another device that emerged from the principles of transduction and benefitted from the development of phonography, and which was to play an important part in the mediation of sound and its deployment. If phonography, through a play of illusion, permitted a sound to appear multiple times, techniques of transmission, and in particular radiophonic devices, diffracted and multiplied the spaces where it could manifest itself.

A product of the twentieth century, the radiodiffusion of sound ushered in a revolution in modes of listening at which the telephone had only hinted. The principal aim of the telephone, from the theoretical works of Charles Bourseul in 1854 and the founding of American Telephone and Telegraph, was to transmit speech in such a way as to allow people to communicate at a distance. It was not a priori a question of a faithful 'restitution' of the interlocutor, as was claimed in the case of the orchestra

---

60.   Didi-Huberman, *L'Empreinte*, 39.

and the phonograph. Certain attempts at applying telephony for other purposes were however implemented with some degree of success—such as the theatrophone (in service from 1881 to 1932), a telephone link communicating between the Paris Opera (and later, numerous Parisian concert halls) and the telephone lines of subscribers, who could thereby join the show's audience from the comfort of their own homes.[61]

This initiative was already an anticipation of radio. But whereas the telephone transmits speech in a closed circuit, radiophony diffuses sound unidirectionally, between a transmitter and receivers, roles which are not technically interchangeable. Where the telephone circulates, as Marcel Duchamp says, from '*isolate to isolate*', radio serves an whole crowd (the listeners) from a single point (the station and its transmitter). Thus what Rudolf Arnheim messianically called 'the great miracle of wireless' came to pass.[62]

Radiophony may not be phonographic, but it is nonetheless a device for sound reproduction. It is a tympanic process augmented by a new technique, the dynamic transmission of the energetic information of sound via radio waves. Although the radio is *almost* instantaneous, we need not for

---

61. Marcel Proust, himself a subscriber, gave his own qualified view on the device in a letter to Georges de Lauris: 'I have subscribed to the theatrophone, which I rarely use, and through which one cannot hear particularly well. But ultimately, for Wagner's operas, which I know almost by heart, I myself make up for the insufficiencies of the acoustics.' M. Proust, *Correspondance*, vols 10–12 (1910–1913) (Paris: Plon, 1983–4).

62. 'This is the great miracle of wireless. The omnipresence of what people are singing or saying anywhere, the overleaping of frontiers, the conquest of spatial isolation, the importation of culture on the waves of the ether, the same fare for all, sound in silence.' R. Arnheim, *Radio*, tr. M. Ludwig and H. Read (London: Faber, 1936), 14.

all that imagine that it is different in nature to phonography.
Both are devices for the reproduction of sound.

What is peculiar to radiophony, though, is the ability to transmit an event that is not yet over but is still in progress, '*in statu nascendi*'.[63] It allows the sonorous testimony of an event to be transmitted *as it takes place*, at distances far exceeding the natural reach of the original sound. Moreover, it is this idea that the radio retransmits sound in its nascent state that gave rise to a misunderstanding concerning the supposed difference in nature between radio and sound reproduction, and led to the radio being placed into the new category of 'transmission' or 'rediffusion'. This is indeed a misunderstanding, for when radio retransmits, it *reproduces* sound and simulates it faithfully, just like a phonograph. It makes no difference that it does so over great distances, without having to fix the sound, and in the very moment of its appearing (or very nearly so). This certainly testifies to what is singular about radio, but indicates no fundamental difference.

It is true, however, that radiophony develops a new way in which sound can be given to be heard. When a sound is transmitted, its *audibility* seems to be assured by the technical device itself, which, by 'processing' it, validates it as sound. The only inaudible sonorous that remains when listening to a radio set will be *background noise* (and maybe a little interference). All the rest will a priori be destined, even predestined, to be heard. Here the recourse to a mythical, echoic tracing, or even an imprint, is no longer really necessary in order to render the sonorous audible (at most, these traces will be superadded, but will not be the true instigators of this bringing-into-audibility). In radiophony sound is *channelled*: it is given to be heard

63.   Ibid., 126–7.

through a specific diffusion channel which compensates for the fugacity of sound with a powerful technical and institutional conditioning. The tracing that takes place here is the work of a configuration that is technical, implicit, and irrefutable. It tells us: 'This sound that is delivered through the radio receiver is not so delivered by chance, and therefore it deserves to be listened to'. Through radiophony, sound acquires, *mechanically*, the first inklings of authority, an authority that is connected to the autonomy of its appearing.

The reproducibility of radio also implies a new way of using sounds. Most sounds produced and diffused by the radio are destined for reproduction from the outset. Thus, as Benjamin remarks of photography, the question of authenticity becomes null and void. For Benjamin, this obsolescence goes hand in hand with a change in the mode of existence of the work of art, which, '[i]nstead of being based on ritual, [...] begins to be based on another practice—politics'.[64] Indeed, it is in this spirit (that of politicizing art, rather than aestheticizing politics) that Walter Benjamin embarked upon his own radiophonic adventure.

Yet radiophony is not an exclusively political device. It has also generated mythological resonances and belief systems. The most striking example is found in a figure who lies at the very origin of radio, Nikola Tesla. In an article where he develops the concept of the *imaginary wavelength*,[65] James Sey recounts how Tesla sought to bring his wave experiments to a culmination by using terrestrial electromagnetic energy as

64. W. Benjamin, 'The Work of Art in the Age of Mechanical Reproduction', in H. Arendt (ed), *Illuminations*, tr. H. Zohn (New York: Schocken, 2007), 224.

65. J. Sey, 'Sounds Like...The Cult of the Imaginary Wavelength', in E. G. Jensen and B. Labelle (eds.), *Radio Territories* (Los Angeles and Copenhagen: Errant Bodies Press, 2007), 23–4.

a global carrier wave, thus proving that the earth itself was a sort of gigantic satellite-dish, a 'cosmic transmitter-receiver'.[66] Although Sey's concept is a little vague, it does attest to an intriguing intuition, in seeking to show that technical and scientific devices, as they established sound as an object of knowledge, also further unfolded it, opening up new and unprecedented arenas of appearance for it, sometimes providing a new medium for beliefs[67] or for a return to ancient traditions with magical sounds—sound once again becoming *mythically bonded* to its medium. Just as in the past breath-sound and air had been inseparable, radiodiffused sound became intrinsically linked to the electromagnetic field. Sound once more conquered etherealized space.[68] Upon which technical and scientific advances appeared not as tools for the abolition of myths, but, quite on the contrary, as leverage for their redeployment, propelling them into new territories.

---

66. '[…] [I]nterplanetary communication has entered the stage of probability. In fact, that we can produce a distinct effect on one of these planets [Mars or Venus] in this novel manner, namely, by disturbing the electrical condition of the earth, is beyond any doubt. This way of effecting such communication is, however, essentially different from all others which have so far been proposed by scientific men. In all the previous instances only a minute fraction of the total energy reaching the planet—as much as it would be possible to concentrate in a reflector—could be utilized by the supposed observer in his instrument. But by the means I have developed he would be enabled to concentrate the larger portion of the entire energy transmitted to the planet in his instrument, and the chances of affecting the latter are thereby increased many millionfold.' N. Tesla, 'The Problem of Increasing Human Energy', *Century Illustrated Magazine*, June 1900.

67. In Sey's words, 'the notion of an imaginary wavelength bring[s] inextricably together the body, the signal, and the aesthetic and scientific possibilities of wavelengths as supernaturally exact media'. Sey, 'Sounds like…', 24.

68. The concept of ether was reborn with the discovery of electricity and electromagnetism.

The electromagnetic ether, where radio waves criss-cross each other, where the sounds of the entire world circulate—those of the living but also, if we are to believe the theories of electronic voice phenomenon, those of the dead—this ether is precisely such a territory. An attractor of belief, a world of sonorous ubiquity, it would also become the theatre of operations for wave warfare, a theatre whose control would be historically decisive. And above all, as emphasized by Gregory Whitehead, one of the pioneers of radio art:

> Radio space is [...] a series of cultural, social and political relations, to be engaged in some way. It seems heretical [...] but radio is not about sound. Radio happens in sound, at a perceptual level, but the guts of radio are not sounds, but rather the gaps between sending and receiving, between transmission and audition.[69]

AREA AND METAMORPHOSES

The treasury of sonorous myths inherited from ancestral beliefs and technical discoveries cluster together to form an imaginary of sound, an imaginary that serves to mark out an area of audibility—the area of sound's appearing and of its *grip*, the area within which it gains traction.

Trace and Milieu

The trace is situated between the sonorous and the audible, and enables 'audible material' to be drawn from the sonorous. It plays the role of a go-between. As for the mark, it is clearly on the side of the audible. In fact, it is hearing itself, as the ambassador of the audible world, that grasps in the sonorous

---

69.   A. Alvarado, 'An Interview with Gregory Whitehead', <http://archive.free-103point9.org/2007/07/13.alvarado_whitehead.pdf>.

the trace that will allow it to *mark* sound—that is to say, to *qualify* it. The trace assists in the prehension of sound; the mark, qua primary qualifying element, establishes the *certain place* whence sound can be convoked, a site that the trace had presupposed and drawn the sonorous toward. A whole process of the marking and delimitation of a space of appearing now comes into play. It is not that the delimitations authorise the marking; rather, it is the marking that generates these plots. Indeed, the mark that makes territory is inherent to 'territorialization':

> The territory is not primary in relation to the qualitative mark; it is the mark that makes the territory. Functions in a territory are not primary; they presuppose a territory-producing expressiveness. In this sense, the territory, and the functions performed within it, are products of territorialization. Territorialization is an act of rhythm that has become expressive, or of milieu components that have become qualitative.[70]

The certain place—this is what the trace permits us to glimpse and toward which it tends; the place of the objectivated sign-sound complex, a stake in the ground. It is the mark that makes the territory. But sonorous territories do not emerge from nowhere; they emerge from an audible world and constitute a *milieu*:

> [T]he notion of the milieu is not unitary: not only does the living thing continually pass from one milieu to another, but the milieus pass into one another, they are essentially communicating.

70. G. Deleuze and F. Guattari, *A Thousand Plateaus*, tr. B. Massumi (Minneapolis and London: Minnesota University Press, 1987), 315.

The milieus are open to chaos, which threatens them with exhaustion or intrusion. Rhythm is the milieus' answer to chaos.[71]

The milieu is the business of the trace; the territory, that of the mark. Tracing is the placing of sound into milieu, its mediation with and toward audibility, whereas the mark makes territory on the basis of this milieu, forming sonorous territories once they have been made audible. The mark that forms the territory is an expressive quality. The milieu is traced, the territory marked.

Like the territory, the mark always has an established relationship to authority. The authority of sound takes shape through its marking, through its belonging to this or that constituted territory. The mark is also the condition sine qua non of communicability. One does not communicate one's perceptions or impressions, one communicates qualities, values. One does not communicate one's experience of sound. One communicates the markers that one has detected in it, markers which, in particular, help to distinguish one sound from another, and *to formulate this distinction*. It is in this way, in the weave of authority and communicability, that markings and territories evolve and flourish.

It falls to the milieu of audibility to initiate a process of the marking of sound that leaves a trace, sound that is audible. And it is from this process of marking that sonorous territories then emerge.

If the mark is the expressivity that forms territory, and if the diversity of such territories corresponds to that of qualitative marks, then we may expect the area of sound (its milieu) to contain polar territories, *extrema* whose matters of expression

---

71.   Ibid., 313.

are opposed to one another. And such poles do indeed exist: they are usually qualified as noise and silence.

Noises, Silences

The problematics linked to silence form a vast world wherein one can easily become lost. To attain what is proper to silence, that is to say its sensible dimension, we must set out deliberately to find it, seek to experience it. In the fifties, John Cage sought such an experience:

> For, when [...] one enters an anechoic chamber, as silent as technologically possible in 1951, to discover that one hears two sounds of one's own unintentional making (nerve's systematic operation, blood's circulation), the situation one is clearly in is not objective (sound-silence), but rather subjective (sounds only) [...].[72]

The numerous commentaries on this experience most often end with the following assertion: 'There's no such thing as silence'.[73]

But silence precisely does *ex-ist*, standing outside of our field of experience. Absolute silence does well and truly exist. In a space where there is no medium for the transmission of sound, in the void, silence reigns. But what Cage's experiment reveals is that no one could ever perceive silence; that silence is properly *inaudible*. We can never have an experience of *the absence of sound*. Silence exists, but not for anyone. No hearing can attain it. An auditor, himself the emitter of

---

72.   J. Cage, *Silence* (Middletown, CT: Wesleyan University Press, 1961), 13–14.

73.   J. Cage, in R. Kostelanetz, *Conversing with Cage* (New York and London: Routledge, 2005), 65.

noise and subjectively responsible for his perception, can never *hear silence*.

Silence is understood as an absence of sound, and Cage's experience shows that this absence is never total. However, it may, sometimes, be *sufficient*. In any given sonorous context, there exists a threshold *of noise* beyond which there is silence— that is to say, beyond which sound becomes inaudible.[74] The ear may be able to hear it, but pays no attention to it. Memory lets it go, it leaves no trace. For the auditor, it never existed as sound, but only as silence. Such silence is sometimes called *background noise*.

Silence is thus always already sound, even as it is, simultaneously, the absolute limit of sound's disappearance. But if silence is always sonorous, if it is always noise, then, as Daniel Charles suggests, 'shouldn't we go all the way and posit *the identity* of silence and noise?'[75]

It is this identity of silence and noise that constitutes background noise, a sound that is already no longer presence, but which is not entirely absent; a noise that does not present itself to hearing because hearing ignores it. But if noise and silence can be conjoined and identified with each other on this ridgeline that is background noise, this does not mean that they are the same in regard to their symbolic, social, or sacred functions.

For example, the combined (ritual, religious, and social) functions of noise often consist in condemning or exorcising phenomena that threaten an established order, as is the

---

74.   We could take the example of musical silence, which, although it does not have an absolute existence, all the same has a certain pregnancy in so far as it is the absence of a musical motif, situated between that which precedes it and that which succeeds it. It is an entirely relative silence, but one which nonetheless functions as silence.

75.   D. Charles, *Gloses sur John Cage* (Paris: UGE, 1978), 65.

case with charivaris, or the clamour with which an eclipse is greeted.[76] The noise generated during a charivari served to denounce what were considered morally-dubious conjugal arrangements (marriage between spouses of overly disparate ages, remarriage of widowers, etc.). As for the uproar occasioned by an eclipse (a ritual which, according to Lévi-Strauss, is observed throughout the world), it aims to frighten off the animal or monster who is devouring the sun or moon. In both cases, noise testifies to the rupture of an established order. In these cases, the function of noise 'is to draw attention to an anomaly in the unfolding of a syntagmatic sequence'.[77]

But even when noise is functionalized, channelled, its becoming is not necessarily constrained by the social framework within which it appears; it can become an instrument of combat[78]—either literally, in the hands of a dominant power (as a psychological weapon), or in those of groups rising up against an established order.[79]

Noises and silences are always relative to a cultural context and to an artistic and/or political usage. They reflect various realities, all of which have a certain validity and pertinence, and carry a certain weight in the process of delimiting the area of sound. And yet noises and silences can sometimes be conflated

---

76.   C. Lévi-Strauss, *The Raw and the Cooked: Introduction to a Science of Mythology: I*, tr. J. and D. Weightman (London: Cape, 1970), 298–9.

77.   Ibid., 289.

78.   One of the latest innovations in non-lethal armaments is the LRAD (Long Range Acoustic Device), which uses ultrasound technology to project extremely loud sounds (beyond the threshold of pain and irreversible damage, generally thought to be 130 dB) within a quite narrow angle of delivery (around 30 degrees). It swiftly picked up the nickname 'sound cannon' or 'sonic bazooka'.

79.   Cf. *Noise and Capitalism* (Donostia and San Sebastian: Arteleku, 2009).

into an a-perceptual identity. In this case, they describe an accursed territory where noise serves only to engender silence:

> We [...] learn that the militants of the RAF [...] were, among other things, subjected to so called 'sensory deprivation' experiments. The subjects were placed in a cell transformed into an achromatic milieu and where all sounds were neutralized (through the device of white noise: the individual no longer hears anything, not even the sounds of his own body, the beating of the heart, breathing, grinding of teeth, etc.; their cries are inaudible). In the medium term, the result of the experiment is the death of the subject (the case of Holger Meins); in the short term, as one of the scientists responsible for the important progress obtained in this branch, Professor Jan Gross, discovered, 'this aspect [the possibility of influencing someone through isolation] can surely play a positive role in penology (the science of punishment), namely, when it is a matter of *re-educating* an individual or a group, and when the utilization of such a unilateral dependency and such manipulation may effectively influence the process of re-education.'[80]

This passage resonates strangely with Cage's experience, during which he heard the irreducible noises of his body. But whereas in that case absolute silence revealed, to he who listened, his character as a living organism, here noise engenders a total absence of perception whose effects are deadly. The irony is that it is by way of total noise[81] that one comes closest to a 'silence effect'. Here we discover a reversal of the role of noise, which, in Cage's experiment, revealed that the auditor was alive, but which, in the hands of disciplinary

---

80. J.-F. Lyotard, *Rudiments païens* (Paris: UGE, 1977), 125–6.

81. White noise 'fills' the totality of the audible spectrum.

torture, becomes an instrument of gagging, of deafness, of the saturation of hearing, and finally of death. The identity between noise and silence is obtained when background noise becomes an ogre.

History of Sound, Stories of Sound

But we cannot reduce the area of sound to a space in which sonorous avatars are magnetized around two poles, noise and silence (sometimes fused with one another). It also contains the clusters of values, beliefs, and conceptions that are articulated with sounds. Moreover, this area is not static, and these clusters change over time, and thus can become objects of study, elements for a history of sound. Indeed, Raymond Murray Schafer, in his research based on the notion of the 'soundscape', which he defines as 'an acoustic environment as a field of study',[82] speaks of a historical responsibility with regard to sounds. As well as writing a history of sounds based on literature, he formulates a programme for the conservation of sounds that are threatened with extinction, concentrating principally on those that are the specific signature of a space, and which he calls 'soundmarks':

> The term soundmark is derived from landmark and refers to a community sound which is unique or possesses qualities which make it specially regarded or noticed by the people in that community. Once a soundmark has been identified, it deserves to be protected, for soundmarks make the acoustic life of the community unique.[83]

82. R. Murray Schafer, *The Soundscape: Our Sonic Environment and the Tuning of the World* (Rochester, VM: Destiny Books, 1994), 7.

83. Ibid., 10.

For Schafer, the soundmark is a sound which, owing to its sin-gular character, becomes the *acoustic* signature of a territory which then becomes associated with it. Thus the soundmark is not an innocuous sound. It must be known and recognized by a community. It must have left a trace and must have precisely marked the place, making a territory of its space of appearing.

Each sound, then, once it becomes audible (once it leaves a trace) and forms a territory (makes a mark), can become the soundmark of a more or less virtual, more or less sensible territory. These are the soundmarks that Schafer proposes to catalogue and to conserve, mostly by way of textual sources (which in fact describe the usage of the sound more than its actual qualities), in order to develop a history of sound.

One might well wonder about an approach that seems unable to accept one of the principal characteristics of sound, its fugacity and its *vocation* of disappearance. This is the double-edged sword of a historicization of sound: it engen-ders a better knowledge of sonorous events, but becomes embroiled in problematics linked to the perenniality of sound when sound, precisely, is precarious.

What is more, in considering this we must better understand the term '[hi]story'[84] in its two aspects: at once as genealogy and as *fiction*, understood in Foucault's sense—that is to say, as the 'weaving of established relations, through the discourse itself, between he who speaks and that of which he speaks'.[85] It would be an illusion to think that the history of sound could be constructed on the basis of sounds themselves, since by

---

84. [The French word *histoire* can mean both 'history' and 'story'—trans.]

85. M. Foucault, 'L'arrière-fable', in *Dits et écrits, I: 1954–1975* (Paris: Gal-limard, 2001), 506.

their very essence they will have definitively disappeared. The history of sound as Schafer understands it is concocted from the traces that sounds have left behind, and from the imprints of them that have been produced. It is through these artefacts, these phantoms of sounds and their relics, that this historical fiction is elaborated. Schafer encourages recourse to rational and statistical methods of observation, analysis, and reportage. But the fact remains that taxonomy—and particularly the taxonomy of 'phantoms'—is always of the order of magical thought; as Lévi-Strauss says, '[c]lassifying, as opposed to not classifying, has a value of its own'.[86]

David Toop, on the contrary, is well aware that sounds fade away, and that a history of sound is possible only by means of traces. Thus he ventures into extra-sonorous artistic domains in search of mute traces that testify to the presence of sound. In his 'Notes toward a History of Listening', embracing the field of art as privileged territory of observation, Toop wonders about our relation to sound, and to a sound art that is homogenizing in its effects:

> What is sound art anyway? Is it simply a style, imprisoned by the precedence of existing work, or is it an open field, defined only by a focus on listening, or a prioritization of listening? The senses can never be separated out into discrete streams of data, so that all we can say about any art form in this respect is that it gravitates more towards one mode of perception than another. What interests me is the life of sound in silent media, its existence as an unspoken, unheard presence in media that produce no sounds that can be measured or felt as physical sensations. By using the

---

86. C. Lévi-Strauss, *The Savage Mind* (London: Weidenfeld and Nicolson, 1966), 9.

eyes as if they were ears, we can allow some air and light into the cramped discourse and confining definitions of sound work.[87]

Through this sketch, these 'notes', Toop exhibits sound's power of evocation and reaffirms the power of myth harboured by sensible traces, thereby arguing for the existence of an inextricable bond between sound and narration. The history of sound is the exhibition of sound's propensity to create (*hi*)*stories* plural, and the demonstration of its intrinsic narrativity. It is the affirmation that, on one hand, every sensible form is always, embryonically, a narrative form; and on the other hand, that all narrativity is always, embryonically, an evocation of the sensible. This is what Robert Walser seems to suggest, in the mouth of his Snowwhite, as he indicates the way in which sound enables an *opaque* narrativity. Refusing to look at her mother, the queen, embracing a hunter, Snowwhite declares to the prince:

No, *you* tell it. What do you see?
And I will gather from your lips
The picture's subtle lineaments.
When you depict it, I am sure,
You'll soothe the harshness of the view
With judgment wise and shrewd. Well? Start.
I'd like to hear instead of watching.[88]

---

87.   D. Toop, 'Notes toward a History of Listening', *Art Press 2*, *L'art des sons*, 15 (November 2009–January 2010), 13.

88.   R. Walser, 'Snowwhite', in *Robert Walser Rediscovered*, tr. W. Arndt (Hanover and London: University Press of New England, 1985), 109.

The narrativity of sound might owe to the peculiar role it plays in the enterprise of narrative, or more exactly the component intrinsic to sound that distinguishes it from any other narrative mode. This peculiarity, upon whose mercy Snowwhite throws herself, relates to the diffuse yet evocative character of sound, to a certain narrative opacity that Snowwhite, in her modesty, seeks to exploit. The history of sound and the narrativity proper to it are more than a mere oral modality of the story or tale. They mobilize the sensible in a very particular way, forming, on the basis of sound itself, a narrative regime that aims not at words, but beyond words, toward what TS Eliot called the auditory imagination, a meditation on sonorous reminiscences.[89]

More than simply the symbolic space across which sound travels, the area of sound is also constituted by the traces that sounds leave behind and the histories upon which they draw. The history of sound and its narrative power ultimately reveal that sounds are always linked to forms of belief, whether mythical or religious. They also demonstrate that this area only becomes constituted through relations between the audible and listening, and never outside of them. For it is these relations which, by way of that which is evoked by sound, form a definable area; and it is they that take precedence over the far too simplistic consideration of a sound in itself and for itself. Nonetheless the question of a *nature* of sound, in particular in terms of its supposed materiality, has been posed continually, during every epoch of its history.

89.　Cf. T. S. Eliot, *The Use of Poetry and the Use of Criticism* (Cambridge, MA: Harvard University Press, 1933).

Sonorous Matter

In 1799, or more exactly in the 16th Brumaire of Year VIII—so, more than a century after Huygens's discoveries had instigated the wave theory—Jean-Baptiste de Lamarck presented his *On the Matter of Sound* to the Institut National. Agreeing that sound is indeed produced by a shock, by an object's being set vibrating, and that this vibration is propagated from sound source to auditor, Lamarck observes nonetheless that sound is transmitted not only through the air but also through liquid and solid bodies. From this he deduces that air is not the fluid matter that is propagated when a sound is emitted, but that there exists a fluid proper to sound:

> The proposition amounts to suggesting that the matter peculiar to sound is not common air, but only the subtle and essentially elastic fluid that permeates the mass of the gaseous composite that constitutes this matter, since this same subtle fluid has the faculty of propagating without resistance through milieus more dense than itself the tremblings which the vibrations of sounding bodies cause within it, and of penetrating, in this state of agitation, all the way to the fleshy matter of our auditory nerve; which produces in us the sensation of sound.[90]

Lamarck calls this fluid *ethereal fire*.[91] Now, ether had survived since antique times, ceaselessly metamorphosizing into

---

90. J.-B. de Lamarck, 'Mémoire sur la matière du son', in *Journal de physique, de chimie et d'histoires naturelles* (Paris, 1799), 408.

91. 'Ethereal fire is a simple matter, fluid in essence, elastic and very compressible, of an extraordinary rarity and tenuity, invisible and even imperceptible to our senses, free, tranquil, naturally cold, and having the faculty to penetrate easily the masses of all bodies'. J.-B. de Lamarck, *Mémoires de physique et d'histoire naturelle*, first article 'du feu éthéré' (Paris, 1797), 136.

different forms. And in fact Lamarck's ethereal fire is quite close to Aristotle's theory of *pneuma*: it is a fluid implicated in the transmission of sound, but which, above and beyond this, animates beings with its heat, and whose substance is 'analogous to that which constitutes the stars, the celestial Ether, sidereal matter, [...] a body assuredly, but a body other than the four elements that we know of, and of a more divine nature'.[92] Just like the *pneuma* of the antique theories, Lamarck's 'ethereal fire' is 'the true matter that bears or forms sound'.[93]

This belief in the relation, or even identity, between sound and its fluid medium never really went away, its last explicit manifestation doubtless being Tesla's discoveries linking the myth of electromagnetic ether to radiophony. This materialist temptation to seek some substance proper to sound is an attempt to render its existence tangible and to legitimate hopes to channel it. And yet it is not strictly speaking an attempt at rationalization. On the contrary, it confers upon the phenomenon of sound all the mysteries and supposed powers of the ether. Tesla, picking up electromagnetic phenomena in the ionosphere, thought he could hear radio signals transmitted from other planets.[94]

Such a *myth of materiality* can also be found in the writings of architect Adolf Loos, in particular an article entitled 'The Mystery of Acoustics'.[95] Taking up arms against the destruction

---

92. A.-E. Chaignet, 'Le pneuma', in *Histoire de la psychologie des Grecs* (Paris: Hachette, 1887), 308.

93. Lamarck, *Mémoirs*, 'du feu éthéré', 136.

94. Cf. Sey, 'Sounds like...', 23–4.

95. A. Loos, 'The Mystery of Acoustics' [1912], in *On Architecture* (Riverside, CA: Ariadne Press, 2002), 193–5.

of Vienna's Bösendorfer Saal, Loos sets out his case by stating his convictions in terms of architectural acoustics. He claims that '[t]he acoustics of a hall does not depend on the spatial design, but on the materials'.[96] For, as he insists, sound gradually modifies the material of the concert hall, a little as a violin develops a fine patina, according to his own example; and these fine modifications progressively transform the acoustics of the place, rendering it absolutely unique. He adds that this acoustics is most fragile, and that playing 'bad' music in the hall could ruin it in a matter of a few days. This kind of reflection belongs more to magical thought than to any scientific discipline. For it speaks of the will to connect up diverse elements in order to return to a register of discourse founded uniquely upon an intuition or a belief. Which does not mean, as Lévi-Strauss has shown in regard to what he calls the 'science of the concrete', that such an assemblage is not possessed of a *certain* reason.[97]

In both Tesla and Loos we have a belief in an invisible communication between sound and matter, a communication that tries to extract sound from its immaterial and spectral condition, but which in fact ends up endowing it instead with an 'ectoplasmic' materiality. This sonorous 'material', in Loos and Tesla alike, ends up harbouring no less mystery than before.

This will to materialize the sonorous highlights the need to give it body—to give it *a* body, even. To give sound this body is to place it into matter, to put it in place, or rather, in milieu. This is the necessary prerequisite in order for sound to exist—that

---

96. Ibid., 193.

97. 'It may be objected that science of this kind can scarcely be of much practical effect. The answer to this is that its main purpose is not a practical one. It meets intellectual requirements rather than or instead of satisfying needs.' Lévi-Strauss, *The Savage Mind*, 9.

is, to be audible—but also in order for sound to make a mark and thus to make a territory of the place. So this body of sound would be the completion of the tracing of the sonorous, and the condition of its marking. It would be the pivotal point in the process of the solidification of sound which, by way of a cluster of values that characterizes it and a materiality that situates it, engenders a proper space for sound, a territory.

The body of sound—which is not a sonorous body, but instead sound as seen through its materiality, as the completion of the audibilizing of the sonorous and precursor to its being territorializing—thus fulfils the function of a 'place-holder'[98] of the incarnation of the audible within its milieu.

The relation of body to sound is always deduced from a simple corpuscular characterization of the sonorous, and is thus articulated around the sound-auditor relation, inscribing in the very listening body itself another 'place-holder' of the sonorous, the final destination of the audible. In every case, from the pneumatic theories to Lamarck's and Loos's intuitions, a body-to-body relation between sound and a receiver-auditor is implied, whether that auditor is human or not. With the theory of *pneuma*, we might even speak of a *body-in-body* relation whereby the sonorous substance infuses the very depths of the auditor and his or her organs.

It is this same relation that sometimes engenders a complete substitution of body by sound, albeit a mythical one. The case of Echo, whose existence, once her body has gone, is manifested only in the sound that she emits, or that of Marsyas, whose virtuosity on the flute cursed by Athena and

---

98. J.-L. Nancy, *Corpus*, tr. R. A. Rand (New York: Fordham University Press, 2008), 67.

the pride he takes in it literally cost him his skin,[99] testify to this bond, this transference between heard body and hearing body. These myths and intuitions draw attention to sound's natural predisposition to implicate bodies, whether through subtle incursions into the intimacy of listening, or through deep roars whose power sets the auditor's stomach resonating.

The embodiment of sound can however manifest itself outside of metaphorical, mythical figures, and even outside of audio-corporeal sensation. It can be actualized in a technical object. Through the tympanic techniques it introduced, Bell and Blake's ear phonautograph,[100] a hybrid bio-machinic construction, realizes and attests to this relation of transference between sound and body, replacing the latter in the very generation of sound. The audible is always stretched out between two bodies, the body that generates it and the body that absorbs it. So that there is indeed a becoming-body of sound, which is deployed on all of its strata of existence and at all the points of observation that encircle it—'a body [being] always ob-jected from without; to "me" or to another'.[101]

THE GRIP OF SOUND

Thus, before being the vehicle of signs, signals, or any semantic information whatsoever, sound bears within itself its own body, its own history, its own marks. It is through these, and not through the sound itself, that it is recognized, that one can know it and hear it—for hearing is always indexical.

---

99.   Marsyas is skinned alive by Apollo following his defeat by the latter in a musical duel. Cf. Ovid, *Metamorphoses*, Book IV, v.

100. Cf. Sterne, *The Audible Past*, 32.

101. Nancy, *Corpus*, 29.

Always, already, the fleeting character of sound, its intangibility and the spectral range of its appearing, from the hyper-intimacy of the 'internal' voice to the gigantic, frightful alterity of thunder, have indicated its excessive character. Excessive it is, in so far as there is no sonorous equivalent of total darkness, but only a penumbra. For as fleeting as it may be, sound is always present to our ear. And through its marks, its traces, its history, it always a *power of evocation*.

We should understand the area of sound, its milieu of existence, as the inescapable space of its possible appearing. This space is also defined by the fact that it is constituted entirely under the influence of sounds, in their grip.

Through a history or a body that we lend them, through the traces that they produce (and which produce them), sounds are constituted into a milieu in which they appear and are identified as such. This milieu, this audible world, is not infinite, though. It is a zone on the near and far side of which sounds are no longer heard and the sonorous no longer becomes audible, no longer achieving the necessary traction to leave a trace. Short of and beyond the audible world, the area of sound, there lies a sonorous limbo.

What lies within this perimeter, this bounded area, is itself fragmented into territories. The marking of sound become audible is the carving-up of the area into territories. Of course, territories can be superimposed on each other, and no delimitation can ever be strict and definitive. The configurations of territories are, as always, a question of authority.

2

APPREHENDING
SOUND

PERCEIVE, HEAR, LISTEN

Sound is not something self-sufficient and isolated within nature. It cannot *be* for itself. So *regardless of whether it is audible or not*, it is always coupled with a listening. The apprehension of sound is always articulated with the listening that corresponds to it, even if this listening is virtual. The reminiscence of sound, the evocation of a sonorous memory, always proceeds via the mobilization of a stance of re-listening. The convocation of sound invariably implies the presence, the possibility, of a listening. This coupling is not univocal, though; which means that we need to distinguish different ways in which listening can be used, different types of listening.

Plurivocal Listening

There is a certain tradition of thought that expresses an intuition as to the origins of hearing and its primordial purpose. This intuition links listening to survival and vigilance against danger. Thus Nietzsche explains the development of the auditory faculty in terms of the need to safeguard against threats, a need itself driven by fear:

> The ear, the organ of fear, could have evolved as greatly as it has only in the night and twilight of obscure caves and woods, in accordance with the mode of life of the age of timidity, that is to say the longest human age there has ever been [...].[102]

A century later, Roland Barthes reaffirms the entanglement of the act of listening with territorial logic. According to him, 'listening is that preliminary attention which permits intercepting

---

102. F. Nietzsche, *Daybreak: Thoughts on the Prejudices of Morality,* tr. M. Clark and B. Leiter (Cambridge: Cambridge University Press, 1997), 253.

whatever might disturb the territorial system; it is a mode of defense against surprise'.[103]

This relation between territory and listening is not unilateral, though. It is a complex, twofold relation. At the same time as listening awakens one's consciousness of the territory, one constitutes for oneself a territorial representation of that which is given to be heard. By virtue of listening, one perceives a territory; but at the same time, in the same moment, one constitutes that territory. It is this double movement whereby, in one and the same instant, the territory gives itself to be heard and listening aggregates the perceived sounds into a spatiotemporal continuity, into a territory, that constitutes the central node of the relation between the audible and the territory.

Primordial listening, the listening of fear, places itself at the centre of a sensory apparatus of survival. But it is only one mode of listening among others. Audition embraces sound in many different ways and, through the plurality of configurations that determine it, generates a vast complex for the denomination, definition, and delimitation of its various forms.

Indeed, numerous theories of listening have been formulated on the basis of a systematic division of audition into different modes. Barthes, for instance, tells us that '*hearing* is a physiological phenomenon: *listening* is a psychological act'.[104]

In proposing this separation, Barthes seeks to distinguish between two 'modes' of audition: brute perception, embodied in the faculty of hearing, and the intentionality of a listening that can only be defined in terms of a 'goal'. For Barthes, the

---

103.   R. Barthes, 'Listening', in *The Responsibility of Forms* [*L'obvie et l'obtus*], tr. R. Howard (New York: Hill and Wang, 1985), 245–60: 247.

104.   Ibid., 245.

existence of different types of goals implies the existence of different types of listening. He distinguishes between three of these: the first bearing upon *indices*, a primordial listening which he qualifies as 'alert'; a second focused on *signs* and which constitutes a 'decipherment'; and finally a third, 'psychoanalytical' listening, operating 'from unconscious to unconscious'.[105]

Furthermore, in opposing the 'phenomenon' of hearing to the 'act' of listening, Barthes characterizes the first as passive, the second as active. Jean-Luc Nancy, on the other hand, reverses this distinction between hearing and listening, making the distinction pivot on the question of 'meaningful' sense:

> If 'to hear' is to understand the sense (either in the figurative
> sense, or in the so-called proper sense: to hear a siren, a bird,
> or a drum is already each time to understand at least the rough
> outline of a situation, a context if not a text), to listen is to be
> straining toward a possible meaning, and consequently one that
> is not immediately accessible.[106]

The distinction between the two is ultimately a question of terminology and differences in regard to what falls under which term; but the intuition of a division between types of listening of different natures is a persistent one. We find it again in other typologies: in Pierre Schaeffer, for example, where it takes the form of a typology specifying four modes of listening:

---

105. Ibid., 252.

106. J.-L. Nancy, *Listening*, tr. C. Mandell (New York: Fordham University Press, 2007), 6.

1. I listen to what interests me.

2. Provided I am not deaf, I perceive aurally the sounds that go on around me, and this whatever my activities and interests are.

3. I hear in relation to what interests me, what I already know and what I seek to understand.

4. After hearing I understand what I was trying to understand, what I was listening for.[107]

Here we find the same opposition between active audition and passive audition that Barthes set out with the distinction between 'listening' and 'hearing'. In Schaeffer, the passive/active distinction operates between 'aurally perceiving' on one hand and 'hearing' or 'listening' on the other. Schaeffer places the identification of indices under 'listening', and confers objectivity upon it. He places the subjective acquisition of 'qualified perceptions' under the heading of 'hearing'. Finally, he calls 'understanding' the mode wherein sounds become signs, with the 'emergence of a sound content and *reference to, encounters with*, extra-sonorous concepts'.[108] In fact, by virtue of this, 'understanding' is common to all of the senses, and consequently cannot constitute a pole that is specific to listening.

If Schaeffer's structuralist approach has the merit of exhibiting the complexity and multiplicity of audition, his penchant for systematic organization has the drawback of creating hierarchies, or at least pecking orders, between the different modes of audition—although he does make it clear that the different modes of listening can be 'practis[ed] [...] in parallel'.[109]

---

107. P. Schaeffer, *Traité des objets musicaux* (Paris: Seuil, 1966), 113 [*Treatise on Musical Objects*, tr. C. North and J. Dack (Oakland, CA: University of California Press, forthcoming)].

108. Ibid., 97.

109. Ibid., 98.

Schaeffer's typology could be adapted to the concepts developed in this book: what we have called the sonorous belongs to the *unheard* (i.e., it falls short of what Schaeffer calls 'aurally perceived'—it is ungraspable sound); the audible, sound that leaves a trace, would be 'aurally perceived'. Listening or hearing, which qualifies the latter, would mark the onset of the audible, which henceforth would be territorialized. One might therefore define three stages in the apprehension of sound: *the unheard, the aurally perceived*, designating any sound that leaves a trace (to perceive is always to immediately remember having perceived); and *listening* or *hearing*, denoting any audible that is intelligible—that is to say, qualified, identified, and evaluated.

Despite the nuances that Schaeffer brings in, and the above attempt at reconciliation, it remains that his typological organization has the drawback of giving us a list of homogeneous functions, more or less combinable with each other, relating to audition and to its modes. The fact is that, even if we accept that these functions exist, that does not mean that they form a discrete network within which one might identify invariable saliencies and therefore defined modes of listening. Rather, they are archetypes of one and the same process, one emerging more than another depending upon the moods of audition, the sounds perceived, the degree of attention (which ultimately is not just a seesaw between active and passive), and any other contextual variable that could potentially exert an influence on perceived or perceiver.

A typical passage from the sonorous to the audible (from the unheard to the aurally perceived and thence to the heard) that illustrates the continuous, gradual character of auditory perception is found in the case of sonorous reminiscence: when a sound which we *did not hear* comes back to us in memory a few moments later. The sound has well and truly been picked up by the perceptual apparatus, but is at first not manifested to the consciousness of the auditor, remaining unheard. It is only later, for some reason or another, that it presents itself to the auditor, who then *hears it* a posteriori. In this case, there is no change in the mode of listening, but only the emergence of a full perception that had at first been ignored, unheard.

Listening therefore should not be defined by and divided into functional modes. It interfaces with that which is perceived according to a plurivocal relation which depends on the context of appearance of the *given-to-be-heard*. Listening is always listening *to* something; and this is always a function of a given situation. It should not be considered as if it were strictly autonomous.

Listening necessarily concerns both that which is perceived (the given-to-be-heard) and the one who perceives it (the auditor)—meaning that all listening is the occasion for, or the activation of, a reflexive process in he or she who always lies at the origin of listening: the auditor.

Being-Listening

In *Listening*, Jean-Luc Nancy poses the following question: 'What does *to be* listening, *to be* all ears, as one would say "to be in the world," mean?'[110] The first element of his response will be that 'to be listening will always [...] be to be straining toward or in an approach to the self'.[111] This stance of listening reveals the auditor to herself as *being listening*, thus bringing into play a conscious grasp of being in the world in its audible dimension,

---

110.   Nancy, *Listening*, 5.

111.   Ibid., 9.

even though she also feels herself to be constituted by this same audible world.

This is the twofold virtue, and the twofold danger, of a listening that is turned both toward the exterior, the given-to-be-heard, and toward the interior, being-listening. In fact, only *auditor zero* could find himself in such a simple and definitive perceptual configuration. There are interdependencies everywhere and transfers of all sorts are omnipresent. However, this auditor zero, in so far as it is a decontextualized, desocialized figure with no history and doubtless no future, makes an interesting model with which to represent a stance of listening that is stripped bare, abstract, a simple thread stretched out between an auditor and that which his or her perception intends.

It is on the basis of this image, this auditor zero, that we can figure being-listening as a pure stance, entirely *intending towards*. Such an approach implies a consciousness of being constantly *in* sound. Such an 'immersive' conception of the perception of the sonorous is also to be found in the contemporary notion of the *soundscape*. But in fact this stance of listening bound up with a consciousness of being constantly immersed in the sonorous allows us to construct a more profound conception of the soundscape. For the soundscape appears to be the phenomenal field of appearing that orients listening toward an intersubjective dimension:

> [T]he sonorous place, space and place—and taking place—*as* sonority, is not a place where the subject comes to make himself heard [...]; on the contrary, it is a place that becomes a subject insofar as sound resounds there [...].[112]

112. Ibid., 17

Thus being-listening, conscious of the audible world that surrounds it, does indeed fabricate a relation between subjects, one listening and the other resonating. So that the sonorous landscape, the soundscape, can be understood as the time-space that unifies all the sounds that present themselves to listening in a given moment and a given place.

This intersubjective rapport, founded on the pivot point inside/outside, as well as *identifying* a uniform sonorous via a sensible, audible appropriation of the world through which one is moving, at the same time finds the listener concentrated as close as possible to his sense and to the organ dedicated to it: the ear. If we are to believe Barthes, it is listening itself, with the assistance of the ear, that implies a *clarification* of the relation between self and world:

> Morphologically, on the species level, the ear seems made for this capture of the fleeting index: it is motionless, fixed, poised like that of an animal on the alert; like a funnel leading to the interior, it receives the greatest possible number of impressions and channels them toward a supervisory center of selection and decision; the folds and detours of its shell seem eager to multiply the individual's contact with the world yet to reduce this very multiplicity by submitting it to a filtering trajectory; for it is essential—and this is the role of such initial listening—that what was confused and undifferentiated become distinct and pertinent—that all nature assume the special form of danger or prey; listening is the very operation of this metamorphosis.[113]

This tendency to argue for a *clarifying listening* sees the soundscape as emerging, in the crystallization of the auditor

---

113.   Barthes, 'Listening', 248.

qua being-listening, as an object of knowledge, and thus follows in the wake of the anatomist and acoustic approaches, whose aim is the acquisition and production of knowledge about the ear and the perception of sound. Although this tradition is as old as humanity itself, it remains alive to this day, and, from Alcmaeon of Croton to the biomechanical project of Bell and Blake, via Gabriele Fallopio, there is a persistent will to comprehend the auditory sense by isolating it and concretizing it around its organ. Peter Szendy, working on the notion of listening in its most intimate dimension, in terms of the personal mythologies that it can generate, evokes the possibility of an organology of listening, emphasizing that 'in this new *organology of our ears*, it becomes more difficult than ever to distinguish between the organ and the instrument'.[114] This 'instrumentizing' of listening resonates with what Bell and Blake accomplished in a clinically literal manner: that is to say, the 'instantiation' of listening, in its organic modality, in a biotechnical circulation where organs and prostheses (phonographs, tape recorders, etc.) are intertwined and together contribute to the modification of the perceptual, auditory system, and that of modes of listening themselves.

In all of these approaches, the necessary recourse to the intimate and to the isolation of listening seems to contribute to the same objective: the pacification of the relation between sensation, its organ, and the sensible world that is destined for it. This path may seem salutary in so far as, in ploughing the furrow of the audible, it generates knowledge by turns objective and subjective, technical and affective, and reveals and authorizes new possibilities for listening, new modalities, or opens the door to a new type of listening. However it also poses

---

114.   P. Szendy, *Écoute. Une histoire de nos oreilles* (Paris: Minuit, 2001), 163.

a risk, one that Merleau-Ponty identifies in his *Phenomenology of Perception* as that of isolation:

> Synesthetic perception is the rule and, if we do not notice it, this is because scientific knowledge displaces experience and we have unlearned seeing, hearing, and sensing in general in order to deduce what we ought to see, hear, or sense from our bodily organization and from the world as it is conceived by the physicist.[115]

Merleau-Ponty denounces an isolation of the senses that deprives them of each other through the action of an ideology and a specific regime of discourse: scientific discourse. To this discourse he opposes an apprehension of the sensible, and in particular of auditory perception, by way of his own experience of listening, observing the sensible transfers for which it can be responsible:

> [...] I hear the hardness and the unevenness of the cobblestones in the sound of a car, and we are right to speak of a 'soft,' 'dull,' or 'dry' sound. Even if one might doubt that auditory perception gives us genuine 'things,' it is at least certain that, beyond mere sounds in space, it offers us something that literally 'sounds,' and thereby it communicates with the other senses.[116]

The audible tells us things, evokes, and *makes us feel* something beyond the sonorous. It contributes to a more general apprehension. Michel Thévoz, a careful reader of

---

115. M. Merleau-Ponty, *Phenomenology of Perception*, tr. D. A. Landes (London and New York: Routledge, 2012), 238.

116. Ibid., 239 [translation modified].

Merleau-Ponty, sums it up in this elegant formula: 'To hear is always to overflow the register of auditory perception'.[117]

Now, if listening overflows auditory perception, it remains to determine the very nature of that which persistently presents itself as proper to the domain of audition, that is to say its inalienable object: sound. What is revealed by the twofold tension we have described, where hearing is at once turned toward the intimacy of being-listening and toward the sensible environment that envelops it, are two possible becomings of the nature of sound: a becoming-phenomenon and a becoming-event.

THE NATURE OF SOUND: PHENOMENON VS. EVENT

The Phenomenological Approach

What do we mean by phenomenology? If phenomenology is the 'study of "phenomena", that is to say (of) that which appears to consciousness, of that which is given,'[118] then a phenomenological approach to sound would aim to determine its nature on the basis of or in terms of the way in which it presents itself, gives itself to the 'consciousness' of the auditor.[119] According to the phenomenological approach, the question of sound can only be broached in so far as sound presents itself to consciousness and in so far as the auditor experiences it. Merleau-Ponty states however that

---

117.   M. Thévoz, *Le Miroir infidèle* (Paris: Minuit, 1996), 120.

118.   J.-F. Lyotard, *La Phénoménologie* (Paris: PUF, 1954), 7.

119.   'Consciousness is always consciousness of, and there is no object that would not be an object for.' Ibid., 43.

[t]he subject of sensation is neither a thinker who notices a quality, nor an inert milieu that would be affected or modified by it; the subject of sensation is a power that is born together with a certain existential milieu that is synchronized with it.[120]

This impersonal nature of the perceiving subject is assumed by phenomenology when it negates the divided relation between subject and external world. The phenomenological subject is not closed up in its interiority; it is a worldly subject:

The world is not an object whose law of constitution I have in my possession; it is the natural milieu and the field of all my thoughts and of all my explicit perceptions. Truth does not merely 'dwell' in the 'inner man'; or rather, there is no 'inner man,' man is in and toward the world, and it is in the world that he knows himself.[121]

This statement aims to rule out both the Augustinian thesis of truth through interiority and the thesis of the a priori existence of a world.[122] The suspension of the thesis of the world and its reduction (*epoché*) to a field of experience or to a 'phenomenon of existence' makes of sound a phenomenal object—that is to say, an object fundamentally taken up in a relation with, and constituted by, an *address*. Faced with the well-known enigma 'Does a tree falling in a forest make a sound if no one is there to hear it?', phenomenological reasoning would respond as follows: 'If every object is an object *for*, there could never be a sound that could not be perceived, in

---

120.   Merleau-Ponty, *Phenomenology of Perception*, 219.

121.   Ibid., lxxiv.

122.   'It is not a matter of knowledge if we perceive the real as it is [...] precisely because the real is that which we perceive.' Lyotard, *La Phénoménologie*, 58.

the sense that it only becomes sound because a subject perceives it. Therefore, not only can the tree not make a sound for no one, and therefore *does not do so*; but what is more, such a thought-experiment, *simulating* the absence of a presence, postulates a *constituted* world—something to which phenomenology cannot subscribe, sound qua intended being nothing but the object of the intentionality of the perceiving, *constituting* subject.'

So this approach does indeed assign a 'nature' to sound, a nature of a phenomenal order, sound only being sound from the moment when it appears in the phenomenal field of an auditor, that is to say once it is intended by that auditor (in so far as the latter has a consciousness, that is to say an intentionality). According to phenomenology, the deep nature of sound is to be a *given-to-be-heard*.

The Evental Approach

Roberto Casati and Jérôme Dokic initially put the evental theory forward in a work entitled *The Philosophy of Sound*.[123] Posing the question of the nature of sound, the authors inspect and revise the traditional beliefs and classical theories on the subject. They claim that sound is a quality that belongs not to an object, but to an event:

> Following the thesis that we wish to defend, sounds *are* events.
> [...] We propose here to identify sounds with *events in the resonant object*; this identification constitutes our Evental Theory.
> At this stage, the crucial point is not to determine whether these events are themselves of a wavelike nature, but to recognise that

123. R. Casati, J. Dokic, *La Philosophie du son* (Nîmes: Chambon, 1994). Translated as *Philosophy of Sound*, <http://jeannicod.ccsd.cnrs.fr/ijn_00420036>.

sounds are firstly concerned with the spatial region occupied by the resonant object, even if there must be in most cases a participation of the environmental milieu in order for us to be able to receive perceptual information about the sound.[124]

In this approach, two strong postulates are opposed respectively to the traditional intuitions that would assimilate sound to a quality and to the classical physicalist theory that would assimilate sound to a wave front moving from sonorous source to auditor. For Casati and Dokic, sound is primarily a localized vibratory event that is not propagated. Where the classical theory identifies sound with the sound wave, the evental theory identifies it with the vibratory event produced by the sounding object, and circumscribes it strictly to this event alone. The direct consequence of this theory is a breaking of the articulation between the generating event (the sound) and that which is given to be heard. In the evental theory, sound is no longer necessarily an *audibilis*.

Taking up the example of synaesthesia, where a sound induces non-audible sensory responses, or those of ultra- and infrasound, where the sonorous event generates waves outside of the frequency response of human audition, Casati and Dokic argue that the sonorous event is independent of any perception we might have of it. Audition may necessarily be provoked by a sound, but this in itself does not define the limits of its existence. Thus, to the same question of whether the tree in the forest makes a sound when it falls if there is no one there to hear it, the evental physicalist theory responds that sounds will be produced, that sound waves resulting from these events will be propagated, and that therefore sounds will be present, even if they remain inaudible, or rather audible by no one.

---

124. Ibid., 38–44.

When there is audition, though, the evental theory assures us that it is indeed the sound itself that is heard, and not the propagation of sound. What we hear is indeed a vibratory event as it is produced, even if it is perceived via the sound waves that propagate it. Just as colour belongs to an object and, when light is present, permits the transmission of information concerning it, so each sound belongs to a vibratory event (and is identified with it) and, given an adequate medium, permits the propagation of wave information concerning it.

In virtue of these observations, Casati and Dokic feel justified in giving the following example:

> [I]n the framework of the Evental Theory, it is possible (but not obligatory) to maintain that the thunder and the lightning are one and the same event. We say 'lightning' to describe the visual aspect of it, the word 'thunder' to describe the audible aspect.[125]

Quite contrary to the exceptional status granted to sound in theories of the soundscape, the evental approach reduces it so radically to a factual event that it seems impossible to find in it any specificity that is *in essence* sonorous.

Phenomenon vs. Event

The principal opposition that arises between phenomenological and evental approaches resides in the very conception of sound. This opposition translates into a divergence in the definition of the appearing of sound. For phenomenology, sound appears—that is to say exists—from the moment when it is targeted by the intentionality of the auditor. It only becomes

---

125. Ibid., 59.

sound through and for some audition. Sound is assimilated to sensation. For the evental theory, sound appears as soon as its event takes place. It exists for and in itself, independently of its sensible address and of any auditor who may perceive it.

Each of the two approaches mounts a critique of the other's theoretical inaudibility: the evental theory critiques the phenomenological approach for its qualitative conception of sound, reproaching it for its subjectivism and its 'counterintuitive consequences',[126] namely that 'two people can never hear the same sound'[127] since sound is essentially subjective. As for phenomenology, it can turn the critique around by showing that since, for the evental theory, a sound is strictly localized to the resonating object, then it is not the sound that one hears, but its *consequences* in *the propagation of waves* which, being deployed in a certain medium, will undergo distortions, however minimal, and will be perceived in as many different manners as there are different auditors. The sound itself, since it is strictly circumscribed to its point of appearing, a point inaccessible to the ear, remains unperceived.

Another critical point raised by phenomenology against the evental theory concerns the very possibility of the existence of sound in itself. For such a theory 'skips over' a question that is fundamental in phenomenology: the existence of the world. The 'natural' attitude that phenomenology questions and critiques consists in accepting the world a priori as existent, whereas phenomenology submits it to a sort of 'examination of conscience'. Since our experience of the world is always based on our perception of it—a necessarily subjective perception—

126.   Ibid., 38.

127.   Ibid.

what phenomenology contests is ultimately the possibility of founding any knowledge *in abstracto*.

It thus appears that the opposition between the evental theory and the phenomenological approach is more a divergence of focus than a descriptive disagreement, in the sense that it concerns the nature of sound *in so far as this nature interfaces with the system of thought in the context of which it emerges*. The physicalist approach is bound to circumscribe the nature of sound as closely as possible to its objective character as an event. On the contrary, phenomenology defines the essence of sound as exactly as possible in terms of the experience that one has of it, that is to say in terms of its sensory modalities.

However, the question of the nature of sound need not be condemned to languish in the balance between a sensation-sound and an event-sound. Another approach does seem possible. It would not attempt to homogenize the two, nor take a relativist stance in regard to them. On the contrary, although an enterprise of deconstruction, it would seek to be constructive. For it seeks to construct and to define the nature of sound without necessarily equating the idea of nature with that of identity (a 'homogenist' approach). This approach, albeit a sort of middle way between physicalism and phenomenology, is not the path of resemblance or of reconciliation. On the contrary, it is the way that consists in assuming their irreconcilable separation. It is the 'schizological' approach.

THE RANGE OF SOUND

The Schizological Approach

By 'schizological' we should understand not so much a reference to Deleuze as a neologism conceived on an etymological basis.

The postulate of such an approach is that the nature of something can be considered not qua unity but qua unsynthesizable multiplicity. From this point of view, sound is considered to be, *by nature*, a *disparate*, since it is, fundamentally, a *separate*.

In this it is opposed to both physicalist and phenomenological approaches, each of which defines, in its own manner, a unitary pole that is designated as *sound* (the event on one hand, the phenomenal object on the other). But the intention of a schizological approach is not to assume the coexistence of different frameworks of focalization of a sound-object, nor to establish a 'cubist' representation of the nature of sound, whose unitary face would be a function of the relativity of perspectives and of the point of view adopted. Rather, the schizological path assumes that these perspectives cannot be reconciled, and takes account of the inherently heterogeneous and divided nature of sound.

This divergence between a unitary nature on one side and a fragmented 'nature' on the other calls for a re-examination of the physicalist and phenomenological theories from the schizological point of view. Now, if the reservations it harbours in regard to a phenomenology of sound are close to those voiced by the evental theory (in particular, the reduction of sound to its phenomenal qualities), schizology also considers the latter to be vulnerable to various objections.

In the evental approach, a sound is localized and is not equated with the wave fronts that it brings about. A sound does not move unless the emitting source, the resonating object, is itself moving. There is no such property as the provenance of a sound, and therefore sounds are not propagated.

By neglecting the role of the propagation of sound in its milieu, the evental theory distances itself from what constitutes the very experience of a sound. This means that the evental theory cannot consider echoes, Doppler effects,[128] or more simply resonances and reverberations of all types to be sounds, but only '*informational perturbation*[*s*] which *depend* on facts relating to the milieu'.[129] Although the schizological approach admits that such effects are not sonorous events and cannot in themselves be considered to be sounds, it defends the claim that these effects modify *the sound itself*. Qua separated, the sound is located both where the vibratory event appears, and where the *propagated consequences* of this event appear—so all modifications in propagation must be considered to be constitutive of the sound itself.

According to the evental logic, every vibratory event can be qualified as a sound; yet it is not so easy to attach every sound to a vibratory event. In limit cases such as that of the sound of the sea or the rumbling of thunder, it is impossible to determine locally 'the sonorous event in the resonant object'. In such cases it is counterintuitive to represent the sound one is experiencing as the summation of a multitude of molecules of water. The sea exists qua sea; it generates another order of reality and is subject to diverse influences as an extended entity (that of the moon on the tides, for example), and not simply as a summation of localized individual atoms.

The other objection that schizology could make to the evental theory goes to the very roots of the identity between sound and sonorous event. Addressing the question of how

---

128.   The Doppler effect is the frequential lag of a wave between emission and reception owing to a variation in distance, at the time of audition, between sonorous source and auditor. The well-known example is that of the change in pitch of the sound of ambulance sirens as they pass by.

129.   Casati and Dokic, *La Philosophie du son*, 51.

we know 'when there is sound', Casati and Dokic take the example of a tuning fork placed in a vacuum:

> A tuning fork vibrates in a jar emptied of air. We introduce air into the jar, and then we take it away again; the sound only begins when there is air in the jar, and stops when there is no more air. But can we say that the tuning fork *itself* begins to resonate and then stops resonating, depending on whether we introduce the air or not?[130]

A schizological approach, a logic of the separated, would be inclined to respond that the tuning fork will only resonate *effectively* in the presence of air. When it is deprived of air, it continues to vibrate in a register of frequency compatible with human hearing, but this vibration will not be propagated and, in the absence of any medium, will not be even potentially audible. In which case the tuning fork does not resonate; it vibrates. This is how we distinguish the sonorous event from sound itself. An infra- or ultrasonic vibratory event is not *physically* distinct from an event that we might qualify as sonorous. And yet the difference is fundamental: one is perceptible, even if only potentially, by the human ear; the other is not. We must therefore be able to discriminate between them: and indeed *sound is this discriminatory notion*.

Ultimately a sound is a sound above all because it is possible that it could be heard. Taking a nominalist approach, we can deduce from this that the terms 'ultrasound' and 'infrasound' were invented precisely to designate events of the same nature as sound, but exceeding sound's field of influence in one direction or the other—indicating in the same gesture

---

130. Ibid., 42.

a central space where the notion of sound is instantiated and dephased. In which case, the field of sound is above all perceptual—it corresponds to the frequency band of human audibility. If there is a near and far side of sound, corresponding to criteria determined relative to the median human perception, it is indeed because the term 'sound' was itself informed by the existence of this perceptual gamut.

Through a rigorous exposition the physicalist approach tries to capture the concept of sound and to bring it into its fold, even though there is already a term that designates quite adequately the phenomenon it addresses, independently of any perceptual connotation: vibration.

The schizological approach locates sound at the meeting point of a vibratory event, a potential audible, and an auditor. A sound cannot do without either one of these terms. We introduced above the distinction between the sonorous and the audible. Although the sonorous may be raw and unheard, we nonetheless have a sensible experience of it. This experience may fail to appear to perception and to intellection, but is nonetheless the object of a retention (think back to the example of reminiscence). With these considerations in mind, schizology holds open a space where sound can shift between perceived and unperceived. This requires that we distinguish between inaudible vibratory events which, in themselves, are impossible to perceive (ultrasonic events, for example) and sounds that are not perceived even though they are potentially perceptible.

On the other hand, the schizological objective is not to reduce sound to a physical-phenomenal composite object. It is rather a matter of considering sound under its twofold aspect of phenomenon and event without ever attempting a synthesis of the two. Sound must be considered as a ubiquitous entity located both in the physical generation of a phenomenon, in its propagation, and in its reception. It is this simultaneous multiplicity of its appearing, not its reducibility to one thing or another, that makes for the richness and the mystery of sound. Sound is irreducible and its nature can only be a nature separated from itself. Rather than a nature of sound, there is a *range* of sound.

Deployment

Most of the time, listening and sound are represented under the auspices of a dualist regime that distributes them according to the axes of transmitter-receiver or object-subject. Indeed, the evental and phenomenological theories, each in their own way, describe a *sound-object* integrated into such a regime. Now, 'the attributes "subject" and "object", "represented" and "representing", "thing" and "thought" mean [...] a practical distinction of the utmost importance, but a distinction which is of a FUNCTIONAL order only, and not at all ontological as understood by classical dualism.'[131] Schizology, assuming the multiplicity and ubiquity of that which *makes sound*, redistributes or reallocates these functions within a heterogeneous regime where the separate has as much of a place as the integrated. What is designated here by 'sound' is not considered as a polar function, but as a range, a thickness, or a deployment.

This deployment extends from the event to the phenomenal object, between pure affectivity and pure appearing, the bounds that delimit the space of sonorous reality. Thus it no longer seems so decisively important to define a homogeneous nature of sound. A deaf person may not hear a sound but can

---

131. W. James, *Essays in Radical Empiricism* (Cambridge, MA: Harvard University Press, 1976).

sometimes feel it (as the body resonates), which makes a case for an extra-audible existence of sound (a thesis defended by physicalism). A victim of tinnitus or someone subject to sonorous hallucinations (acousma) will hear sounds that have as their origin no 'event in the resonant object', but which are no less appreciable for the unfortunate auditor. The reality of the sonorous encompasses these extrema of auditory experience, ranging from the experience of the vibratory to perceptual auto-generation.

Sonorous illusions and 'peri-sonorous' vibratory events are so many demonstrations that a comprehension and a global account of sound cannot be accepted, either to the detriment of the actuality of sound (i.e., affirming that sound is *only* produced 'in the head' of the auditor, and therefore that it is *I* who produce the sound) or to the detriment of sound as perceived phenomenon (i.e., affirming that the subject and the milieu play no role in the perceptual 'becoming' of the sonorous event). The perception of sound is thus an empire with two faces, one turned toward the interior, the other toward the exterior. The fact that these two faces communicate does not *necessarily* imply a change of nature in that which belongs to one or the other. The two faces remain separate; they do not fuse into one another.

What the regimes of phenomenology and physicalism contest is an entire relation to the world, a way of determining that which is in-itself and that which is outside, that which ex-ists. But listening to a sound always supposes an internal-external interfacing, a space of synchronization between object and perception that exceeds any simple dualism:

> Each time that I experience a sensation, I experience that it does
> not concern my own being—the one for which I am responsible

and upon which I decide—but rather another self that has already sided with the world, that is already open to certain of its aspects and synchronized with them.[132]

This interfacing is thus of a prepersonal nature. In this sense, it exceeds the subject-object distinction. This prepersonal character testifies to a structural unknowability of that which is perceived by the subject:

> Between my sensation and myself, there is always the thickness of an originary acquisition that prevents my experience from being clear for itself.[133]

If there is indeed a 'prepersonal' which, in perceiving, synchronizes itself to the world, there is always a 'thickness' that ultimately prevents the subject from 'becoming conscious' of it. We could define this thickness as the space where synchronization is impossible, or as asynchronous space. Asynchronous because it is in constant and unstable desynchronization with the fragmentation of 'sensory selves', each the subject of a sensation which 'begins and ends with it'. Asynchronous space: the space of the indecipherability of the self by the world and of the world by the self, the thickness of a frontier between personal space and the prepersonal space that is synchronized with the world.

Asynchronous space is therefore the 'enharmonic' wake (effective, but impalpable) that cannot but be a space in becoming, even while being pure *schizz*, ceaselessly marking the gap between *ipse* and this self stretching out toward the

---

132. Merleau-Ponty, *Phenomenology of Perception*, 224.

133. Ibid.

world, tirelessly shifting like a haunted shadow, concealing itself at all costs.

Strategies for dealing with this state of affairs that presides over internal-external interfacing in perception divide into two major tendencies: one seeks to establish a structure of thought that parcels out the functions and roles of each in the process of interfacing, making of experience one of these functions and integrating the emission-transmission-reception paradigm into a veritable mechanics of perception; while the other, placing experience at the centre of the interfacing, accepts that this means living with irreconcilable residues, at the risk of losing one's bearings in the interfacing, at the risk of a dissolution of the subject-object frontier and an abandonment of the subject in favour of a *molecularized* 'being-in-the-world'.

These two major tendencies find a resonance in the following texts:

> But now on the sea, 'the ear cannot be filled with hearing,' the boat rides ever new waves, and an 'equal thirst takes hold of me.' I may plunge into it, feel a wave across my body, but where I am the sea is not. If I want to go where the water is and have it, the waves make way before the swimming man. I may drink in the saltiness, exult like a porpoise, drown myself, but I still won't possess the sea: I am alone and distinct in its midst.[134]

> As he swam, he pursued a sort of revery in which he fused into himself with the sea. The intoxication of leaving himself, of slipping into the void, of dispersing himself in the thought of water, made him forget every discomfort. And even when this

---

134. C. Michelstaedter, 'On Persuasion', in *Persuasion and Rhetoric* [1910], tr. R. S. Valentino (Cambridge, MA: Harvard University Press, 2004), 10.

ideal sea which he was becoming ever more intimately had in turn become the real sea, in which he was virtually drowned, he was not moved as he should have been: of course, there was something intolerable about swimming this way, aimlessly, with a body which was of no use to him beyond thinking that he was swimming, but he also experienced a sense of relief, as if he had finally discovered the key to the situation, and, as far as he was concerned, it all came down to continuing his endless journey, with an absence of organism in an absence of sea.[135]

In Michelstaedter, it is the impossibility of becoming one with the world, which he identifies with an accession to truth—the impossibility, therefore, of being *persuaded*—that presides over his relation to this same world. There he remains, 'alone and distinct'. For some this feeling of solitude, this experience of an individuality impermeable to the world that surrounds it, may imply a will to the *decryption* of the world, an explanatory approach. This was not the case for Michelstaedter, who, suspecting such enterprises, supported by *rhetoric*, as being a game of dupes and an illusory consolation, and presenting them as such, made the choice to confront the *true* impossibility of being in the world, and ended up taking a pistol to his head.

In Michelstaedter there is a constant dual relation between the individual and the world that he cannot possess. Such a meagre and unsatisfying realization, according to Michelstaedter, can only be of consolation through the artifice of a blinkered system, and through the establishing of narcotic discourses.

---

135. M. Blanchot, *Thomas the Obscure*, tr. R. Lamberton (New York: Station Hill Press, 1988), 8.

In Blanchot's text, the frontier between the world and the individual, between the personal and the prepersonal, begins to give way on the occasion of 'a sort of revery'—that is to say, upon the relaxation of *reason*. The individual no longer seeks to possess the world, it is the world that possesses him and destitutes him of himself. This is the experience, the affective experience, that then becomes central to the establishing of an immersive relation to the world, a dynamic and disseminatory relation.

PERCEPTION-CONTINENT

The sonorous field, whether considered as a phenomenal field or as a constellation of sonorous events interlacing and agglomerating around listening, accords well with the image of an ocean of sounds. Two attitudes, one tending toward the expression and structuration of the internal-external difference, the other, on the contrary, toward its dissolution, play a fundamental role in the clarification and determination of listening. Cartography of the sonorous field by the individual, or molecularization of the individual within that field: here is the alternative which any consideration of our relation to sound must face up to, an alternative whose resolution must in a certain sense, in every case, be a preliminary to any *intentionality of listening*.

Listening is always deployed through strategies of listening. As Casati and Dokic note, 'the audition of sounds cannot be reduced either to the thinking of sounds, nor to the formation of beliefs concerning them'.[136] Apprehending sound is a disparate enterprise; in apprehending sound oneself and one's

---

136. Casati and Dokic, *La Philosophie du son*, 20.

perception are like a continent bordered on every side by the ocean, perceptual multiplicity against perceived multiplicity.

3

FORM AND *VOICE* OF SOUND

From Sensible Object to Sound Object

A sound object is not a given object. We cannot suppose it to already be there. 'The object,' Jean Oury tells us, 'is first and foremost that which we encounter. It is an "event". The object, in the traditional sense, is the combination of this encounter (*tugkanon*) and the sayable (*lekton*)'.[137] What remains, then, is to understand how sound can—and *must*—become an object, and why. Equally, it remains to be determined how it becomes *objectum*, throwing itself before perception so as to become audible. None of this goes without saying. However, Aristotle already postulates the object as being indispensable to sensible perception, envisaging it as essentially external to the perceiving individual.

In Aristotle, the sensible object gives itself to be perceived—that is to say, delivers itself in act to the senses. Sensation appears when a sensible object 'imprints' with its quality the sense to which it corresponds. Aristotle uses the analogy of the imprint of a ring pressed into wax which takes on its form without there being any transfer of matter, and without the metal being assimilated into the wax. The sensible object is considered to be the mediating element that translates a sensible quality for a given sense. This is what Aristotle means when he says that 'to smell an scent is to have a sensation of it, but the air, at the moment when it undergoes the action of what is odorous, then becomes a sensible object'.[138]

---

137.   J. Oury, 'L'objet chez Lacan', <www.revue-institutions.com/articles/oury_objetlacan.pdf>.

138.   Aristotle, *Of the Soul*.

Thus the air is constituted as a sensible object when it is permeated with the odorizing quality of the object that emits the scent. The place of the sensible object is therefore twofold: it is comprised both in the medium permeated with the sensible quality and in the emitting object. This confusion becomes even more marked when Aristotle talks about the sonorous object. Faithful to a 'post-pneumatic' approach to audition, he emphasizes the fundamental role of the air in the diffusion and the auricular perception of sound. We might expect that the sensible object proper to the ear—that is to say, the sonorous object—would be formed when the air was set in motion, as was the case for odours. But Aristotle defines the sonorous object from a physico-causal point of view:

> Thus a sonorous object is one that is capable of exciting motion
> in a mass of air continuously one as far as the ear.[139]

Here the sonorous object is indeed above all the 'resonant' object, that is to say the object that provokes the sound and instigates vibration. This amalgamation of the source of the sensation and the element that imprints itself on the corresponding senses testifies to Aristotle's tendency to discretize sensible experience.

Although the Aristotelian theory is ambiguous as to the twofold status of the perceived object (designating both the emitting object and the medium responsible for sensible transmission), it nevertheless does posit the mechanism of perception as a discrete dual relation in which the sense is articulated in terms of both its organ and the sensible object, circumventing the vexed question of the medium (air, for

139. Ibid.

example) by conferring upon it, along with the sensible qualities of the emitting object, the status of object for itself. What this reveals, once again, is the twofold reality of sound, as reflected in the concept of the sound object as at once physical and intentional object.

Pierre Schaeffer is the first to have conceptualized the sound object as a purely intentional object as opposed to the physical object, the emitter-object. Michel Chion defines this Schaefferian sound object as

> any sound phenomenon or event perceived as a whole, a coherent entity, and heard by means of a *reduced listening* which targets it for itself, independently of its origin or meaning.[140]

But the object, as we have said, is not given. It must, at some moment or other, appear and present itself as such to perception. Chion understands the object as a 'coherent entity', but he does ask how this coherence is distinguished within and extracted from the phenomenal field, from a sonorous field. In an alpine metaphor, he shows that the sound object can be considered only as a kind of protrusion that emerges from a continuous, and much vaster, field:

> The mountains are [...] very special objects; we realise that, after all, it is only man who has isolated these geological ensembles as objects. Physically speaking, a peak of the Mont Blanc mountain chain does not exist, and the act of presenting a point that is higher than its surrounding environment has no special meaning,

---

140. M. Chion, *Guide des objets sonores* (Paris: INA-GRM-Buchet/Chastel, 1983), 34 [*Guide to Sound Objects*, unpublished translation by J. Dack and C. North, 32] [translation modified].

or in any case does not make it a 'unit' in itself, isolated from the rest. All I mean to say is that sounds belonging to a chain of sonorous events often tend to be these kinds of objects, and are only objects in so far as they are presented under a certain aspect when confronted by human perception.[141]

If sound is not an object *in itself*, then the becoming-object of sound, its *conditioning* into an object, must depend upon a specific process, a process of the extraction and constitution of sensible saliencies, and of their integration into an objectal logic. For Schaeffer, the decomposition of a sonorous field into discrete elements, into objects, is constitutive of listening itself—so the becoming-object of a sound is instigated by a listening that is always already discriminative, a process of identification that is already underway.[142] This suggests a particular perceptual relation between sound, which is not an object *in itself*, and listening, which would consist *essentially* in lying in wait for sounds to be identified and drawn off from an uninterrupted sonorous field. How does this function operate? How, within the sonorous, does the object come to appear? According to Chion, 'sound is an object only under certain conditions. It is an object that is constituted culturally, through an act of attention and nomination'.[143]

---

141. M. Chion, 'Comment tourner autour d'un objet sonore', in P. Szendy (ed), *L'Écoute* (Paris: L'Harmattan/Ircam-Centre Pompidou, 2000), 54.

142. 'But if I stay still, with my eyes closed and my mind empty, it is highly probable that I shall not continue to listen impartially for more than an instant. I locate noises, I separate them, for example into close or distant noises, coming from outside or in the room, and, inevitably, I begin to prefer some to others.' Schaeffer, *Treatise*, 89.

143. Chion, 'Comment tourner', 55.

Thus 'sound become object' is not so much Oury's 'that which we encounter', but more of an autonomous entity fashioned by a listening, siphoned off from a sonorous flux into which that listening cuts. The becoming-object of sound harbours a mystery of transmutation, as the meeting point of the conditionality of the sound object's appearance—that is to say, its contingency—and the permanence of a dissociative process embedded in the act of listening, as Schaeffer suggests.

In Schaeffer, listening is rational: it functions like a *sieve* that retains only individuated elements, objects extracted from an unformed substrate, a kind of nothingness. Listening, in Schaeffer, begins with the abrupt sonorous occurrence, an acoustic disturbance breaking a supposedly originary silence; only to accede to the *intellection* of sound, a quasi-linguistic decoding of sound, via an intermediary step during which procedures of qualification and evaluation are carried out. Between the lines of this sequential, rational conception Schaeffer glimpses the possibility of a listening that would target sound 'for itself', and the possibility that sound might be constituted into a sound object. It is on the basis of his coupling of objectivated and rational listening, a sort of *perceptual given* [*étant donné*], that Schaeffer is able to imagine a new 'method' of listening, leading him to develop the concept of a reduction of listening.

Object and Structure

Reduced listening is 'the stance of listening that consists in listening to sound *for itself*, as *sound object*, abstracting from its real origin or from the meaning that it may bear'.[144] In Husserl, reduction—*epoché*—designates the bracketing-out of the thesis of the world and the a priori postulation of its existence,

---

144. Ibid., 33.

in favour of the apprehension of the world as *phenomenon of existence*. Thus the world in which 'I' live is no longer the world that 'I' know, but that which 'I' apprehend. The objects that compose it are no longer absolute objects, but silhouettes (*Abschattungen*) which 'I' perceive.[145]

Schaeffer seeks to carry out this reduction on the sonorous world, bracketing out any supposed knowledge in order to focus on the sound itself qua phenomenal object. Indeed, for Schaeffer, it is only on condition of this reduction that we may properly speak of a sound object:

> There is a sound object when I have achieved, both materially
> and mentally, an even more rigorous reduction than the acous-
> matic reduction: not only do I keep to the information given by
> my ear (physically, Pythagoras's veil would be enough to force
> me to do this); but this information now only concerns the sound
> event itself: I no longer try, through it, to get information about
> something else (the speaker or his thought). It is the sound itself
> that I target and *identify*.[146]

Here Schaeffer takes up the example of the acousmatic situ-ation, a listening situation in which the emitting source of the sound is invisible. The term 'acousmatic', exhumed by Jérôme Peignot, originally related to the pupils of Pythagoras, who listened to the teaching of their master without being able to

---

145. 'Thus the thing can never be given to me as an *absolute*, and hence there is an "infinitum imperfect [...] as part of the unanullable essence of the correla-tion between 'physical thing' and perception of a physical thing."' Lyotard, *La Phénoménologie*, 23 [Lyotard's citation is from E. Husserl, *Ideas Pertaining to a Pure Phenomenology and to a Phenomenological Philosophy, First Book*, tr. F. Kersten (Dordrecht: Kluwer, 1983), 94—trans].

146. Schaeffer, *Treatise*, 241 [emphasis mine].

see him, since he was hidden behind a curtain that screened him off from his audience. The reference to the Pythagorean acousmatic situation is purely metaphorical, though; for reduced listening is defined as an *acausal* listening, targeting the sonorous phenomenon *for itself*; a listening dissociated from any semantic information that might be conveyed by the sound, and one that voids any relation to the emitting source—which, of course, was not the case for Pythagoras's pupils.

Through the reduction of listening, the sound object that Schaeffer's rational approach to audition presumes is realized as a formal and evental unit. The intentional object targeted by reduced hearing corresponds implicitly to an energetico-formal physics. That is, reduction cannot extract just any sound from the sonorous continuum, since '[t]*he sound object is the coming together of an acoustic action and a listening intention*',[147] and thus presupposes that this 'acoustic action' is formally identifiable.

Schaeffer conceives this 'identifiability' as the complex that links a form to its cultural shaping and to a structural assemblage of sound objects. In Schaeffer the object always supposes structure, and vice versa. Moreover, the dialectic that he sets up between object and structure goes way beyond the phase of identification alone, forming a veritable 'object-structure chain' (to take up Chion's term) in which every object can be considered as a structure itself composed of objects, and every structure can be envisaged as an object.

The couplet object/structure has a certain resonance with the processes of *identification* and *qualification*. The function of identification is to isolate an object from the sonorous continuum and to individuate it; whereas qualification consists

---

147.   Ibid., 243.

in describing and characterizing a sound object according to its internal formal qualities. Thus identification targets and extracts the sound object qua sonorous unit emerging from a structure, while qualification apprehends the object as a structure composed of formal qualities.[148]

The articulation of these two processes conditions Schaeffer's whole analytical architecture, in particular his typo-morphology, which pivots on this twofold coupling:

> [M]orphology tends towards describing sound, whereas typology fulfils the need to identify objects. Morphology receives from typology fragments taken *haphazardly* from the sound continuum, for the purpose of evaluating and qualifying them.[149]

Both in the dialectic object/structure and in the relation between typology and morphology, what we observe is a certain reversibility denoting an uncertainty, a vacillation as to the solidity of the concept of the sound object. If object and structure can exchange roles as a function of the focus of listening and the granularity of analysis, then where does the sound object reside qua object of perception? And if identification (typology) furnishes the elementary fragments for qualification (morphology), then equally, morphology (qualification) imposes *formal criteria* that typology (identification) needs in order for it to extract what it needs—so we are still no nearer to understanding what it is, in perceptual experience or in the analytical method, that informs the objectivation of sound, and how the one communicates with the other.

---

148. Cf. Chion, *Guide*, 58–9 [58–60].

149. Schaeffer, *Treatise*, 359 [emphasis mine].

Schaeffer tries to overcome this difficulty by tempering it. Although he admits that the identification of sound into objects is contingent and relative, he nonetheless turns to psychophysiological knowledge in order to establish a framework of 'morphological' criteria that are supposedly perceptible to all human audition. Sound itself must be predisposed to the play of identification, and must present sufficiently *formed* characteristics to be able to be *used* for typo-morphological ends. It is on the basis of this kind of contract with the sonorous that Schaeffer introduces the concept of the 'suitable object'.[150]

The sound object, qua intentional object, appears to listening by virtue of a certain pregnancy. But this pregnancy is marshalled by criteria understood and recognized within the typo-morphological system itself. Thus constituting the object allows one to validate its structure, to accede to a systematic approach, and thereby to establish a new musical system. For, as Schaeffer recalls, we must keep in mind that 'objects are made to serve [...] that, once they are grouped into structure, they forget themselves as objects, and each bear a value only in relation to the whole'.[151] It is as a function of this principle and this intentionality or targeting that an object will be determined as 'suitable' or not, depending upon how

---

150. '1) Sound objects are called suitable when they seem to be more appropriate than others for use as a musical object. For this they must fulfill certain criteria:
   · be simple, original and at the same time easily "memorable", with a medium duration; therefore be balanced typologically;
   · lend themselves easily to reduced listening, therefore not be too anecdotal or too loaded with meaning or emotion;
   · finally, combined with other sound objects of the same genre, *be capable of producing a predominant and easily identifiable musical value*.'
Chion, *Guide*, 97 [106] [emphasis mine].

151. Schaeffer, *Treatise*, 33.

well it integrates into a system of classification and how well it responds, formally, to the conditions of human perception, and thus becomes identifiable.

Reduced listening, which is a formal listening, targets the suitable object not like a perceptual sieving that picks out the sound object, but more like an active process that itself, according to predefined criteria, instigates the *formation* of sounds into objects. In which case identification is not so much the search for pre-existing formal units (the supposed 'sound objects') as the very construction of these units, these sonorous identities predisposed to slot into a structure. Given all of this, it becomes relatively straightforward for Schaeffer to say that 'sound objects [...] can be described and analyzed quite easily. We can gain knowledge of them [and] transmit this knowledge'.[152]

When the intentional object becomes suitable it exceeds its status as mere object of perception, becoming a systemic, calibrated object. It is at once a phenomenal object and the object of a musical system. The suitable object testifies to this servomechanism (in the cybernetic sense) slaving the object targeted by listening to the object upon which the musical system depends. The 'theorem' of the suitable object may thus be stated as follows: 'In defining a system, I define the objects that I need in order for it to run; and by defining these "suitable" objects, I condition my perception, configure it to identify such objects and to invalidate others.'

If we consider the object in the sense of an object of knowledge, a *scientific* object, we can understand better the pathways and the entanglements that lead the experience of the sonorous toward typo-morphology—in the sense that,

152. Ibid., 81.

if we are to believe Niels Bohr and Werner Heisenberg, 'one cannot radically separate the scientific "object" discovered at the end of the research process from the pathway of thought and the operational procedures that led to its revelation and its construction'.[153]

THERE IS NO REDUCED LISTENING

Meaningful Listening

Reduced listening, as a noncausal listening that places the aesthetic experience at the heart of its protocol, seeks to establish a non-*indexical* relation to sound that does not target *anything else* through sound, but targets sound itself, for itself. But then the notions of sound object and suitable object seem to distort this enterprise somewhat: setting up the notion of suitable object draws listening into a perceptual current concerned more with the validation of a pre-established system (typo-morphology) than with a spontaneous exploration with no 'object' other than sound itself. If suitable objects exist, they must be targeted by compatible modes of listening— which comes down to saying that listening itself must become 'suitable'—and if a disposition of listening is predetermined by and oriented toward a specific kind of object, then it cannot be said to target nothing through sound. On the contrary, through audition, suitable listening aims to establish a system coupled with a framework of values.

In his book on listening, Nancy emphasizes the way in which the meaningful and the sensible are closely entangled in the very act of listening:

153. J. Garelli, 'Introduction à la problématique de Gilbert Simondon', in G. Simondon, *L'Individu et sa genèse physico-biologique* [1964] (Grenoble: Éditions Jérôme Millon, 1995), 8.

The ear is stretched [*tendue*] by or according to meaning—perhaps one should say that *its tension is meaning already, or made of meaning*, from the sounds and cries that signal danger or sex to the animal, onward to analytical listening.[154]

Listening always *produces* meaning by identifying it in the sounds that it picks out. This means that it is impossible to disentangle a pure sensible from a pure meaningfulness. In this sense, an objectified sensible is already meaningful, or, in other words, is already a *sign*. According to Ferdinand de Saussure:

> [T]he linguistic sign unites, not a thing and a name, but a concept and a sound image. The latter is not the material sound, a purely physical thing, but the psychological imprint of the sound, the impression that it makes on our senses. The sound-image is sensory, and if I happen to call it 'material', it is only in that sense, and by way of opposing it to the other term of the association, the concept, which is generally more abstract.[155]

Even though the sonorous is fundamentally not a language, the listening that targets it seeks, and has always sought, to identify within it signifying information that is in part conventional and thus arbitrary.[156] Meaning that the musical object, 'constitut[ed] culturally through an act of attention and of

---

154. Nancy, *Listening*, 26 [emphasis mine].

155. F. de Saussure, *Course in General Linguistics*, tr. W. Baskin (New York, Toronto and London: McGraw-Hill, 1966), 66.

156. 'The bond between the signifier and the signified is arbitrary. Since I mean by sign the whole that results from the associating of the signifier with the signified, I can simply say: the linguistic sign is arbitrary. The idea of "sister" is not linked by any inner relationship to the succession of sounds s-ö-r which serves as its signifier in French.' Ibid., 67.

nomination', is also arbitrary. We might well expect the Saussurian theory of the sign to yield some precious information as to the formation of sound into an object, then:

> Speech phenomena, in themselves, are certainly *concrete*, yet they are incapable of signifying anything at all, except by virtue of being the same or not the same as each other. The fact that a certain person says *aka* at a given place and time, or a thousand people in a thousand places and times produce the sound sequence *aka*, is the sole given fact. It remains, however, that only the ABSTRACT fact of the *acoustic sameness of these aka* goes to create the *acoustic entity aka*. There is no point in looking for a more tangible primary object than this abstract primary object.
> (The same goes for any acoustic *entity*, in fact, because it is subject to time; (1) takes *time* to occur, and (2) reverts to nothing after this time. For example a musical composition compared to a painting. Where does the musical composition *exist*? This is the same as asking where *aka* is. In reality the composition exists only when it is performed; but to see this performance as its existence is false. Its existence is in the *sameness* of its performances.)[157]

Saussure himself makes the point: the principle of identity applies to any acoustic entity. Any acoustic entity, any sound object, in the very moment that it is constituted—that is to say, identified—through its recognition takes on a meaning, even if only an embryonic one: it is already meaningful as individuated sonorous entity that is part of a signifying system.

---

157. F. de Saussure, *Writings in General Linguistics* [1857–1913] (Oxford: Oxford University Press, 2006), 16.

Reduced listening and the object it targets, the sound object, is thus located at the originary point of articulation between the meaningful and the sensible. In becoming a sound object, sound does not yet become meaning. It is, according to Giorgio Agamben, a *voice*—in the sense that, without signifying anything whatsoever, the sound object shows that it contains meaning or at the very least that it is an 'intention to signify',[158] or in short that it exists within and participates in a system in which it makes sense. This limbo, where meaning is reduced to intention, but where the object already emerges out of the sonorous flux, offers us an 'experience that *is no longer* mere sound and is *not yet* meaning'.[159]

The Aporia of Reduced Listening

Even as it liberates itself from the causal character of sound, reduced listening, once it places itself in the service of a typo-morphology, condemns itself to remaining unfulfilled—distanced, so to speak, from itself. The only possible motivation for a phenomenological-type reduction is to return 'to the things themselves'. But reduced listening targets something other than the sonorous itself. It targets an object, a formally determined entity that is identifiable according to a predefined framework of identification.

There is no reduced listening properly speaking: under the regime of objectivated sound, signifying intention survives in a formal mode. Form informs, instructs, reassures. It speaks. It is a *voice* in Agamben's sense. So the structure of organization proper to reduced listening, typo-morphology, is the heir of a

---

158. G. Agamben, *Language and Death: The Place of Negativity*, tr. K. E. Pinkus with M. Hardt (Minneapolis: University of Minnesota Press, 2006), 33.

159. Ibid [emphasis mine].

veritable codex in which is inscribed the sound object whose 'suitable' character is a pledge of allegiance—making listening nothing but a *pretext*.

The role of form, then, is to give listening identifiable access to a signifying intention. As Saussure shows, it is the identity or non-identity of a sound that grants it a signifying status. Indeed,

> [a] signifier (in general) must be recognizable in its form despite and across the diversity of the empirical characteristics that can modify it. It must remain the *same* and be able to be repeated as such despite and across the deformations that what we call the empirical event makes it necessarily undergo.[160]

This formal identity 'necessarily implies a representation'.[161] That is, formal identity appears when there is identification and recognition of an entity that is re-exhibited in a way that is necessarily different, but sufficiently identical for one to be able to assimilate it to that which is primordial. 'Repetition is the power of language';[162] but repetition is only the revelation of *form*. Indeed it is in fact form that fertilizes the germs of language, that bears within it the premises of signification. The sound object thus appears as a *formal resonance* that is *recognized* by reduced listening.

Although it promised freedom, the setup of reduced listening, from the outset, read the given-to-be-heard through prior determinations, with reason taking priority over experience.

---

160. J. Derrida, *Voice and Phenomenon*, tr. L. Lawlor (Evanston, IL: Northwestern University Press, 2011), 42–3.

161. Ibid., 43.

162. G. Deleuze, *Difference and Repetition*, tr. P. Patton (London and New York: Continuum, 2004), 363.

Now, experimental protocol dictates that method and objectives should have priority over the experiment itself. Thus sound is channelled, and one observes only its 'suitable' manifestations. Meaning that if, by reducing listening, Schaeffer liberates it from a sclerotic causal field from which it can only be extracted with great difficulty, he does so only to immediately reassign it to a formal field. Reduced listening is thus the occasion for a causal desemantification of sound in favour of a formal 'meta-semantification'.

In fact, the aporia of reduced listening resides in its very definition. To seek 'to listen to sound *for itself*, as *sound object*' is precisely to introduce formal determinations, 'powers of language', into the enterprise of reduction. In listening to the sound 'as object', one precisely does *not* listen to the sound for itself.

The act of listening is fundamentally an act of deviation, in the sense that it operates via the diversion of attention. Attention is withdrawn from the sound itself in order to focus on the identifiable signifying resonances that it produces. Something else is always targeted through the sound object, and for good reason; listening is always *a stretching toward*, and never stops at sound. It traverses it, goes through it, so as to arrive at something else, something that still belongs to the domain of sensation but also, already, that of language. In setting forth a formal musical system, Schaeffer only gives meaning a new handle on sound, where the electroacoustic context of presentation had amputated it from its causal character.

Sound always speaks to us. There is no reduced, pure, consummate listening. Such a listening targets the *voice* of sound, and not sound itself.

Form and Trace

The sonorous, in order to be audible, must *make* a trace. The idea of a pure reduced listening directly implies the effacing of every trace and the return to sound itself, that is to say to the sonorous. Yet if the sonorous is precisely that which is unperceived, it cannot be targeted by any listening whatsoever. Reducing one's listening so as to accede to sound 'as object' comes down to targeting the sonorous and thus rendering it audible. In this sense, in reduced listening, form is at once the object of identification (the identifiable trace) and the object of qualification (the mark).

The notion of form, which acts as the pivot of the twofold function of identification/qualification, does indeed succeed in articulating the sonorous in terms of object/structure, thus actualizing its becoming-language. As we have seen, such a becoming, such a form, only appears through the sensible activation of differences and identities, something Derrida formulates in the following way:

> On the one hand, the phonic element, the term, the plenitude that is called sensible, would not appear as such without the difference or opposition which gives them form. Such is the most evident significance of the appeal to difference as the reduction of phonic substance. Here the appearing and functioning of difference presupposes an originary synthesis not preceded by any absolute simplicity. Such would be the originary trace.[163]

---

163. Derrida, *Of Grammatology*, 62.

Derrida articulates the relation between trace and form via difference, or more exactly via the notion of *différance*. Furthermore, within the space of a single page he gives us these two complementary propositions: '*The (pure) trace is différance*' and 'Différance is the formation of form'.[164] Incorporating the two into a syllogism, we might therefore propose the following formula: *the trace is the formation of form*. This formation of form is a making-available, an always-already present supplement which *becomes* active. Now, if form is indeed 'the power of language', 'intention to signify', then we can conclude that '[t]*he trace is in fact the absolute origin of sense in general. Which amounts to saying once again that there is no absolute origin of sense in general*'.[165]

The notion of the trace implies two interdependent points: the first is that the trace is 'instituted'—that is to say that it has no natural link with the signified, or that the signifying power that emanates from it is not essentially linked to it (here we meet again Saussure's notion of the arbitrariness of the sign). The second point, a direct corollary of the first if we examine it closely, is the non-originary character of the trace. The trace is not the origin of the audible, it is its *means*. It is in this sense that Derrida, upon declaring that the absolute origin of sense is the trace, goes on to indicate that 'there is no absolute origin of sense in general'.

Listening makes a trace in sound. The trace is but the result of a *trace-making*—that is to say, the accomplishment of an intention. This observation also confirms the schizological approach, which considers audible sound as a point of

---

164. Ibid., 62–3.

165. Ibid., 65.

convergence rather than as a phenomenal projection immanent to the auditor or a strictly transcendent physical event.

The audible has no reality without one or the other of these terms: the immanent and the transcendent. Even if it is necessary to distinguish between the two, sound is *both* event (the sound appearing) and sensible manifestation (the appearance of sound). However, if the audible is the sonorous as 'formation of form', the sonorous should not simply be considered as the undifferentiated magma of a raw acoustic material.

For it would be erroneous and unfortunate to append a hylomorphic schema to the sensible distinction between sonorous and audible, unperceived and perceived. According to Derrida, once again:

> [T]he hyle is a real but not intentional element of the experienced. It is the sensate (experienced and not real) material of affect before any animation by intentional form. It is the pole of pure passivity, of the nonintentionality without which consciousness could not receive anything other than itself, nor exercise its intentional activity.[166]

The sonorous does not respond to this definition of *hyle*, for although it is indeed real and is not a priori subject to a listening that intends it, nonetheless it cannot be considered to be a homogeneous and passive entity. The sonorous stands for the limbo of sound, always already activated, always present in the audible itself. In the same way, the relation between aurally perceiving and listening does not respond to a hylomorphic schema that would take one to be raw sensible matter for the

---

other to draw off and form. Taking account of this, we shall adopt Gilbert Simondon's position:

> There is not a sensation that would be a matter constituting an a posteriori given for the a priori forms of sensibility [...] [T]he a priori forms of sensibility are neither a prioris nor a posterioris obtained via abstraction, but structures of an axiomatic which appears in an operation of individuation.[167]

The process of identification is always supplementary: it super-adds itself to the object, rather than being its origin. Functioning via differentiation, identification is always external to the object that it identifies (unlike individuation, which is internal to it); not so much because a process cannot be the very object that it processes, as because a differential cannot be implemented exclusively on the basis of one or other of the terms it solicits.

Autonomy and Reification

Sound does not individuate itself, and is never already individuated. So it acquires autonomy only through the external action of an *individuating intention*. Reduced listening is precisely such an intention: it realizes the autonomization of sound by making it thinglike. When reduced listening is employed, the sound object brings about a relation that both exceeds and degrades the purely phenomenal acceptation of the term 'object', suggesting an at once more 'thinglike' and more tangible character.

The concept of the sound object as coined by Schaeffer to imply an individuation or autonomization of sound, refers to a

---

167.   Simondon, *L'Individu*, 28.

signifiant fabric that is external to it. Sound perceived 'as object' is always a *formal index*, a potential sign. A sound considered as autonomous, whether or not it is qualified as a sound object, is thus always an *audibilis*. It is always the result of a listening, it always belongs to a field of audibility, and always falls under the influence of signifying regimes. Form does not liberate the sonorous, it channels it, 'audibilizes' it:

> It is always tempting to arrest a form. Form is the temptation of discourse. It is in taking form that it develops, is fixed, and makes itself recognized.[168]

Form is the lever that propels the sonorous toward recognition, hence toward permanence, and finally toward audibility. This process of the individuation of the sonorous, this becoming-object of sound unleashed by an intention, by a listening, is none other than the process of reification. It sets out from a misunderstanding, a misguided dualism between sonorous form and the signifying indices that emanate from it, when sound itself is nothing but an emanation in which the sensible and the meaningful are already commingled.

The concept of reification is quite applicable to the domain of perception, even if its original context was different.[169] Beyond reference to strictly interhuman relations, to strictly social factors, the home soil of Lukácsian 'historical' reification, it can very well be employed in considering the perceptual pole

---

168. G. Didi-Huberman, *La Ressemblance informe* (Paris: Macula, 2003), 19.

169. According to Axel Honneth, 'the concept of "reification" [...] demands that we account for the possibility of a reifying perception not only of our social world, *but also of our physical world*'. A. Honneth, *Reification: A New Look at an Old Idea* (Oxford and New York: Oxford University Press, 2008), 61.

of human experience. Although reification originally described a glaciation of human relations in the era of the commodity, a generalized apathy or a 'disaffected' relational situation that favours a 'thinglike' mode of interaction, it ultimately implies more than this. For, considering that listening is partially determined by cultural factors, it may well find itself entering into a thinglike relation to the world, reducing the sensations it receives to mere objects.

Reification is the name of the global process that constitutes sensible objects, isolates them, autonomizes them, renders them thinglike. It is reification that establishes them in a regime of permanence, extracting them from their *hic et nunc*, from their auratic existence. Walter Benjamin shows us the pitfalls attendant upon the *placing in perpetuity* of that which is reified:

> The peeling away of the object's shell, the destruction of the aura, is the signature of a perception whose sense for the sameness of things has grown to the point where even the singular, the unique, is divested of its uniqueness.[170]

The great principle of reification reveals itself under the pressure of Benjamin's critique, and assumes the aspect of identification. Therefore we can propose a status for the sonorous that has been identified, that has become object but not yet sign: that of *reified sound*. In constituting objects in this way, reification excises them from the global sensible experience to which they belong, removing from them their proper existence,

---

170. Benjamin, 'Little History of Photography', 519.

plunging them into a kind of 'forgetting' or oblivion.[171] It fabricates autonomous objects which are ultimately empty objects.

The understanding of the sonorous universe as being always already fragmented insinuates itself by way of a two-way tautological circle: it fuels a targeting of listening, a listening setup that targets sound qua fragmented, and thus forestalls listening while simultaneously finding confirmation and legitimation in it. This circle may be reduced to the following formula: 'When I hear an object that I have targeted qua object, I obtain confirmation that it was indeed an object that I should have expected to perceive.'

The object is the product of a reifying perception that is none other than the reification of sensation itself; because in order for objects to be extracted from it, sensation must in the first place be approached as a finite entity. It is only through one's own sensible experience, and through the reification of one's sensations, that one can construct finite, defined, partial objects.

The autonomization of sound can only be apprehended by contrast, in the sense that it is only enabled, triggered, through a chain of processes gravitating around sound. Autonomous sound is the consequence of a drawing off or an extraction that is enabled by a discontinuity—that is to say, by an exteriority that superintends the objectivation of the sound. The protocol of autonomization is established outside of sound; autonomous sound only makes sense for and from an exterior position.

---

171. 'For all reification is forgetting: objects become purely thing-like the moment they are retained for us without the continued presence of their other aspects: when something of them has been forgotten'. T. W. Adorno and W. Benjamin, *The Complete Correspondence 1928–1940*, tr. N. Walker (Cambridge, MA: Harvard University Press, 1999), 321.

The passage from sonorous to audible, the extraction of the sonorous from its limbo, immediately implies an autonomy, a finite, formed character; which itself engenders a *voice*, an intention, or an availability for signifiance. As it becomes autonomized, sound ultimately ends up being enslaved to the regime of signs that has called it up.

Refrain

This becoming-autonomous, this becoming-object of sound, is revealed through the primary sound object in the modern history of listening, the object that incarnates the very paradigm of reproducible, recorded sound: looped sound, imprisoned in the locked groove of a record, and later a length of magnetic tape, itself looped.

Becoming captive of its own infinite repetition, looped sound seems to lose its fugacity and to acquire a pseudo-tangibility, in the sense that it can no longer extract itself from listening, as the playback device ceaselessly re-presents it. Like everything that is reproducible, it then becomes a potential object of study:

> [W]e slowed the sound right down and located the zone of interest. We cut a piece of sound out of this zone, appropriately dilated, and 'looped' it. Once it was speeded up again it found its tessitura and played itself over and over again. Of course the samples retained a certain dynamic, and it was difficult to 'homogenise' a loop like this properly, i.e. cancel out its form. Nevertheless, we must say that despite these imperfections it enabled the experimenter to grasp a slice of listening and a temporal element of its form.[172]

172. Schaeffer, *Treatise*, 378.

To speak of a 'slice of listening' amounts to confessing to having reified the sensible, to having rendered the sonorous phenomenon intelligible. The becoming-object of sound, realized by its reproducibility and its newfound ability to make an imprint, redoubles its becoming, concretizes its twofold destiny as at once object of knowledge and object of enjoyment. And yet the looping of a sound does not absolutely correspond to its identical repetition. On one hand, replaying only simulates the sound by reinstantiating it, each time identically *to the nearest infra-thin*;[173] while on the other hand listening itself, by *integrating* the preceding playback, opens itself up to the perception of an accumulation of repeated presentations of the sound, engendering a very specific regime of listening:

> There is, in particular, the apparently paradoxical phenomena that re-listening in itself does not incite one to pay attention to the sound, quite on the contrary. Firstly, it is in fact usually re-hearing rather than re-listening. Re-listening would mean that our attention was always alert; re-hearing, that something imprints itself in successive layers in our memory, but something we do not know what to do with. Often, the more we hear it again, the less we listen, since we 'pre-hear' the broad outline of what is going to happen, without for all that being any the better equipped to describe it.[174]

The 'repetitive-static' phenomenon that Chion describes, a phenomenon associated with the autonomization of sound

---

173. Here the infra-thin emerges in the internal (mechanical, electronic) fluctuations of the playback apparatus, but also by way of the context of presentation, which inevitably alters over the course of time.

174. Chion, 'Comment tourner', 60.

through looping, bears *perceptual* witness to this same auton-omization: the loop, qua loop, participates in a placing into stasis—that is to say a placing into sign—of sound, to the detriment of sound itself; attention is distanced from 'sound appearing' in favour of 'the appearance of sound'. In becom-ing a sound object, an object of knowledge, sound already no longer addresses itself entirely to auditory perception.

Thus the twofold destiny of sound opens up the possibility of a divergence within sound itself: the more that reified sound becomes an object of knowledge, the more it seems to lose any ability to be a direct sensible source of enjoyment. 'Everything that is attained is destroyed', as Henri de Montherlant wrote. To come to know a sound, with the help of its indefinite repeti-tion, is to identify in it all the formal and signifying saliencies that will permit one to represent it and to integrate it into a determinate system of thought (psychoacoustical, musico-logical, linguistic, etc.). The reification of sound into an object helps to locate it within a network of values and signs, within a determinate space.

Looped sound is sound always returning, sound turning on itself. It is, in this sense, the very principle of the refrain, its substrate. Deleuze and Guattari call a refrain

> any aggregate of matters of expression that draws a territory
> and develops into territorial motifs and landscapes (there are
> optical, gestural, motor, etc., refrains). In the narrow sense, we
> speak of a refrain when an assemblage is sonorous or 'dominated'
> by sound,[175]
> The refrain is rhythm and melody that have been territorialized

---

175.   Deleuze and Guattari, *A Thousand Plateaus*, 323.

because they have become expressive—and have become expressive because they are territorializing.[176]

The refrain is expressive in so far as it establishes territories. Thus we return to Deleuze's proposition that 'repetition is the power of language', and can now appreciate it in its full sense. The expressivity of the refrain is the recognition of its form become mark. Yet the refrain is not univocal because, although it does indeed figure the process of the autonomization of sound, at the same time it calls into question that from which sound is extracted and autonomized:

> The territorial assemblage implies a decoding and is inseparable from its own deterritorialization [...] Just as milieus swing between a stratum state and a movement of destratification, assemblages swing between a territorial closure that tends to restratify them and a deterritorializing movement that on the contrary connects them with the Cosmos.[177]

The refrain thus proceeds according to a twofold movement of migration, always extracting itself from its territory in order to re-form it once again; it is at once a conquest of territory and an evasion of territory. In fact, Deleuze and Guattari distinguish two types of refrain: a first type that expresses and territorializes, a second that deterritorializes and flees.

The second type of refrain—deterritorialized-deterritorializing sound—finishes up as a pure becoming that abstracts itself from itself. Now, a formed sound, a reified, objectivated sound, is first and foremost a sound marked out for a particular usage.

176. Ibid., 317.

177. Ibid., 336–7.

The territorial marking that it realizes is in a certain sense a meta-function revealing that, as a utile sound belonging to a determinate system, it is itself the delimitation or limiting of the space in which it is realized and utilized as object.

So if 'the territorial assemblage implies decoding', the deterritorializing movement directly and implicitly engenders an appeal to recoding. Here the objectivation of sound, its autonomization, is amalgamated with a reifying process. The autonomy of sound is a means, it is the condition of the identification of sound and the *vector* of its formation. By virtue of this, it is inseparable from a dynamic of signification. In seeking to extract the sound object, in trying to send it outside of the space of signs—that is to say, in trying to deterritorialize it—one also extracts its dark side, its *voice*, that which isolates and fixes it, that which assures its formal determination and therefore offers it up to a new process of designation, initiating a new territorialization. Autonomized sound always already comprises frontiers, and forms a territory.

Reified sound does not speak, though—or rather, it raises its voice, but has nothing to say. In fact it declares only one thing: 'I am object'. Autonomous, objective sound is an identity. It has been designated as such. It is true that it is a limited designation, in so far as the meaning emanating from the object-sound is an empty meaning which does nothing but affirm its objectal status. The persistence of signifiance in objectified sound is of the order of a tautological affirmation—'as object, I am object'—but it is also a paradoxical assertion that is a condition of autonomy: 'I am an empty object whose proper signification is to be without signification'. We must not lose sight of the fact that the reifying process is therefore a process of detachment and of apathy.

This 'hollow' meaning which affirms the object only by and through itself is the 'formal sense', the 'formation of form', of the object-sound. It is the liminal and irreducible sense of every identifiable sound. Now, this limit meaning needs to be fertilized. It is not an external limit beyond which everything becomes meaningless; on the contrary, it is an internal limit short of which a sound cannot be formed, cannot be identifiable, cannot exist. Autonomy should always be understood as a principle of existence. It only makes sense in relation to an exteriority, and is constituted according to that exteriority:

> [T]he object does not await in limbo the order that will free it and enable it to become embodied in a visible and prolix objectivity; it does not pre-exist itself, held back by some obstacle at the first edges of light. It exists under the positive conditions of a complex group of relations.[178]

By targeting sound, listening participates in its reification. Subsequently, reified sound creates territory once it is marked, that is to say reinvested in a system of signs; once its form, becoming expressive, constitutes it as sign-sound. Sound then enters into a register of representation. The object-sound is the formal condition of the existence of sound, of its becoming as an element of representation and as an imaginary production. It is the condition for sound's taking up its place in modes of discourse.

This is a question of territory and nothing else. Fragmenting the sonorous continent, marking out regions, establishing criteria, are so many strategies devised in order to know it as

---

178. M. Foucault, *Archaeology of Knowledge*, tr. A.M. Sheridan Smith (London: Routledge Classics, 2002), 49.

a whole, to identify it, it and it alone, once and for all. As the young Otto Weininger wrote:

> It is only in obedience to the most general, practical demand for a superficial view that we classify, make sharp divisions, pick out a single tune from the continuous melody of nature.[179]

BELIEFS AND PERCEPTION

> Perception is—among other things—a mechanism for the generation of beliefs, and these beliefs can surely differ according to the sensory modes involved in their formation.[180]

What underlies this observation by Casati and Dokic is that at one end of a listening there is always an auditor, a subjectivity. Belief is precisely that which is incommunicable, dwelling as it does in the meshwork of intimate conviction, deeply embedded in that which constitutes, and elaborates itself as, subjectivity. One can suggest a belief, catalyze it, exalt it, or even provoke it—that is to say, induce it in someone else; but in no way can one communicate it or transfer it to them. One can only modulate the beliefs that they themselves hold. In this sense, belief is always a last bastion impregnable to knowledge.

In a certain sense, it is in order to check this subjectivity intrinsic to perception, in order to render it communicable— that is to say, objective—that the path of the reduction of listening was taken. By constituting a sound object one obtains a communicable whole, a medium both of sensation and of

179. O. Weininger, *Sex and Character* (London: William Heinemann, 1906), 3.

180. Casati and Dokic, *La philosophie du son*, 25.

self-referential discourse—that is to say, a medium all of whose necessary signifying material is contained within itself; a safe and secure formal deposit.

The objectivation of the perceived can therefore be considered as an authoritarian development, aiming at an ordering, a system, seeking to establish a communicability of the sensible. It is in this sense that the marking of sound, a necessarily qualitative marking, *makes* territory.

To seek to communicate beliefs is not to fabricate a reality, but to construct a mythology. Thus 'there is a history of perception which, finally, is the history of myth'.[181]

---

181. W. Benjamin, *Gessammelte Schriften*, ed. R. Tiedemann and H. Schweppenhauser (Frankfurt am Main: Suhrkamp, 1987), vol. VI, 67.

4

DESIRING-LISTENING
AND
FETISHISM OF LISTENING

DESIRING-LISTENING

Roland Barthes says that listening is 'finally like a little theatre on whose stage those two modern deities, one bad and one good, confront each other: power and desire'.[182] The induction of the sonorous into the audible, the audibilizing of sound, is the activation of a regime of discourse that takes sound as its object. This regime may take a mythological or religious form, but equally may adopt a rational approach that singles out sound as an object of knowledge. Moreover, as shown by the case of Raudive's electronic voice phenomena and that of Tesla's electromagnetic ether, these two types of discursivity (scientific and religious) can very well exist alongside one another. In fact Barthes qualifies the targeting of sound—listening, that is—as 'religious *and* deciphering'.[183]

Likewise, essentialist, physicalist, and 'reductionist' enterprises, each in their own way, and without being fully conscious of it, have demonstrated that the true motor that drives them is a will, a *desire*, to fully grasp sound. Whether this is achieved by identifying it with the sensory subjectivity of the auditor, with a local physical event, or with a formal object targeted by a listening, the same thing is at stake: the definition and delimitation of what is designated by sound, and its *utilization*. The objective is to divest sound of its fugitive character, to *capture* and *possess* it. Beneath their discursive elaborations which seek to possess sound, all of these modes of listening are themselves driven by this desire for possession—they are all forms of *desiring-listening*.

Desiring-listening is the listening that perceives in the object that it targets a certain promise. This promise is unspeakable

---

182. Barthes, 'Listening', 260.

183. Ibid., 250.

because it augurs both the realization of the object and the accomplishment of the goal, the fulfilment of listening. As Pierre Klossowksi notes,

> the instrument is as inseparable from the object that it pre-supposes, manufactures, and exploits, as perversion is from the fantasy it engenders. Both act as constraints upon the usage of their products. Whoever wants the object wants the instrument.[184]

Listening as Promise of Jouissance

The primordial object of all listening is sound or, more precisely, the audible. The audible is a given-to-be-heard; it already integrates within it an address, and thus supposes a 'consciousness' of being oriented toward the auditor. But sound has no consciousness. This 'consciousness of', this address, cannot come from sound itself. Rather, it is perception, targeting, that determines what can or cannot be heard. Listening does not depend upon an audibilizing of sound—it *produces* this audibilization, it constitutes sound as an *audibilis*.

The object that listening fabricates always supposes a cut, always presupposes a sieving that defines it. By virtue of this, the sound-object must be understood at once as the object formed by listening—as the condition of the audibility of sound—and as the *objectal projection* of listening's desire. Listening is not neutral and apathic. It is always a will to listen, a desire to listen. Sound, as we know, is always present. The distinction we have established between the sonorous and

---

184. P. Klossowski, *Living Currency*, tr. J. Levinson, <http://anticoncept.phpnet.us/Livingcurrency.htm>.

the audible resides precisely in the articulation, in the very constitution, of this presence.

The audible is sound formalized by listening, the result of a targeting or an intention, a commitment on the part of listening. The audible exists, whereas the sonorous languishes in limbo. The sonorous is that which reaches the ear but does not penetrate it, does not imprint itself upon it. It is the unheard. As we know, the ear has no equivalent of the eyelid—sound continually floods into it. Listening, which is above all a perceptual targeting, an organ of selection and identification, makes up for this absence of a physical barrier. Thus listening is always driven by a will to listen, a desire. In a certain sense, then, listening is its own intentional floodgate. It is at once listening and intention to listen.

The objectivation of sound must therefore be considered as both result and means of the listening process's mode of desire. This objectivation tends to fix the inherent fugacity of sound, to confer upon it a tangibility, whether symbolic or mythical, or to establish it as an observable and measurable object of knowledge. Yet for all that, such procedures do not constitute a 'materialist' approach to sound: they do not aim to abolish sound's power of evocation, so much as to take possession of it and to reconfigure it for their own ends and according to *their own story*.

> For any object whatsoever, in fact, the reality principle may be bracketed-out. *No sooner does an object lose its concrete practical aspect than it is transferred to the realm of mental practices.* In short, behind every real object there is a dream object.[185]

---

185. J. Baudrillard, *The System of Objects*, tr. J. Benedict (London and New York: Verso, 1996), 117 [translation modified].

The sound-object considered as object of desire plays the role of the dream object beyond perception, beyond intentionality—that is to say, at the level of intention. The object of desire as dream object testifies to a superior reality that is constitutive for it: it is always associated with lack. The object is a point of fixation that zeroes in on lack through representation and expression. The object is literally the representative of lack. Yet such lack must not be envisaged as a stable point, but rather as a low-pressure system, an attractor driven by the void.

'The ear is not filled with hearing', we read in *Ecclesiastes*; and listening is always stretched out toward the new promises harboured by sound. The objectivation of sound is in a certain sense an interfacing between that which is given-to-be-heard and that which is modulated through it: what we desire to hear, or rather what we desire to *hear again*. For the object is always constituted by *recognition*; it always functions by way of retention, and is always ambivalent. It is the point at which the real, the symbolic, and the imaginary are articulated. Or better still, it is the condition of possibility for this articulation.

The sound-object is reified-represented sound that resists its actual fugacity, drawn along by a desiring process and drawn into that process: we must not forget that sound has always, through the intermediary of listening, been a source of pleasure, of *jouissance*.

Jouissance is not only the attainment of sensual pleasure, but also that of joy. So we must not limit the notion of desire strictly to the sexual sphere (just as it would a mistake to try to entirely distance it from that sphere). Desiring-listening must be embraced as a whole, in its full extent, attending to all the gradations of its libidinal investment.

Listening as promise of jouissance may thus be addressed as a vector of joy, at once means and end. In the following passage, through the narration of his character Peter Camenzind, Hermann Hesse describes one of those moments when the experience of listening is a joyous one:

> [...] I yodeled madly, exultantly, with every possible break and variation, into the shimmering evening. When I stopped, he started to say something, then just cocked his ear in the direction of the mountains. From a distant peak there came a reply, soft and long-drawn-out and swelling gradually, a herdsman's or a hiker's answer, and we listened quietly and happily to it.[186]

Listening is always listening *to* something; it supposes, modulates, and depends upon a relation. The joy of hearing is the joy of being in-relation. Such a joy in listening is felt by Hesse's character: a joy that finds in the reception of the responding yodel the sensory confirmation of being linked to something or someone else. As one of the two terms of oral communication (the other being speech), listening always presupposes a strong relational character between that which sounds and that which listens. In any case, it is predisposed to an experience of a *specifically* relational type. It is in this sense that we may say of sound that it *speaks*.

But we must clarify in what sense 'sound speaks'. The only sound that can 'speak' is sound targeted by listening; it is listening that *makes it speak*. But here, to make listening speak is the same as to speak. In the end, it is listening itself

---

186. H. Hesse, *Peter Camenzind: A Novel*, tr. M. Roloff (New York: Picador, 2003), 52–3.

that establishes sound within discursive power. '*Listening speaks*,' Barthes wrote; and perhaps, ultimately, he is right.[187]

Desiring-listening should therefore be represented as a listening that speaks for the sound that it captures, but which develops this *voice* within a *fictional* register. It thus speaks for sound and auditor alike, and reveals the appearing of sound in this same auditor's field of existence. *The fiction includes the auditor within the scenario of his own perception.*

In Hesse's text, Camenzind creates a fiction on the basis of his listening, but not by hearing something that has not taken place—the yodel sung in response does indeed exist; someone far away in the mountains has *actually* sung in reply. The fiction emerges when the character elaborates, *through his listening*, a sensory story of which only he knows the affective import and the signifying framework within whose perspective it is understood. In this example, fiction is overlaid onto listening in two ways. The first way is manifested in the focalization of listening, as it stretches out towards the response, suspending all other auditory experience. Indeed, the narrator's friend falls silent when he hears the response, the better to enjoy it. By only letting one sound at a time 'speak', listening *fictionalizes* the relation to the audible in the sense that it intentionalizes it. The second mode of fiction at work in the listening of Hesse's character lies in the *projection* that he operates upon the object of his listening (the object here being simultaneously the singer, 'herdsman', or 'hiker', and the song itself—all of which form, *at the level of listening*, one and the same entity); it is this projection that reveals the dream object of listening beyond the real object.

---

187.   Barthes, 'Listening', 252.

In Camenzind's joyous exaltation one does indeed sense listening overflowing any simple function of recording, of sensory capture. What is revealed here is another destiny of listening, a parallel destiny that determines it as an organ of desiring-production. Once more, listening cannot be assimilated to a pure function of knowledge; it forges within itself the *destiny* of its own desiring-process.

> It is commonly accepted amongst authentic libertines that the sensations communicated by the organs of hearing are the most flattering and those whose impressions are the liveliest.[188]

It is on the authority of such an observation that the fornicators of the Château of Silling—Durcet, Curval, the Duc de Blangis, and his bishop brother—in order to ensure the success of their expedition, decide to engage four storytellers who will be charged with enflaming their imaginations.

One might object that, in this case, listening is only a support or medium for the narrative. One might suggest that the desiring-process thereby activated is not at all correlated with auditory sensation or determined by it, but only conditioned by a placing in communication, that is to say by an intellectual function that is independent of perception. In order to convince ourselves otherwise, we might once more turn to the example of Robert Walser's *Snowwhite*, which illustrates the existence of a narrative modality of sound. Snowwhite suggests that she might hear of the frolics of her mother and the hunter from the prince's mouth, so as not to suffer the raw *unveiled reality* of the act. By way of listening, of oral narration, Snowwhite is able

---

188. D.A.F. de Sade, *The 120 Days of Sodom* [1785], tr. A. Wainhouse and R. Seaver (New York: Grove Weidenfeld, 1966), 218.

to represent to herself a vaguer, more chaste image. Inversely, Sade's characters are able to imagine and arrange according to their own fantasy the scabrous tales narrated to them.

A story told is not a story read. It supposes a community. Orality, or more exactly oral transmission, reaffirms listening as relational process. The narrative function mobilized by it is ultimately nothing but the fulfilment of the relational modality of listening. In fact, one might suggest that the narrative modality and the relational modality proper to listening are one and the same, in so far as they both participate in the same state—one in which intimacy and fiction are mutually entangled. For both Snowwhite and Durcet (but fundamentally the same goes for Camenzind), listening is a vehicle whose specific qualities foster a particular imaginary fulfilment, realizing a phantasmatic immediacy between listening and sound (which is never a pure semantic content contained in sonorous vibrations nor, inversely, those same vibrations as pure phenomenal qualities, unshackled from all signification). Listening projects and assembles phantasms and imaginary worlds that are established far away, only to be actualized in the intimate confines of the auditor.

Vision posits distances, assumes obstacles. It stakes out space. Sound moves through obstacles, flees, and is propagated for kilometres. Even a distant sound, as it is apprehended, can be heard *right inside the ear*. Listening realizes the intimacy of the faraway, the intimate embrace of the distant. It can transcend space, or at least change our relation to space. It reconciles two poles without ever merging them into one another, bringing about a proximity or intimacy superposed on a distance or a distancing. Hence it is also the organ of the secret, of confession. Here again, listening speaks; it speaks *as close as can be*.

The pleasure we seek in listening is a pleasure sought for its power of evocation, an interfacing between the most intimate and the most faraway, between the unknown and the immediate, configuring itself, through this back-and-forth, into a signal promise of jouissance.

Desiring-Listening

This reality of listening and of sound, scrambling the frontiers between sensible and sense, event and phenomenon, intimate and external, offers a new understanding of audition, testifying to a density and a thickness which scientific and philosophical rationalism have passed over in silence, and bringing into play a subterranean but omnipresent component of sound: the dimension of desire.

Even so, are we to suggest, on the example of the scopic drive, that there is a *listening drive*? Lacan was the first to sketch out the concept of the invoking drive [*pulsion invo-cante*], which takes the voice as its object—Freud mentioned no such thing when he talked about partial drives. What is specific to this drive, as a consequence of the fact that the ear can never close, is that it is a 'pure going into the Other or of the Other, and thus a gap without return'—and that it therefore occupies a privileged place 'closest to the unconscious'.[189]

The typical illustration of the invoking drive is the experience of Ulysses, as he willingly submits to the irresistible song of the sirens. As mythical tradition recounts, only two crews managed to escape from these bird-women: that of Ulysses, and that of Jason. On board the Argo, salvation came from

189. Cf. S. Chraïbi, 'Fétichisation de la pulsion invocante en pulsion audio-pho-natoire', in *Psychologie Clinique 19: La voix dans la rencontre clinique* (Paris: L'Harmattan, 2005), 129–40.

Orpheus, who, singing and strumming his lyre, pitched his own music against the bewitching voices of the sirens.[190] As for Ulysses and his crew, they employ a ruse in order to resist giving in to the calls, falling into the mortal peril of totally abandoning themselves to the siren's voices: the ever-industrious Ulysses comes up with the idea of sealing the ears of all the crew members with wax, except his own. Wishing to enjoy the song of the sirens without running any risk, he orders himself to be chained to the mast, and for his orders and pleas to be ignored until the ship is far enough from the sirens' isle.

In a short text, Franz Kafka, sceptical of the success of this subterfuge, reworks the myth into a new version where the supernatural nature of the siren song relates to the desire that it can awaken, thus conferring upon desire itself a supernatural, irresistible force:

> To protect himself from the Sirens Ulysses stopped his ears with wax and had himself bound to the mast of his ship. Naturally any and every traveller before him could have done the same, except those whom the Sirens allured even from a great distance; but it was known to the entire world that such things were of no help whatever. The song of the Sirens could pierce through everything, and the longing of those they seduced would have broken far stronger bonds than chains and masts. But Ulysses did not think of that, although he had probably heard of it. He trusted absolutely to his handful of wax and his fathom of chain, and in innocent elation over his little stratagem sailed out to meet the Sirens.[191]

---

190. Cf. Appollonius Rhodius, *Argonautica*, book V.

191. F. Kafka, *The Complete Stories*, tr. W. and E. Muir (New York: Schocken Books, 1995), 431.

According to Kafka, if Ulysses was able to resist and to survive the song of the sirens, it was precisely *because they did not sing*. But Ulysses was able to convince himself that they had sung 'and that he alone did not hear them'—unless, that is, he 'really noticed [...] that the Sirens were silent, and opposed the aforementioned pretence to them and the gods merely as a sort of shield'.[192]

For Kafka, the jouissance ultimately lies not so much in the voice itself (the sirens do not sing) as in the desire to hear—in the tension that precedes listening, conditions it or even, as in this case, fantasizes it. The voice-object, being absent, nonetheless triggers the invoking drive via the *anticipation* of listening. But this absence is also the point around which the drive pivots: rather than an invoking drive, it now becomes simply a listening drive.

The listening drive is a pure tension towards an audible object that ultimately is only *the medium* of the drive, not its real object. Sound, becoming a mere pretext, thereby finds itself sucked into a contraband economy where it exists less *for itself* than in the service of a desiring-production. Here again, sound is reduced to the state of a thing, a tool, or a working part, whose only role is be exceeded in the direction of a desiring-production of listening.

Yet this desiring-tension is not only in play in the fulfilment of a jouissance such as that coveted by Ulysses. The desiring-production that issues from listening is not necessarily a promise of pleasure. It has no inherent direction or orientation. It can just as well contribute to the neurotic collapse of the desiring subject as its conquest of pleasure. Indeed it is the common denominator and the instrument of a certain

---

192. Ibid.

indistinction between the two. Listening qua desiring can also be troubling, frightening. It can be a vector of anguish:

> Finally, my breast so constricted that I could not breathe the life-giving air quickly enough, my lips opened slightly and I uttered a cry...a cry so piercing...that I heard it! The shackles of my ears were suddenly broken, my ear-drum cracked at the shock of the sounding mass of air which I had expelled with such energy, and a strange phenomenon took place in the organ condemned by nature. I had just heard a sound! A fifth sense had developed in me! But what pleasure could I have derived from such a realization? Since then, no human sound has reached my ears without bringing with it the feeling of grief which pity for great injustices arouses. Whenever anyone spoke to me, I remembered what I had seen one day above the visible spheres, and the translation of my stifled feelings into a violent yell, the tone of which was identical to that of my fellow-beings! I could not answer him; for the tortures inflicted on man's weakness in that hideous red sea passed before my eyes roaring like scorched elephants and brushing with their burning wings against my singed hair. Later, when I knew mankind better, this feeling of pity was coupled with intense rage against this tiger-like stepmother whose hardened children know only how to curse and do evil. The brazen lie! they say that evil is the exception among them! That was long ago; since then I have not spoken a word to anyone. Oh you, whoever you may be, when you are beside me, do not let any sound escape your vocal cords; do not with your larynx strive to outdo the nightingale; and, for yourself, do not on any account attempt to make your soul known to me by means of language. Maintain a religious silence, uninterrupted by the least sound. Cross your hands humbly on your breast, and lower your eyelids.[193]

---

193. Lautréamont, *Maldoror*, tr. P. Knight (London: Penguin Classics, 1978), 86–7.

Maldoror experiences the end of his deafness as a curse. It connects him, unwillingly, to all of humanity. Above all this newfound audition exposes his sensibility to the speech of his peers, who, for him, are peers only in name. And then it refers him back to his own voice and to its identity with the voices of all those others. Maldoror dreads and execrates his own listening, for he cannot control access to it—it is a floodgate open forevermore, subjection to which he finds utterly intolerable.

Here Lautréamont very literally puts his character's misanthropy to the test of his sensations. He pitches Maldoror into the sensible, sonorous experience of his aversion to human beings. The most minute sound emitted from any human's mouth is enough—more through what it *evokes* than what it is—to cause intolerable pain. It is not the acoustic characteristics of the sounds themselves that are the irritant, but rather that which they *designate*, and that which sound itself *presupposes*. And yet we should not think that the register of listening is here overridden by misanthropy itself.

There is actually a condition that comes close to what Lautréamont describes here: it is called *phonophobia*. Phonophobia, a psychological condition, must be distinguished from hyperacousia (an abnormally elevated sensitivity to sounds). Although it is certainly an auditory hypersensitivity, phonophobia is not occasioned by the spectral characteristics of sounds, but by that which they evoke, that with which they are identified. It is a disorder that afflicts listening not at the physiological level, but at the level of its evocative function. It is a negative confirmation, a confirmation through denial, of this highly-charged function.

Listening and sound, as outlets for drives but also as anxiogenic, cut their own paths through the empire of desire, simultaneously freeing themselves from the tangible objectivity into which one tries to mould them, and opening onto affects, fears, and jouissance.

This listening, bared to the four winds of desires and fears, is brought to bear 'from unconscious to unconscious, [...] from a speaking unconscious to another which is presumed to hear'.[194] It is the 'panic' listening of Maldoror, the listening that speaks—that screams, even ('my ears screamed', writes Bataille).[195] Desiring-listening is the listening that invests itself in every place, in every circumstance, disseminates itself; it is the listening that opens up 'all forms of polysemy, of overde-termination, of superimposition, [and provokes] a disintegration of the law that prescribes direct, unique listening'.[196]

Schaeffer's reduced listening, a formal and univocal listen-ing, seems like the inverted double of this multiple listening, this collecting duct for a polymorphous desiring-flux. Yet these two modes of listening are not diametrically opposed. For we must not forget that the *epoché*, the bracketing-out of the thesis of the world, is also a psychoanalytical protocol that seeks to establish a privileged access to internal fantasy worlds.

The negation of the causal information carried by sound and the reduction of listening to a pure sonorous manifesta-tion are abstractions. Schaeffer's error was to believe that behind the abstraction we find only reason—when there, as everywhere, we also find desire and fantasy. So reduced listening does not lead us to a homogeneous, rational space; it opens onto an *abstract* space—that is to say, a potentially heterogeneous space, but still a desiring-space.

---

194. Barthes, 'Listening', 252.

195. G. Bataille (Lord Auch), *Story of the Eye*, tr. J. Neugroschal (London: Penguin Classics, 2001), 31 [translation modified].

196. Barthes, 'Listening', 258.

Bringing together the objectivation of sound and the revelation of listening as desiring-listening, we can glimpse the existence of other protocols that structure audition, and where the desiring process is directly integrated with perception. The complex of listening and object, the relations that it supposes and through which it functions, resonate particularly strongly with one of these possible protocols: that of fetishism.

LISTENING AND FETISHISM

Detour: Fetish, Fetishism

The word 'fetish' comes from the Portuguese word *feitiço*, meaning 'spell' or 'magical charm', and which itself comes from the Latin *factitius*, which gives us the English 'factitious' and the French 'factice' (artificial, false). The term 'fetishism' itself was coined by Charles de Brosses in 1760 to designate the cult of objects known as fetishes. In fact it is only with the appearance of this term that a distinction is made between the object and the behaviour that relates to it.

A generic definition of the term 'fetish' might be as follows: a material object that refers to *something* immaterial. This definition is further refined by Sophie Gosselin's observation:

> An object becomes a 'fetish' when a power of signification that
> it does not contain in itself is endowed upon it by man; when
> man projects into an indifferent object a meaning that is then
> believed to emanate from the object itself.[197]

---

197.   S. Gosselin, *Atelier philosophique* 5 (29 October 2003): 'Le fétichisme, de Michel de Certeau à Karl Marx', <www.apo33.org>.

Originally linked to anthropology, where it was used to designate the religious modes of thought of certain animist traditions, the concept of the fetish came to be transferred into two other domains: economics and sexuality.

In political economy, the notion of fetish was introduced by Karl Marx in an early section of *Capital* entitled 'The Fetishism of the Commodity and its Secret'. And in fact, in economics, the term 'fetish' would subsequently be used only in reference to Marx. In Marx, the notion originates in the concepts of *use-value* and *exchange value*, and more exactly in the passage from one to the other. Use-value is the value given to an object as a function of its utility, of the needs to which it responds; exchange-value is a value 'detached' from the object, a value that transcends the object, and which emerges when it is considered as a product of labour. For all products of human labour have

> the same phantom-like objectivity; they are merely congealed
> quantities of homogeneous human labour, i.e. of human labour-
> power expended without regard to the form of its expenditure.
> All these things now tell us is that human labour-power has been
> expended to produce them, human labour is accumulated in
> them. As crystals of this social substance, which is common to
> them all, they are values—commodity values.[198]

In theories of sexuality, the fetish object is an object of desire that plays a mediating role between the subject and the hidden object of his or her desire; it is an object of desire because it is an object that places the subject in communication

---

198. K. Marx, *Capital Volume I* [1867], tr. B. Fowkes (London: Penguin Classics, 1990), 125.

with the real object of desire, or rather with the reality of desire itself.

Jean-Martin Charcot was the first to study cases of sexual fetishism. At the time, the fetishist was thought either to be suffering from a nervous illness or to be a madman. It is only with Freud that sexual fetishism becomes more complex and begins to suffuse sexuality as such, to the point where it becomes inescapable. For Freud, the sexual fetish proceeds via substitution and overvaluation of the sexual object:

> What is substituted for the sexual object is some part of the body (such as the foot or hair) which is in general very inappropriate for sexual purposes, or some inanimate object which bears an assignable relation to the person whom it replaces and preferably to that person's sexuality (e.g. a piece of clothing or underlinen). Such substitutes are with some justice likened to the fetishes in which savages believe that their gods are embodied.[199]

Sexual overvaluation is the motor of this fetishistic substitution, in so far as the latter 'cannot be easily reconciled with a restriction of the sexual aim to union of the actual genitals and it helps to turn activities connected with other parts of the body into sexual aims'[200] (but also activities connected with objects). For Freud, then, there is fetishism in sexuality wherever there is a deviation, however slight, from the straightforward sexual goal. So that from this point on every

199. S. Freud, 'Three Essays on Sexuality', in J. Strachey (ed), *The Standard Edition of the Complete Psychological Works of Sigmund Freud*, vol. VII (London: The Hogarth Press, 1953), 153.

200. Ibid., 150–51.

sexual fantasy, every staging of a sexual encounter, belongs to some degree to the world of the fetish.

This exploration of the concepts of fetish and fetishism within the context of the different domains wherein they first appeared, albeit brief, enables us to extract the underlying substrate—that is to say, to outline the mechanisms in play in fetishism regardless of the particular domains within which the concept originated. It is in this synthetic spirit that Jean-Michel Ribettes arrives at the following proposition as a definition, in general and multiple terms, of the concepts of fetish and fetishism:

> The fetish is defined as a magical object—the visible substitute for an invisible spirit, for an absence, a lack—to which worship, value, desire become attached: fetishism is the mental process that fixes belief, lust, or libido upon this 'magical' object. [...] It can be seen that the register of values that is common across the three fetishisms [religion, the commodity, sexuality] is indeed that of *belief*.[201]

Belief, in the broadest sense, is the 'raison d'être' of the fetish—the role of the latter being not only to materialize, to channel the link between man and the object of his belief, but also to perpetuate it. The fetish is thus both an instrument of mediation with belief, and a guarantee of the existence and validity of this same belief.

Value, desire, meaning, divine principle: here is an incomplete list of possible terms to designate that which the fetish

---

201. J.-M. Ribettes, 'Dans le défaut de l'objet religieuse, économique et sexuel', in *Fétiches & Fétichismes*, catalogue of the exhibition at Passage de Retz (Paris: Passage de Retz/Éditions Blanche, 1999), xxviii, xxvi.

conceals and reveals, that which the fetishist seeks. But the different terms ultimately correspond only to various 'thematic colourations' relating to different fetishisms, which themselves are only modulations, variants, of one and the same fetishizing process. What the fetishizing process conceals and reveals is a *charge*. The charge is that which the object, in being constituted as a fetish, precisely is charged with; that which it contains, that which the fetishist seeks and tries to attain through it.

So the fetishizing process is above all a process of 'charging' which calls for a 'discharging'—a process that always loops back on itself, with every discharge (every time the fetishism is expressed, is satisfied) tending to reinforce the potency of the fetish, the intensity of its charge, rather than defusing it.

Fetishism, then, can be seen generically as a process of the *transference* and *inscription* of a *charge* onto an *object*. The fetish thus constituted then becomes an interface of *mediation*, but also of *masking*.

The Sensible and the Fetish

In 1938 Theodor W. Adorno wrote 'On the Fetish-Character in Music and the Regression of Listening'. Although Adorno himself was unsatisfied with it, this work would play a pivotal role in the initiation and development of his theory of cultural 'goods'; for the first time it would permit the systematization of the concept of fetishism across a whole cultural domain, namely that which Adorno calls 'contemporary musical life'.[202]

---

202. T.W. Adorno, 'On the Fetish-Character in Music and the Regression of Listening', in A. Arato and E. Gebhardt (eds.), *The Essential Frankfurt School Reader* (New York: Continuum, 1985), 270–99: 278.

What appears for the first time with Adorno is the possibility of considering an immaterial object as a fetish, where the latter had previously been designated as a tangibly existing object. Whether it was the boot in psychosexual fetishism, the idol in anthropology, or the manufactured product in Marxist economics, the fetish always involved a manifest materiality—it was above all a *thing*.

In Adorno, the fetish is no longer strictly a material object that refers to something immaterial: a musical tune, for example, can claim fetish status. And a tune cannot be reduced to its pure sensible manifestation, to its pure acoustical properties: it is a vector of signs, values, or references that are properly immaterial.

Here the fetish is no longer constituted around a thing, but around a phenomenon; the fetish is no longer an object, it is a *character*. Adorno remains attached to the Marxist tradition though, and the fetish-character of music he describes is a direct descendent of Marx's commodity fetishism. Consequently he is confronted by the 'double destination' of fetishism, at once sociological and 'symptomatological'.[203] For the Adornian fetish-character turns out to be accountable at once to its socioeconomic dimension as pure product of commodity capitalism, and to its sensible implications, as fetishizing process penetrating into the deep structures of listening.

In fact, Adorno's analysis privileges the social and economic aspects of the fetish character, describing the becoming-commodity of musical works, works that 'fall completely into the world of commodities, are produced for the market, and are aimed at the market'.[204] And yet here and there he puts

---

203. P.-L. Assoun, *Le Fétichisme* (Paris: PUF, 1994), 5.

204. Adorno, 'Fetish-Character of Music', 279.

forward concepts such as that of the 'regression of listening', or that of 'commodity-listening', where he exhibits, in a minimal way, the sensible implications of musical fetishism for listening itself. In doing so, Adorno initiates a new theatre of operations in which fetishism intervenes; a space that is neither simply speculative nor simply libidinal, but is precisely the space of the sensible.

Thus, if commodity fetishism applied to cultural goods furnishes the conditions of possibility for a generalized fetishism in the domain of music, specifically through the constitution of musical works as cultural commodities, it overlays and masks a whole folio of mechanisms that are mobilized in the process and which, from detection by the senses to the emission of a value judgment, model perception and sensation, conditioning them and subjecting them.

What Adorno did not see was that over and above the fetish character *in* music—that is to say, the expression of a fetishist behaviour officiating over 'musical life'—is superimposed a fetishism *of* listening where the expression of beliefs flourishes through an intention of listening that targets an objectivated, thinglike sound.

The fetish is an 'instrumental' object: it serves as a substitute for the real object of desire or worship. It has an operational character and is not defined in relation to itself, but always in functional terms, in terms of the relation that it allows to be established with the targeted object beyond it. It only *is* in so far as it is useful. It embodies, materializes, the presence of the real object of belief. It *incarnates* that object. The choice of 'incarnating' object, although it is fundamentally arbitrary in the Saussurian sense—it is not unmotivated or purely fortuitous. This is what prompts Marcel Mauss to say that it is not just 'arbitrary' in the sense of being culturally undetermined:

The object used as a fetish is never an arbitrarily chosen, common object: it is always defined by the code of magic and religion.[205]

The possibility of a fetishism of sensations, of listening, sheds light on the existence of sensible fetishes, or at least of a fetish-character inherent to sensible objects. By virtue of this, and following Mauss's remark, it appears once more that, although the objectivated sensible may be constituted arbitrarily, it is nonetheless well defined and determinate. For it must offer some assurance that it is capable of playing the role of medium or support. 'Fetishized' sound never comes from nowhere, and never for no reason.

As we have already said, the introduction of the sonorous into the audible necessarily takes place by way of some process, and this process simply *is* listening. It takes place via a delimitation of sound, its objectivation—that is to say, via reification. Just like the fetish, reified, audible sound becomes a medium and a substitute. The substitute-sound is sound become pretext, 'henchman [*suppôt*]' and medium for the *power of discourse*. As substitute, it is called up, modelled, and utilized so as to *manifest* this power of discourse.

But sound is not the only element in the act of listening that can be seen as analogous to the fetish: as is often the case in fetishism, the auditor is at once fetishist and fetishizer. He himself produces, so to speak, his own objects of worship. So that even if substitution is ultimately always oriented toward 'the apparition of sound', it can be diffracted into

205. M. Mauss, 'Art and Myth According to Wilhelm Wundt', in A. Riley, S. Daynes, C. Isnart (eds.), *Saints, Heroes, Myths and Rites: Classic Durkheimian Studies of Religion and Society* (London and New York: Routledge, 2016), 17–38: 17.

multiple more or less tangible objects: desiring-listening can project into certain voices, into certain musicians, into certain instruments manufactured by illustrious luthiers, into certain technical devices, or particular audio media, or even into the ear itself, promises of the most intense and most incontestable auditory jouissance.

Once more, this cannot be a question of assimilating the act of listening to a fetishistic pathology. What is important here is that we consider fetishism generically (seek its substrate, in a certain sense) and identify the precise functions that it incorporates into the process of listening.

If we consider fetishism as a strategy of substitution and mediation within desiring-production, whereby an object fulfils the role of support and medium for a belief, we immediately detect analogies with the formation of the audible through listening: namely, the advent of sound as fetish corresponds, *in a phantasmatic register*, to the becoming-object of sound, its audibilizing.

The object is central to fetishism. It is the object that mediates and crystallizes *the transfer of signifiance* that is truly at stake in fetishism. In this sense (and this sense only) the fetish is similar to Lacan's *objet a* or Winnicott's transitional object. By way of substitution it mediates, represents, and replaces an *unattainable*. As we have already seen, such mechanisms are present in the act of listening—in particular, in Schaeffer's enterprise of reduced listening.

Reduced listening is not a focussing on sound itself. It is a focussing on sound *qua object*. The concept of *epoché* that Schaeffer adopts is not simply the condition of a causal rupture between the sound and its source; it is also an opening onto a phantasmatic world. The *epoché* does not do away with a regime of belief; *it reinitiates the regime of belief*.

Reduced listening apprehends sound through its objectivation. Now, an object that is the medium of a phantasmatic process responds to the definition of the fetish. If ultimately there is no reduced listening, this is because what it targets—sound— eludes it, but is modified by the very fact of this targeting, and becomes fetishized by means of its objectivation. Sound, 'for itself', is never the object of a listening, whether reduced or otherwise.

The object is not the fulfillment of the desiring-production of the sensible. It is the motive for and the instrument of this production. It suffers the consequences of this, and itself becomes other. As Villiers de L'Isle-Adam said, 'the use that we make of a thing rebaptizes and transfigures it'.

Exaltations

If the fetishistic light we have shed upon listening is not meant to be understood from a pathological angle, it also should not be seen as a way of invalidating this or that way of listening in favour of a supposedly virginal listening free of all 'perversion'. On the contrary, it would appear that the fetishistic exalta- tion of the sensible can be the source and vector of the most compelling experiences:

> Isn't fetishism an opportunity for intensities? Doesn't it attest to
> an admirable force of invention, adding events which could not
> be more improbable to the libidinal band?[206]

The relation to sensations is not inevitably degraded by the mechanism of fetishism—a mechanism which, moreover, is

206. J.-F. Lyotard, *Libidinal Economy*, tr. I.H. Grant (Bloomington, IN: Indiana University Press, 1993), 110.

not a 'perversion' of that relation. Fetishism participates in the elaboration of sensation, and can even become a source of exaltation. Pushed to the point of paroxysm, there is a veritable refinement involved in 'machining' the sensible, in *augmenting* it or furnishing it with a new veil of illusion. The most perfect example of this comes from the imagination of Joris-Karl Huysmans, in his story *Against Nature*, which describes the life of a most singular person, a fetishistic aesthete who pushes the art of the factitious and of illusion to the furthest limits of the decadent spirit; an unworldly being responding to the name of Des Esseintes:

> There, by salting your bathwater and mixing into it, according to the formula given in the Pharmacopeia, sodium sulphate, hydrochlorate of magnesium, and lime; by taking from the tightly closed, screw-topped box, a ball of twine or a tiny piece of rope specially purchased in one of those huge ship's chandlers whose enormous warehouses and basements reek of sea-tides and sea-ports; by sniffing those fragrances which will still cling to the twine or piece of rope [...] finally, by listening to the moaning of the wind gusting under the arches of the bridge, and the rumbling of the omnibuses as they cross the Pont Royal just a few feet above you, the illusion of being near the sea is undeniable, overpowering, absolute.[207]

Reading Huysmans and observing Des Esseintes brings to mind this passage from Baudelaire, which was cited by Walter Benjamin:

---

207. J.-K. Huysmans, *Against Nature*, tr. M. Mauldon (Oxford: Oxford University Press, 1998).

I would rather return to the diorama, whose brutal and enormous magic has the power to impose a genuine illusion upon me. I would rather go to the theatre and feast my eyes on the scenery, in which I find my dearest dreams artistically expressed and tragically concentrated! These things, because they are false, are infinitely closer to the truth.[208]

What Benjamin singles out in Baudelaire—and it stands just as well in the case of Des Esseintes—is an inversion of the principle of authenticity which leads to the dissolution of the aura, a dissolution that takes place precisely in the very attempt to reproduce the aura, to reinvoke it by artificial means.

In both Des Esseintes and Baudelaire, the assumption is that sensation is no guarantee of authenticity, or in any case that it is not fated to serve as such a guarantee; and that sensory potency can be manufactured, suggested. Equally, both of them insist that the recourse to artifice is no degradation or degeneration of the human spirit, but that on the contrary it constitutes 'the distinguishing characteristic of human genius'.[209]

The exaltation of sensations has need of an artificial procedure. *It cannot but have recourse to such a procedure.* Moreover the artificial, refinement, is nothing more than the discursive setting-in-motion of desiring-tensions; it is nothing but the *utilization* of fantasies, their mobilization. And therefore the exaltation of sound by listening cannot correspond only to the discursive investment in desiring-listening. Here listening is approached quite unequivocally as a sensitive instrument

---

208. C. Baudelaire, 'The Salon of 1859', in *The Mirror of Art: Critical Studies by Baudelaire*, tr. J. Mayne (New York: Doubleday Anchor, 1956), 289.

209. Huysmans, *Against Nature*, 107.

of jouissance. One must not think that recourse to artifice, to refinement—that is to say, to the power of representation, and ultimately the power of discourse—vouchsafes only intellectual pleasures. On the contrary, this is mental elaboration in the service of a sensible erethism. Here again, the reference to fetishism is a fertile one. It allows us to take account of the powerful link between discursive elaboration, representation, and the formation of sensual pleasure. And this pleasure has nothing in common with a purely mental jouissance: 'I defy any lover of painting to love a picture as much as a fetishist loves a shoe', as Georges Bataille proclaims.[210]

Desire has need of objects, of protocols; and it has recourse to artifice, to fabrication. Sound is a quarry mined by the machinery of listening. Sounds extracted, turned into objects, pass through the screen, the sieve of perception. They are identified, evaluated, designated, classified, selected. We must not fail to recognize this industrious aspect of desire:

> Though the gods were the first promoters of the manufacture of objects, by which means manufacturers were to justify their continued subsistence, starting from the time that the manufacture of idols began to be considered useless, there began a long era of ignorance about the specific commodity character of the instinctual life in individuals, that is, a lack of knowledge about the different forms that pathological utility can take.[211]

---

210.   G. Bataille, 'The Modern Spirit and the Play of Transpositions', in D. Ades and S. Baker (eds.), *Undercover Surrealism* (Cambridge, MA: MIT Press, 2006), 241–3: 242.

211.   Klossowski, *Living Currency*.

The recourse to utility, to instrumental practice, is not apathic and sober. It has no firm, solid base. It is like a tension, an extension, every part of which is overflowed by desiring-processes. Lyotard, discussing the structure of speech, insists upon the way in which the modalities of desire invest a systematic construction such as that of language:

> Don't forget to add to the tongue and all the pieces of the vocal apparatus, all the sounds of which they are capable, and moreover, the whole selective network of sounds, that is, the phonological system, for this too belongs to the libidinal 'body'.[212]

If listening is a complex machinery within which are sedimented and intertwined numerous mechanisms for the management of the audible, it cannot be entirely governed by the implacable logic of the automatic. If it is indeed a machine, it remains first and foremost a desiring-machine, modulated, scanned, and amplified by cultures, discourses, and affects.

BEYOND SOUND

Overvalued Sound

In Freud, the source of fetishism is sexual overvaluation. There is overvaluation as soon as one *represents* the sexual act, which is already then no longer entirely 'for itself'. Perception, being inseparable from the act of representation, or even proceeding via representation, is revealed as an enterprise of the overvaluation of the sensible.

Thus the object of listening, the audible, exceeding the sonorous in so far as it overvalues it, is itself sound overvalued,

---

212. Lyotard, *Libidinal Economy*, 2.

embellished with values and powers of evocation that it does not possess, but which are lent to it precisely when it is constituted as an object. Saint Augustine's *voluptates aurium*, the 'delights of the ear', are illustrative of such an overvaluation.[213] For the pleasure of listening, a sensual pleasure that Augustine acknowledged feeling when listening to religious songs, is not purely a corollary of the acoustic characteristics of the sounds emitted by the singers. Pleasure is taken neither from the harmonious character of the singing voices, nor even from the sentiment of piety garnered by listening to sacred texts, but from their *conjunction*.

Indeed, Augustine declares that it is precisely because this pleasure is found in such a conjunction that he feels he is sinning:

> But this contentment of the flesh, to which the soul must not be given over to be enervated, doth oft beguile me, the sense not so waiting upon reason as patiently to follow her; but having been admitted merely for her sake, it strives even to run before her, and lead her. Thus in these things I unawares sin, but afterwards am aware of it.[214]

However, reason is never absent in the production of jouissance. It is reason that sublimates the sound of song through the piety that it evokes and invokes. It is the trace, that supplementary cloud that gravitates around sound, that fuels the concupiscence of the auditor. This trace is the manifestation of and the ingress for the overvaluation of sound. It is the go-between, the ford that permits the sonorous unknowable

213. Saint Augustine, *The Confessions*, Book 10, part 2, XXXII (tr. E.B. Pusey).

214. Ibid.

and ineffable to be drawn off into an audible that can be more easily managed, observed, and manipulated. Saint Augustine had an intuition of the utile character of the sensible, even if he perceived its ambivalence: if sensual pleasure presents the danger of opening the door to sin, it can also introduce one to the religious inclination:

> Thus I fluctuate between peril of pleasure and approved whole-someness; inclined the rather (though not as pronouncing an irrevocable opinion) to approve of the usage of singing in the church; that so by the delight of the ears the weaker minds may rise to the feeling of devotion.[215]

Sound, as overvalued sensible form, is a vehicle, a bearer of sense that aggregates around regimes of discourse, embedding itself in them. Overvaluation is nothing other than that 'driving principle' that ushers the sonorous into the audible, a kinetic principle that drives the sensible into discourse. Overvaluation is a driving principle, a dynamism. In Freud, it is the compensation for a lack—the sexual act's lack of any reflexive or representative character. Overvaluation, qua *refinement*, is indeed that placing into representation, into words, into images, of the act—so as to compress it, refine it, pervert it (that is to say, alter it). In this sense, the principle of overvaluation is that of being continually in search of alteration:

> Nor is any life ever satisfied to live in any present, for insofar as it is life it continues, and it continues into the future to the degree that it lacks life. If it were to *possess* itself completely

---

215. Ibid.

here and now and be in want of nothing—if it awaited nothing
in the future—it would not continue: it would cease to be life.[216]

What Michelstaedter describes here, this phenomenon of
life being drawn along by a 'lack of life', is not without a certain resonance with Schopenhauer's conception of human
existence:

> All satisfaction, or what is commonly called happiness, is really
> and essentially always *negative* only, and never positive. It is not
> a gratification which comes to us originally and of itself, but it
> must always be the satisfaction of a wish. For desire, that is to
> say, want, is the precedent condition of every pleasure; but with
> the satisfaction, the desire and therefore the pleasure cease;
> and so the satisfaction or gratification can never be more than
> deliverance from a pain, from a want.[217]

Marc Fumaroli, in his introduction to *Against Nature*,[218] brings
together what we might call *Schopenhauer's curse* and the
fate of Des Esseintes, caught between sorrow and jouissance,
between refinement pushed to the extreme *in order to move
forward* and melancholic disarray, spleen. Des Esseintes turns
to artifice, to the elaboration of *sensible representations*, simulations. The relation to desire is a relation to lack, it establishes
the object of desire as intrinsically insufficient; and this lack
can be remedied only by the use and instrumentalization of
external or externalized objects.

---

216. Michelstaedter, *Persuasion and Rhetoric*, 9.

217. A. Schopenhauer, *The World as Will and Representation*, vol I, tr. E.F.J.
Payne (New York: Dover, 1969), 319.

218. J.-K. Huysmans, *À Rebours* (Paris: Gallimard, 1977).

This is the deep reason for the principle of overvaluation, a principle that is active whenever desiring-production is at work, a principle located on the frontier between the actual and fantasy; a principle, finally, that bears within it all the seeds of a phantasmatic production, an entirely phantomatic production of the empty object of desire.

Listening, in so far as it is driven by the desiring activity of the auditor, is, like any enterprise of overvaluation, subject to tensions that push it onto a crest line where sensible manifestations and mental productions can no longer be distinguished from one another. And so, when audition suffers the turbulence of desiring tensions, it becomes liable to *produce* the very object of its listening.

Hallucinated Listening

We must clarify what is implied by the idea of a listening that both produces and receives one and the same sensible object, the idea of a circuit of listening in a state of *feedback*. Listening is constantly, to various degrees, under the influence of desiring-tensions. So it entertains a complex relation to perceived sounds, in so far as it projects onto them a sheaf of phantasms which, like a cloud surrounding the sounds, modify their aspect and model them in such a way as to bring them into accord with the auditor's expectations and desiring-projections. Listening, which was the auxiliary of hearing, now becomes an agent for the resorption and fulfilment of desire. As Barthes writes, 'when listening is oriented toward assuaging fantasy, it immediately becomes hallucinated: I believe I am really hearing what I would like to hear as a promise of pleasure'.[219]

219. Barthes, 'Listening', 248.

The incorporation of fantasy into perception *modifies* it from within, in the sense that perceived objects and fantasized objects enter into a regime of indistinction where the sensible object is haloed with characteristics that are projected onto it for the purposes of jouissance, or the verification, validation, and legitimation of that jouissance.

In fact, auditory fantasy functions both as a *will to hear* and as the confirmation of that will to hear through the production of an artifice that culminates in such verification. Such is the desiring-feedback of listening: a pursuit of the object of jouissance, the elaboration of that same object, and jouissance in the conquest of the object once attained.

Desiring-listening is a mechanism with a dual trigger. First of all, the production of fantasy seeps in *on the edges* of listening. In the preliminary stage when listening is focussed on an object, it orients and modifies *perceptual intent*, preparing it, conditioning it, so that listening is in a state of 'autosuggestion', a moment when one believes that one is 'really hearing what [one] would like to hear as a promise of pleasure'.

The second trigger consists simply in the fact that, when it is unable to focus on a sensible object capable of appeasing its desire, listening will actually fantasize it, hallucinate it, using sound as a medium for its reverie. The prescience of listening then becomes a faculty of invention.

Moreover, within the general empire of sensations, such a disposition can become a mode of sensual stimulation for those who, like Des Esseintes, can take their pleasure only through artificial mental constructions:

> The main thing is to know how to set about it, to be able to
> concentrate your attention on a single detail, to forget yourself

sufficiently to bring about the desired hallucination and so substitute the vision of a reality for the reality itself.[220]

This same phenomenon is discussed, somewhat less com-
placently, by the positivist Auguste Comte, who, in a text
precisely dedicated to fetishism, perceives this hallucinatory
relation to the real as an obscure brake on the development
of what Bachelard would later call the 'scientific spirit'. He
describes fetishism as being

> a sort of permanent common hallucination whereby, through
> the exaggerated empire of affective life over intellectual life, the
> most absurd beliefs can profoundly alter the direct observation
> of almost all phenomena.[221]

What is not quite clear is what Comte means by 'direct observation'. Are we to oppose to desiring-listening, phantasmatic
and screened by drives, a 'direct', apathic, rational listening?
Everything that has been said thus far tends to suggest
that such a direct and apathic listening—a reduced listening, in short—simply does not exist, and that listening is
always *animated*.

What is more, it is only by virtue of this internal animation
and the affects that traverse it that listening can generate such
pleasure and such disquiet. For, once more, desiring-tensions
and phantasmatic productions are not uniquely destined
for pleasure. They are never univocal, and are always active
whether or not one wishes them to be so. They are also present

---

220. Huysmans, *Against Nature*, 36.

221. A. Comte, *Cours de philosophie positive*, 52nd lesson, quoted in Pouillon,
'Fétiches sans fétichisme', in *Objets du fétichism*, 135.

in the rude irruption of sounds, their unsolicited invasion. Then they are the 'henchmen' of a panic listening, able to awaken both marvel and fear in the auditor taken off-guard, capable of ushering him toward jouissance or nervous collapse.

This is what happens to Lenz during his mountain walk:

> Only sometimes when the storms tossed the clouds into the valleys and they floated upwards through the woods and voices awakened on the rocks, like far-echoing thunder at first and then approaching in strong gusts, sounding as if they wanted to chant the praises of the earth in their wild rejoicing, and the clouds galloped by like wild whinnying horses [...] and then like the murmur of a lullaby or pealing bells rose up again from the depths of ravines and tips of fir trees and a faint reddishness climbed into the deep blue and small clouds drifted by on silver wings and all the mountain peaks, sharp and firm, glinted and gleamed far across the countryside, he would feel something tearing at his chest, he would stand there, gasping, body bent forward, eyes and mouth open wide, he was convinced he should draw the storm into himself, contain everything within himself....[222]

Lenz's experience of listening is dense, intense, precisely because it is hallucinatory—it is *excessive*. The artificial production of listening, when it is no longer solicited or when it becomes excessive, that is to say when what is produced completely takes precedence over what is received, or in short *when the clouds begin to whinny*, becomes a hallucinated production. Upon which listening itself enters into a regime of hallucination.

---

222. G. Büchner, *Lenz* [1879], tr. R. Sieburth (New York: Archipelago Books, 2004), 68.

There is hallucination from the moment when affect inflects perception and subjects it to its empire. At that point, the essential sensations perceived by the subject are no longer received from without, but are produced by the subject's own fantasies, even if these internal productions may be stimulated or catalyzed by external elements. Affects, desires, and phobias act directly upon perception, subjecting it to their own prerogatives.

For example, it is guilt, reinforced by a manic disposition, that leads Edgar Allan Poe's character to hear again and again, ever more loudly, the heart of the man he has killed. In the short story 'The Tell-Tale Heart' Poe describes the murder of an old man, with the murderer himself as narrator. The latter exposes his crime, with the intention of showing that he is not mad, as some claim, but of sound mind.

The narrator, endowed with great sensory acuity, is horrified at the sight of one of the eyes of the old man with whom he lives, an eye that he compares to that of a vulture, 'a pale blue eye, with a film over it'.[223] He hatches a plan to get rid of his roommate. Night after night, he watches him as he sleeps and, with the aid of a dark lantern, sheds light on the old man's eye. But the eye is always closed, thus defusing all malice in the murderer-to-be.

On the eighth night, the protagonist, repeating his ritual, awakens his victim when he opens up his lamp. There follows a long and anguished wait:

> I kept quite still and said nothing. For a whole hour I did not
> move a muscle, and in the meantime I did not hear him lie down.

---

223. E.A. Poe, 'The Tell-Tale Heart', in *Tales of Mystery and Imagination* (Ware: Wordsworth Classics, 1993), 221.

> He was still sitting up in the bed listening; —just as I have done,
> night after night, hearkening to the deathwatches in the wall.[224]

This waiting occasions a veritable circuit of anguished listening. The old man, watchful, racking his brains to work out what could possibly have caused the noise that awakened him, betrays his anguish with faint groans and the sound of his racing heart. His fear is transmitted to the listening murderer. This listening of fear makes a profound impression on the protagonist and will ultimately be the end of him. Both of them, silent, are all ears: a listening rendered sonorous in the old man by the terror that transpierces him; a silent listening on the part of the assassin, whose anguish mounts as the heart of his prey drums harder and harder, leading the murderer to fear that the noise will alert his neighbours.

Finally the deed is done, the old man is crushed by his own bed. The narrator then dismembers his victim and hides the sawn-up body under the floorboards. Soon afterwards three police officers arrive at the two men's home, alerted by a neighbour who heard a shriek.

The murderer, quite sure of himself, lets them in, reassures them, and sits them down in the very room where the dismembered body is hidden. Initially at his ease, the assassin perceives a low muffled sound, growing ever louder. Convinced that the sound is perfectly perceptible, he begins to suspect the policemen—who do not seem to hear anything, who display no *consciousness* of the sound, no sign of suspecting his crime—of playing tricks on him. In a state of nervous exhaustion, no longer able to bear this 'steadily increas[ing]' noise, he ends up confessing his deed, absolutely certain that

224. Ibid., 222.

the policemen must also hear the victim and the 'beating of his hideous heart'.[225]

In this text Poe lays out panic listening in its full complexity. From the alertness of the two protagonists to the inculpatory hallucination of the murderer, by way of the whole mental process of the old man as he resorts to *all that he can imagine* in order to *decide on* the origin of the perceived sound,[226] everything in this text points to the manifestation and expression of a listening *governed* by fear. Hallucination is but the consequence of such a listening.

During his walk in the mountains, Lenz, a veritable *homo natura*, as Deleuze and Guattari say, hallucinates through the prism of his schizophrenia. The murderer of the *tell-tale heart* hears the beating of his victim's heart persist and grow louder as his paranoiac delirium grows. And yet, although auditory hallucination can be invested by the pathological field (as in acousmia), *it cannot be reduced to it*.

Hallucination, of whatever sort, is not the sole prerogative of madness. Each of us can experience it more or less lucidly. Hallucination does not refer only to the voice of the Virgin who whispers a message to the saint, or the voice that orders the madman to kill. It is entirely of a piece with the *production* of listening, the modification of the sensible object.

---

225. Ibid., 224, 225.

226. We should emphasize here the reference to what are known in French as 'clocks of death' [*horloges de la mort*]—deathwatch beetles, whose larvae live in wood. They have an unwelcome tendency to hit their head against the walls, producing a series of percussive sounds from which their French name originates. These sounds are mostly heard at night, when all is quiet; they have sometimes been compared to the manifestation of poltergeists—one more illustration of the phantasmatic temptation to which listening falls prey when it is deprived of causal information.

It is the overinterpretation of a Raudive, mentally *kneading* the captured sounds in order to make them into the elements of a signifying language, even going so far as to combine many languages together so as to attain a convincing result. It is the ecstatic manifestation of the yogi or the shaman, the apparition of 'mystical sounds'. But it is also, more simply, the imagination running away with itself when confronted with the experience of listening.

What else could repetitive sounds heard inside the walls at night be, if not the tick-tock of the clock of death? In the throes of anguish, listening does not *seek* the cause of the mysterious sound—it *finds* it, even if it means hallucinating the sound itself in order to make it correspond *to what it has chosen to hear*. Acousmatic listening, then, builds on listening's pre-existing propensity to cross over into the properly hallucinogenic. All listening is listening to some thing—or rather, all listening *must* be listening to some thing.

The spectrum of hallucinated sound is broad and gradated; it is manifested and traversed in various ways: from neurotic delirium to mishearing, passing through altered states of consciousness and mystical transports. Hallucination is also manifested during reveries, moments of the loosening of consciousness.

Indeed, one of the first theorists of dreams, Léon d'Hervey de Saint-Denys, understanding hallucination in a generic sense, does not especially distinguish it from dream. For him, hallucination, like dream, is 'the representation to the eyes of the spirit of the object that occupies thought, when there is complete isolation from the external world'.[227]

---

227. L. d'Hervey de Saint-Denys, *Dreams and How to Guide Them* [1867], tr. N. Fry (London: Duckworth, 1982), 87 [translation modified].

In fact, in introducing the concept of the lucid dream, within which one becomes conscious that one is dreaming and can orient oneself to some extent within one's own dream, Hervey de Saint-Denys affirms that there is continuity between wakefulness and sleep, and that there are intermediate states wherein consciousness and perception are altered:

> As the body gradually loses its animation, and reality is forgotten, the mind sees more and more clearly the tangible images of the objects with which it is preoccupied. If we think of a person or place, the person's face and clothes and the trees or houses that are a part of the images gradually lose their vague outline, attaining a new crispness of form and colour. I even suggest in parenthesis to all who suffer from insomnia that, as they may often have noticed, their long-sought sleep is usually on the way when, as they doze off, fairly clear images begin to appear. In fact these moments of clear vision are already moments of true sleep. The transition from reverie to dreams of the greatest clarity takes place without any interruption in the train of ideas.[228]

In affirming this continuity between sleeping and waking states, Hervey de Saint-Denys in fact implies an intimate entanglement of perception and imagination, in particular by emphasizing the apparently paradoxical fact that a greater 'sensible' acuity comes over one as consciousness gives way to sleep, 'as reality is forgotten'. One form of perception is gradually replaced by another. But if this perception that occurs in dreams is essentially imaginary, virtual, it can also be conditioned by actual perception, gravitating once again into the sphere of the real. Hervey de Saint-Denys himself gives

228. Ibid., 36.

of phantasmatic perceptual processes:

> I had gone to take a bath, being tired after an evening spent at a
> dance. I dozed off in my tub. The sounds of a distant piano held
> my attention; and, as I went to sleep, I tried to catch the connec-
> tion between the loudest musical phrases, which, because of the
> distance of the instrument were the only ones that reached my
> ears. Soon I fell completely asleep, and I dreamed I was seated
> near a piano, watching a young woman of the neighbourhood
> whom I had often seen pass with a scroll of music in her hand,
> and I was listening as she played. Now I could hear every note ,
> every nuance of interpretation. A slight noise woke me suddenly
> from this brief sleep. I continued to hear the music which had
> guided my dream in the distance, but now I heard it only at
> intervals and very imperfectly, as I had done before I went to
> sleep. My perceptions were obviously less acute than when I
> had been momentarily asleep. I received only the sound waves
> that were strong enough to act upon my organs of hearing in
> their normal state.[229]

Lucid dreaming is midway between sober perception and
hallucination as it is normally defined. It is an altered state
of consciousness, much like those induced by other means
(ecstasy, delirium, drug use). What it reveals is that there
is no sudden leap between clear perception and hallucinatory perception, but a continuum across which perception
undergoes various degrees of alteration. Like Des Esseintes,
Hervey de Saint-Denys employs this faculty for the purpose
of jouissance, orienting the course of his dreams according

229. Ibid., 99–100.

to his wishes, proof that will and self-consciousness can be placed in the service of fiction and artifice just as well as that of clear vision and cognition—notwithstanding Auguste Comte and what therefore turns out to be *his own* fantasy of 'direct observation'.

Hallucination is a mode of perception inseparable from perception itself, not a deregulation or an exception to it. It is, in more or less dilute forms, the rule of perception. Nor is it uniquely dependent upon states of consciousness or physiological changes (fatigue, distraction, etc.). It depends above all on the cultural apparatus within which the auditor has grown up since birth: the impact of a civilization on an individual is a hallucinatory vector in so far as it catalyzes, modifies, and transforms his or her perceptual apparatus. As Jean Oury says,

> painters change the world before our eyes: we no longer see the same clouds since Turner, the same women after Watteau, the same lemons after Braque. Art, as we know, does not imitate nature so much as nature imitates art.[230]

Still, can this education of perception, this acculturation of the sensible, really be understood in terms of hallucination? If we set out from the strict definition of the latter, certainly not. But if we consider hallucination as a gradual process to which the name 'hallucination' only fully applies in its final stages, then this opens up certain new perspectives on the way in which cultural and perceptual factors join forces in the desiring-representation that is the hallucinatory tendency.

---

230. Jean Oury, citing Jean Paulhan, in *Création et schizophrénie* (Paris: Galilée, 1989), 174.

On the other hand, to demonstrate the potential of the hallucination of listening is not to disqualify it or to imply that all value judgment resulting from it is null and void. It is rather to show that listening is a sensory oscillation, holding in balance, depending on the moment, context, and situation, two extremes: an apathic capture of stimuli, and a hallucinated production catalyzed by affects and desires. In thus demonstrating that listening is not a fixed pole but a drifting, moving perceptual target, we also explain why discursive rigidification seems so necessary. To firmly establish a discourse around sound and listening is to struggle against both the fugacity of sound and the inconstancy of listening.

Hallucination must be considered as a mode of perceptual activity that is not necessarily the result of nervous collapse (although it can be, and then becomes pathological) but which gradually, insidiously distils itself drop by drop, by virtue of the perception of ill-defined objects. Thus hallucination plays the role of a *phantasmatic verification of certainties*.

Purities

The desiring, fetishistic, or hallucinatory process of listening establishes perceived, objectivated sound as 'henchman', substitute, or go-between. Sound is a pretext for the expression and activation of an entirely other desire or disquiet (the confirmation of life after death in Raudive, the wholesale possession of the world through its molecularization in Lenz, etc.).

Sometimes the object of desire is sound itself, in so far as it has become the object of the expression of values. This is the case with the belief in a purity of sound—which is also a *purist*, even puritanical, approach to sound. Here again, sound is overvalued (Freud was not able to see that modesty is also a kind of sexual overvaluation, catalyzing the excessive aspect of sex by setting up a moral framework in opposition to it). The purity of sound corresponds to a moment where the phantasmatic apparatus folds in on itself, and where sound becomes at once the object and medium of fantasy. Sound is crystallized, and takes on all the authenticity that is attributed to ineffable and ungraspable things.

In this autonomous regime of sound, there arises a great temptation to establish a 'panacoustic' discourse as counterweight to the hegemony of vision in our cultures and its panoptical grip upon us. Indeed there is such a discourse, which emerged around the concepts developed by Murray Schafer, the creator of acoustic ecology.

In *The Soundscape*, Schafer introduces two concepts, clear hearing and schizophonia, which are most indicative of what we might consider an aporetic stage in the overvaluation of sound: the stage where sound is confined within an autonomy that is both preferential treatment and gilded coffin.

Clear hearing, 'clairaudience', 'refers to exceptional hearing ability, particularly with regard to environmental sound'.[231] This concept circulates implicitly throughout Murray Schafer's theoretical work, which seeks to set in train, through a clear and deliberate hearing, the reacquisition of a harmonious relation to the acoustic environment that supposedly existed before the advent of the industrial age. In addition, Schafer develops a curious distinction between 'hi-fi' and 'lo-fi' soundscapes,[232] a distinction that depends on the notion of 'masking', and which is structured around the couplets town/country and past/

---

231. Schafer, *The Soundscape*, 272.

232. 'Applied to soundscape studies a hi-fi environment is one in which sounds may be heard clearly without crowding or masking.' Inversely, 'a lo-fi environment is one in which signals are overcrowded, resulting in masking or lack of clarity' (ibid).

present, making of the countryside of the past the nec plus ultra of hi-fi, and presenting the cities of today as archetypal noisy lo-fi environments, veritable acoustic Babylons.

To this degradation of the environment linked to the development of industry and the urban mode of life Schafer adds another source of the destitution of listening: mediation. At this point he introduces the concept of *schizophonia*, which relates to 'the split between an original sound and its electroacoustic reproduction'.[233]

Schafer's concept is somewhat reminiscent of Benjamin's observations on the loss of the aura of works of art owing to their mechanical reproducibility. But where Benjamin exhibits a new problematic, with its own risks, promises, and symptoms, Schafer simply cries wolf, deploring

> the overkill of hi-fi gadgetry [which] not only contributes gener-
> ously to the lo-fi problem, but [...] creates a synthetic soundscape
> in which natural sounds are becoming increasingly unnatural
> while machine-made substitutes are providing the operative
> signals directing modern life.[234]

Schafer sets up his opposition between natural and artificial without bothering to define them, no doubt thinking that such a distinction speaks for itself. Natural sound, in Schafer, is not limited to sound produced by what is commonly called 'Nature': he would surely consider the sound of village church bells, for example, to be natural. For Schafer the term 'natural' no doubt comprises the idea of a unity of space and time, the

---

233. Ibid., 273.
234. Ibid., 91.

hic et nunc of Benjaminian authenticity; and the artificial no doubt arrives with the dislocation of the appearance of sound:

> Originally all sounds were originals. They occurred at one time in one place only. Sounds were then indissolubly tied to the mechanisms that produced them. The human voice traveled only as far as one could shout. Every sound was uncounterfeitable, unique. Sounds bore resemblances to one another, such as the phonemes which go to make up the repetition of a word, but they were not identical. Tests have shown that it is physically impossible for nature's most rational and calculating being to reproduce a single phoneme in his own name twice in exactly the same manner.[235]

Here again, there is a confusion between the appearance of sound and sound's appearing. The sound that appears is always *produced*, generated by a vibratory event. The electroacoustic 'reproduction' of sound precisely does not reproduce it. It re-presents it by producing a sound from its imprint: a new sound which is identical to the nearest infra-thin, and which therefore, as we have said, is *different*. It is the appearance of sound, its phenomenal character, that is sufficiently similar for the ear to be able to identify it, like a *trompe-l'oreille*, with the originally appearing sound. Now, if the sound is different, then there is no dislocation of sound, and there is no schizophonia. The only schizz here is precisely that which distinguishes the appearance of sound (that which is given to be heard by the auditor) from the sound's appearing (which includes the cause, context, and *situation* of the appearing of the sound).

---

235. Ibid., 90.

It is because he believes that sound has a homogeneous and immediate character, an essential character, that Schafer understands the electroacoustic reproduction of sound in terms of schizophonia. Whereas in fact what the reproduction of sound attests to and manifests is simply the composite nature of sound; of a sound that consists of vibratory events, perceptual and symbolic traces, and an audition that actualizes them. In itself, then, reproduction invalidates the idea of a pure and autonomous nature of sound, a nature which Schafer reproaches it with violating and soiling by trying to duplicate it. Schafer's schizophonia is nothing other than a scornful recognition of the fragmented, schizological natures of listening and of sound.

Oscillating between an alarmism deploring the sonorous nuisances of modernity and a will to safeguard sounds on the verge of extinction, Schafer's approach is clearly under the influence of the syndrome of paradise lost, a phantasmatic space that is ultimately nothing less than a panacoustic empire. The pure, clear relation to sound advocated by Schafer is articulated around a nostalgia that resonates on two planes, situating itself both as a defence of a 'traditional' sonorous environment and, in reference to an originary sound, as an affirmation of primordial sound.

For example, when he makes the dubious claim that 'if cannons had been silent, they would never have been used in warfare',[236] Schafer speaks for an idealized relation to sound and listening that has no real basis. This idealization by way of the supposed purity of sound is in fact only the vehicle for a pastoral and millenarian tradition, an eminently utopian one. In his idealized panacoustic empire, Schafer dreams of an

236. Ibid., 78.

omnipotent sound capable of determining everything, even the use of war machines.

Such a space of 'everything audible' is ultimately what Schafer calls a 'soundscape'. Now, although emphasizing the sonorous component of a landscape is a laudable intention, the use of a dedicated term for it turns out to be pernicious. For it only increases the alienation of sound and its exclusion from the sensible environment, as Tim Ingold points out in a text explicitly entitled 'Against Soundscape':

> [T]he environment that we experience, know and move around in is not sliced up along the lines of the sensory pathways by which we enter into it. The world we perceive is the same world, whatever path we take, and each of us perceives it as an undivided centre of activity and awareness. For this reason I deplore the fashion for multiplying -*scapes* of every possible kind. The power of the prototypical concept of landscape lies precisely in the fact that it is not tied to any specific sensory register—whether vision, hearing, touch, smell or whatever.[237]

The final stage in the overvaluation of sound is its autonomization and its complete detachment from the sensible world. This is the risk courted by approaches linked to acoustic ecology, and is precisely what Ingold deplores—all the more so given that the relation between environment and auditor goes in both directions. For the theory of the soundscape accords a great importance to the *circulatory* relation between individual and environment (each auditor being himself a producer of sounds, he fashions in turn the environment that fashions him).

---

237. T. Ingold, 'Against Soundscape', in A. Carlyle (ed), *Autumn Leaves* (London and Paris: CRiSAP/Double Entendre, 2007), 10.

Indeed, it is the awareness of such a relation between indi-vidual and sonorous environment that opens up the possibility of an acoustic ecology—that is to say, of a stewardship or management of the sonorous context within which one lives. Here once again, such a reflection seems natural and legiti-mate, and yet one might wonder how a stewardship of sound defined according to the soundscape perspective might work. As suggested by the subtitle of Schafer's book, *The Tuning of the World*, what is at stake here is in fact not so much becom-ing aware of the sonorous environment as organizing it so as to act upon it, to discipline it—precisely to 'tune' it.

In fact, what we find at the source of this growing aware-ness of being a listener in a ceaselessly changing sonorous field are the residues of a culture of the musical apprehension of sound; and this ultimately involves the implication, within the conceptual construction of the soundscape, of an organized, or organizable, nature. This can be seen clearly when Schafer uses the notion of the 'keynote' in the analytical framework suggested for listening to a soundscape.

The fact that what is at stake in Schafer is ultimately musi-cal transpires through the idea that each sound should be in its place and that all sounds should be perceived (which responds to the definition of the hi-fi soundscape—a suitable, *appropri-ate* soundspace). The overvaluation of sound thus draws the ecological approach toward a disciplinarity that brings it close to musical ordering. The overvaluation of sound, the faith in a pure and natural sound that must be defended, ends up as a mere pretext for the expression of a *vision of the world*.

MUSIC AND CRYSTALLIZATION

Through his ecological approach Schafer engenders a *harmonic* relation to sound. His conception of the world is that of a world in order, in the most 'antique' sense—a Pythagorean sense, so to speak. So soundscape must already be considered as a 'musical' notion which, with this harmony, betrays its most radical nature, the deep origins of its whole genealogy.

Music, as understood since the modern epoch, is ultimately nothing but the stewardship and development of this harmonic relation by man and his 'genius'. Jules Combarieu, in his rather dialectical definition of music, exhibits the whole spectrum across which it is deployed, aiming to establish it in its objective existence, all the while assuming its avowedly ungraspable nature which, however, he continually tries to circumscribe:

> The interpreter and creator of deep psychical conditions, the delicate emanation of the mind, the subtle force of the moral life, it is at once feeling and thought. Into the enchantment of sounds it puts logic for the intelligence, a language of love for the heart—an art of construction and of form for the imagination. It is the meeting-point of the law of numbers which rules the world, and the unfettered fancy which creates the possible. Although hemmed in on every side by its relation to ordinary life, it is yet a glorious example of that spontaneity of the reason which attains 'to greater heights than theology or philosophy' (Beethoven).[238]

What we should retain from Combarieu's definition is the architectural element of music, its inclination toward construction,

---

238. J. Combarieu, *Music: Its Laws and Evolution* (New York: D. Appleton and Company, 1910), 2.

but also its faculty for elevation 'to greater heights than theology or philosophy'.

Pierre Schaeffer distinguished the sound object from the musical object on the sole basis that the musical object *has been designed* for music. The sound object becomes musical when it is integrated into a musical structure. Before Schaeffer, a musical sound had to respond satisfactorily to criteria of pitch, timbre, and duration. After him, the traditional criterion of an easily identifiable pitch definitively loses its pertinence. Noises now invest the field of music, and themselves become musical objects. The distinction between musical sound and noise, founded on a tradition that established a sound as noise on the basis of criteria such as absence of identifiable pitch or excessive level of acoustic pressure, now becomes blurred. And yet music and musical sound remain; it is noise that has been integrated into the musical, and not the other way around.

Combarieu writes later on that 'music is the art of *thinking in sounds*'.[239] Now, to 'think in sounds' is to convoke (musical) listening and place it in the service of a (musical) discourse. So, to be entirely exact, Combarieu's formulation calls for a tautological addition, becoming: 'Music is the art of thinking in sounds *musically.*' The prism of music in the modern epoch merges with and loses itself in the nascent rationalism that shapes it, makes it conform to the ideal, affirming that the sublime, the divine, can only be attained through the reasoned and ordered expression of things.

---

239. Ibid., 7.

Organized Sounds

Everyone will tell you that I am not a musician. That is correct. From the very beginning of my career, I classed myself as a phonometrographer. My work is completely phonometrical. Take my *Fils des Étoiles*, or my *Morceaux en Forme d'une Poire*, my *En Habit de Cheval*, or my *Sarabandes*. It is evident that musical ideas played no part whatsoever in their composition. Science is the dominating factor.

Besides, I enjoy measuring a sound much more than hearing it. With my phonometer in my hand, I work happily and with confidence. [...]

I think I can say that phonology is superior to music. There's more variety to it. The financial return is greater, too, I owe my fortune to it. At all events, with a motodynaphone, even a rather inexperienced phonometrologist can easily note down more sounds than the most skilled musician in the same time, using the same amount of effort. This is how I have been able to write so much. And so the future lies with phonometrology.[240]

Erik Satie is a master of irony, but through this irony the internal conflicts of music are revealed and rub up against one another. In claiming to create works in which 'musical ideas [play] no part whatsoever', he inaugurates the principle of nonintentional composition that we will find later in John Cage. If he ushers in the figure of the genius-composer, in particular with his furniture music and his *Vexations*, Satie also attacks the rigorism of musical systematics. As Diedrich Diederichsen has written—and this is particularly true in the

---

240. E. Satie, 'Memoirs of an Amnesiac', tr. N. Wilkins in *The Writings of Erik Satie* (London: Eulenburg Books, 1980), 58.

case of *Vexations*—'in Satie there is already a bringing into play of timbre as autonomous metasign, in part directed by compositional construction'.[241]

In asserting that his works express nothing and in ironically proclaiming himself a phonometrographer, Satie evokes the paradox of the musical, at once a conventional system and an expressive element issuing from the subjectivity of the composer—a paradox that governed the academicism of the time, which precisely sought to reconcile the normative and the expressive through the promotion of a music that was systemic, organized, and thus conventional, but at the same time expressive and brilliant. Such a music sets itself up as the systematization of an opportunist intersection of romantic humanism and the modern ideal.

But in fact, music, qua musical matrix, is more than a system—it is a metasystem, or a metastable system, which tends toward a potential generalized musicalization of all sound. The music of noises, invented by Luigi Russolo and rationalized by Pierre Schaeffer, is proof of this: music has the capacity to integrate an infinite number of sounds. Any sound whatsoever can accede, one way or another, to the status of musical sound.

What is paradoxical is that this openness, this adaptability of the musical system, is not always accompanied by a drive to liberate sound. The criteria of musical validity exceed the qualitative criteria that belong to sound itself. They also include its usage and its integration into the musical system, into musical discourse.

---

241. D. Diederichsen, 'Entendre la couleur—Le *big band* de Matthew Herbert', in *Argument son—De Britney Spears à Helmut Lachenmann: critique électroacoustique de la société et autres essais sur la musique* (Dijon: Les Presses du Réel, 2007), 21.

Music always, and sometimes for the better, proceeds via restraint. Taking the example of free improvisation, Diederichsen arrives at the conclusion that, with a few exceptions, even the most 'free' improvisations remain inflexible with regard to the idea that it must be practiced by *musicians*. This observation leads him to observe that

> it is therefore possible to state that music, even music stripped of its tonality and composition, still abounds with so many prior conditions that what we need first is a musical practice of the dismantling (of music) in order to fabricate a true communication, beyond music.[242]

We must understand that music has gradually passed from being a *constituted* element to being a *constituting* element,[243] and that, in this sense, it now proceeds tautologically. A sound is only musical in so far as it is integrated into a musical structure, meaning that a set of sounds can be annexed by music and can thus be qualified as musical because something of the musical is found in them—with the essence of the musical itself remaining opaque.

Music is this process of the integration of sonorous elements activating, through *musical* listening, an organizing function. Thus, even where there is no clear and explicit musical intention in the production of sound, it can very well be reinvested a posteriori by listening. It is this kind of reinvestment

---

242. Diederichsen, 'Entendre la couleur', 45–6.

243. Music remains a constituted element in so far as it remains functional, i.e., in so far as it responds to one of the functions assigned to it. Once it becomes autonomous, that is to say once one decides to define it not through its usage, but through its nature, and it acquires a capacity for self-determination, then it becomes a constituting element.

of musical intention in listening that permits humans to speak of 'birdsong'.

This organizing function has long manifested itself through musical notation, and continues to do so today. Notation is definitively not constitutive of the organizational function of the musical; yet there can be no doubt that it acts as a catalyst for this function, particularly through the unification and smoothing out of the musical vocabulary:

> [T]he history of musical notation is that of an increasingly rigorous mathematicization, highlighting the generalized standardization of signs in the system of representation. The score is to music what linear perspective is to painting, [...] a regulative placeholder that reacts upon its referent by subjecting it to a codified symbolic logic.[244]

Sublimated Sound and Cosmic Harmony

Music is closely associated with the idea of order. This order can be determined sociologically, but can also claim a universal status in so far as it is founded upon cosmic laws. The origins of codified music go back to antiquity. They are founded on the principles of harmony and their connection to the universe itself—in particular, the attempt to define musical intervals in correspondence with the distances between the planets:

> Pythagoras, employing the terms that are used in music, sometimes names the distance between the Earth and the Moon a tone; from her to Mercury he supposes to be half this space, and about the same from him to Venus. From her to the Sun is a tone and a half; from the Sun to Mars is a tone, the same as from the

---

244. Thévoz, *Le Miroir infidel*, 116.

Earth to the Moon; from him there is half a tone to Jupiter, from Jupiter to Saturn also half a tone, and thence a tone and a half to the zodiac. Hence there are seven tones, which he terms the diapason harmony, meaning the whole compass of the notes.[245]

On the basis of this harmony of the spheres, which we also find in Plato,[246] a privileged relation between the musical and the 'universal' develops, generating both a reasoned approach to music, and the development of a discourse legitimating the musical via its 'cosmic' destiny. It is this conception of music that allows Leibniz, for example, to say that 'music is a hidden exercise in arithmetic, of a mind unconsciously dealing with numbers'.[247]

It is indeed a question of the expression of conceptions or beliefs and their legitimation. Music is never—or only on very rare occasions and only since the twentieth century—a pure mathematical development. It is always compromised by a practical, aesthetic residue. The most important compromise is the temperament of the scale, an alteration of harmonic perfection for the benefit of a justness of which only subjective and culturally-determined listening can be the judge. One may think here of La Monte Young's piece *The Well Tuned Piano*, and the startling sonority of the piano tuned to just intonation, that is to say according to a purely mathematical harmonics.

In this work, Young takes a twofold approach, a rather original combination of avant-gardism and mysticism—not a

---

245. Pliny the Elder, *Natural History* (tr. J. Bostock).

246. Cf. G. Pelé, *Inesthétiques musicales au XXe siècle* (Paris: IDEAT-CNRS/ Université Paris 1/L'Harmattan, 2007), in particular 152–64, 'À la recherché de l'harmonie [In Search of Harmony]'.

247. G.W. Leibniz, Letter to Christian Goldbach, April 17, 1712, *et passim*.

rather a *harmonic* and immanent mysticism, in the sense that
the aim of his music is less to evoke a universal harmonic order
than to experience it from within:

> God created the body so that the soul could come to earth to
> study music so that it could have a better understanding of
> universal structure. Music can be a model for universal structure
> because we perceive sound as vibration and if you believe, as
> I do, that vibration is the key to universal structure you can
> understand why I make this statement.[248]

Music is never isolated. It is part of a system of values and of
representation that each individual develops in experiencing
the world and his or her relation to it. The 'musicalizing' tension of listening acts as a desiring-tension—one listens musically to that which promises to be musical. It thus transfers
onto sound the values that are attributed to the musical.

Music, as formalization of desiring-listening, crystallizes
sound, which is at once sublimated and placed in tension by
the structural framework within which it is thus fixed. Once
it becomes musical, sonorous material already belongs to an
ordered world.

Even if 'desire cannot be assumed, accepted, understood,
locked up in names = nomenclatured',[249] nomenclature, and in
fact order, can certainly become an object of desire. For desire
is not necessarily the breath of liberty, and we must take into

---

248. La Monte Young, cited by David Toop in *Ocean of Sound*, 178. See also
the interviews with Young in D. Caux, *Le Silence, les couleurs du prisme et la
mécanique du temps qui passe* (Paris: L'éclat, 2009).

249. Lyotard, *Libidinal Economy*, 20.

account that 'representing is desire, putting on stage, in a cage, in prison, into a factory, into a family, being boxed in are desired'.[250]

FICTION-LISTENING

Listening is always predetermined by *intentions* that fuse with it. These intentions, these tensions, orient its power of focalization, its faculty of transforming the sonorous, the unheard, into the audible. Listening, mobilized by these tensions and driven by them, constitutes sound objects by determining them formally or symbolically. They identify and constitute a trace as affirmation and supplement of existing sound. Sound is thereby reified, rendered tangible. It is invokable, convokable, utilizable. Like a fetish, it serves as a medium for the desiring tensions that invest perception, enslaving the latter so as to make it an instrument of jouissance. The desiring process is never the assumption of a state, but its attenuation, its repression, or its annihilation. Thus sound is submitted to desire as a dead branch is to the current of a river. It is oriented, it is immersed, and it re-emerges, all as a function of dynamic contingencies.

Listening is never directly connected to sound: there is always a pretext, a context, a conduit, which predetermine it. It is the 'henchman' of a discursive scaffold whose duplicity often involves a claim to return to sound itself, when in fact it only establishes sound in a utile relation; when it only produces listening in order to hear it speaking words that it itself has put into its mouth.

And so listening is a matrix of fictions, but

> [f]iction is not the creation of an imaginary world opposed to
> the real world. It is the work that operates *dissensuses*, which

---

250. Ibid., 12.

changes modes of sensible presentation and forms of enunciation by changing the frames, the scales, or the rhythms; by constructing new relations between appearance and reality, the singular and the common, the visible and its signification. This work changes the coordinates of the representable: it changes our perception of sensible events, our way of relating them to subjects, the way in which our world is peopled with events and figures.[251]

Fiction-listening submits the sensible to the power of discourse, conditions it in a process with neither beginning nor end; a process which, looping back on itself, generates a dual trigger mechanism acting on two distinct moments of audition. Hence the fictionalization of listening is deployed in an at once proactive and retroactive manner. Proactive, first of all, as a suggestion of the sensible, of the type that Des Esseintes elevated to the rank of art, conditioning his perception in advance by assigning it a determinate axis of focalization. Such a stance develops an a priori discrimination of sensible experience, de facto atomizing it and submitting it to the force of the imagination, to the force of representation—that is, to the force of discourse.

And then retroactive, qua *verified* listening: there is a part of listening that always involves a verification and validation of itself. Once again, this verification is determined by the sheaf of pre-existing values, systems of discourse, and representations. And here, once again, what we observe and auscultate is a reified, crystallized audible.

---

251. J. Rancière, *Le Spectateur émancipé* (Paris: La Fabrique, 2008), 72.

5

AUTHORITARIAN LISTENING

DISCOURSE AND THE ANCHORING OF SOUND

As we have seen, for Barthes listening is the theatre of operations for the struggle between desire and power. But desire and power are not simply two opposing terms: each excites and stimulates the other, each one is by turns means and end of the other. Power is desirable, but it is also an instrument for the deployment of desire.

Power has another ability which desire does not have at its disposal, though. Or rather, it is a placeholder for the perfect attainment of that which desire seeks above all: order. Power is the setting in motion, in rhythm, of an order which is simultaneously the very expression of power.

Discourse and Doctrine

It is for this purpose—the expression of order—that discourses are fabricated and aggregated. But what is a discourse? Discourse is not a passive space, and '[i]t would be quite wrong to see discourse as a place where previously established objects are laid one after another like words on a page'.[252] Foucault refuses to see discourse as a mere receptacle articulating already-signifying elements. He insists that discourses are not 'groups of signs (signifying elements referring to contents or representations) but [...] practices that systematically form the objects of which they speak'.[253]

Discourse is a 'practice' that acts upon objects. But as we recall, objects themselves, qua 'objectivated' or 'formed', are already discursive forces. They 'call for' discourse as lungs call for air: they presuppose it and are destined for it. So discourse

---

252. Foucault, *Archaeology of Knowledge*, 47.

253. Ibid., 54.

develops at the intersection of desire and power, and is 'not simply that which manifests (or hides) desire—[but] also the object of desire'.[254] Neither is it 'that which translates struggles or systems of domination, but is the thing for which and by which there is struggle, discourse is the power which is to be seized'.[255]

The very production of discourse is subject to mechanisms of control and regulation. A discourse is never established according to margins of mobility or degrees of freedom; it is established according to protocols. Among these protocols Foucault identifies three systems of exclusion: the *prohibited*, which determines what may and may not be said at the moment when discourse appears; *madness* or senselessness, which immediately invalidates the discourse and its authors; and the *will to truth*. By virtue of such exclusion, a discourse is a system of expression and representation that affirms itself as being a priori valid.

To these three systems of exclusion Foucault then adds procedures of internal control (for example, the commentary, which acts as an instrument for the reactualization and smoothing-out of discourses) and procedures of regulation whose object is no longer discourse itself, but its enunciation. This new prescription brings with it the question of the authority of that which conveys the discourse. If the discourse is seen as valid, that which enunciates it, he or she who enunciates it, must *be an authority*:

---

254. M. Foucault, 'The Order of Discourse', in R. Young (ed), *Untying the Text: A Post-Structuralist Reader* (Boston, London and Henley: Routledge and Kegan Paul, 1981), 51–78: 52.

255. Ibid., 52–3.

No one shall enter into the order of discourse if he does not satisfy certain requirements or if he is not, from the outset, qualified to do so.[256]

All of these procedures, then, come together in the establishing of a system of subjection to a discourse, a system that regulates it, makes it circulate, distributing and determining the roles and functions of those who make use of it so as to assure its validity, its recognition, and its authority.

The use of discourse, in so far as it is regulated and shaped, is necessarily doctrinal. The more discourse tries to consolidate itself, to legitimate itself, the more regulated its use becomes, the more doctrine will take precedence over discourse. Discourse is never neutral: it distributes roles and duties throughout its site of appearing.

Discourse and Apprehension of Sound

In every case, at every moment, it seems that listening renders the sonorous audible through recourse to functions of focalization, identification, and designation. What listening grasps in sound so as to render it audible is its trace. In fact, listening does not simply grasp this trace, but establishes it. The trace is nothing other than the power of discourse, but at the same time is already its object.

Discourse intervenes in listening by turning the perceived object into an object that can be spoken of, described, classified, linked to this or that other object—that is to say, by making it communicable. Discourse introduces heard sound into a community. But here we are speaking of a highly developed second-order discourse. Discourse in embryo, potential

---

256. Ibid., 61–2.

discourse, is already there, flush with listening itself. At once more and less than a discourse, it is a discursive seed. It is that which, as yet silent, provokes listening, determines an aim for it, a reason. It is that through which listening generates objects. It is that which forms the audible object. Residing in it already are the becomings of discourses, of fictions. It is already there when desire grows, already there when the real asserts itself. Lyotard writes that '[r]eality and desire are born together at the threshold of language'.[257] This seed, also, is located at the threshold of language.

An object, whatever it may be, *qua targeted object* is always an object of discourse. Any pebble lying on a road somewhere, once it is seen as a pebble, is the bearer of a discourse, albeit the most primitive one. Thus discourse is the space of the appearing of objects. Subsequently, as Foucault shows, discourse establishes itself as unitary in so far as the objects it constitutes cannot possibly disrupt this unity:

> [the] formation [of objects] is defined if one can establish such
> a group; if one can show how any particular object of discourse
> finds in it its place and law of emergence; if one can show that
> it may give birth simultaneously or successively to mutually
> exclusive objects, without having to modify itself.[258]

Listening is doubly subject to discourse: in its internal functioning first of all, in so far as it is piloted by that structuring force of language, that discursive seed; and then in its *becoming*, in so far as it is enslaved to usages determined by specific

---

257. J.-F. Lyotard, *Discourse, Figure*, tr. A. Hudek and M. Lydon (Minneapolis, MN and London: University of Minnesota Press, 2011), 123.

258. Foucault, *Archaeology of Knowledge*, 49.

discursive regimes. It is by turns a listening that is indexical, musical, a reduced listening, a panic listening, etc., while being, at every moment, all possible listenings. If listening speaks, it is because it is made to speak; because it is always transpierced, through and through, by the discursive traits that are continually soliciting it.

To apprehend the sonorous is not yet to listen. To listen is already to be in a position of decoding, to already perceive the audible beyond the sonorous; it is almost to already capture the intelligible beyond the audible. The sonorous surroundings in their totality reach the ears; but only that which is audible is listened to. Or more precisely, only that which is listened to or heard (for it is the same thing) becomes audible.

Discourse takes hold of the apprehension of the sonorous in order to make a listening of it; and through this apprehension, it takes hold of the sonorous in order to make it audible, once it has been atomized into objects. Once more, discourse is never passive. It acts anywhere and everywhere it can. Consequently, as Foucault says,

> we must not resolve discourse into a play of pre-existing significations; we must not imagine that the world turns towards us a legible face which we would have only to decipher; the world is not the accomplice of our knowledge; there is no prediscursive providence which disposes the world in our favour. We must conceive discourse as a violence which we do to things, or in any case as a practice which we impose on them; and it is in this practice that the events of discourse find the principle of their regularity.[259]

---

259. Foucault, 'The Order of Discourse', 67.

The power of discourse is an active power, always a con-quering power that seeks to bring sensible experience in its entirety under its regime. But if this power is deployed by doing violence to experience, experience itself is a consenting victim, and desires to be set in order.

Carlo Michelstaedter explains this need for order, for the structuring of experience, in terms of the inability to experi-ence the world immediately and totally, the impossibility of being *persuaded* by it. Out of reach, persuasion then becomes occulted by discursive systems and apparatuses, by a *rhetoric*, which serves as narcotic and palliative for a life that cannot possess itself fully: 'thus *rhetoric flourishes alongside life*. Men put themselves in a *cognitive attitude and make knowledge*.'[260]

The sensible is the foremost thing at stake in the struggle for knowledge. It is the territory that must be possessed and administered in every last one of its corners. Power has always distrusted anything that could reconfigure the sensible or alter it (the arts, drugs, madness).

Walter Benjamin says that the 'world of perception' is 'one of the supreme strata of language';[261] and it is through this community between sense and the sensible that discourse comes to invest the latter. In the context of listening, it is clear enough what is at stake here: it is a question of making the ineffable sayable, making the fugitive permanent. Sound, in itself, always escapes. By targeting it, reifying it, identifying it, designating it, and qualifying it—in short, by bringing it into the world of discourse—it can be fixed, anchored. '*The more sharply defined, the more fully formed, a complex of percep-tions is, the easier it is to reproduce*.'[262]

---

260. Michelstaedter, *Persuasion and Rhetoric*, 69.

261. W. Benjamin, *Fragments* (Paris: PUF, 2001), 74.

262. Weininger, *Sex and Character*, 101.

This anchoring of sound rests upon the fact that the structures of language penetrate down to the very lowest levels of perception, that they are always present. However, it is not enough to say that listening proceeds via anchoring, fixation, objectivation: it turns to discourse in order to go further. Discourse is a second way of locking down sound which makes up for the imperfections of the discriminative functions of listening, and develops the structuring that is presupposed by objectivation. What is at stake in this discourse is the ability to *deduce* the other objects that belong to this structure (that are *appropriate* to this structure) and to *recognise* them when they appear. Discourse qua structure applied to sounds and to listening thus becomes an instrument for the evaluation, validation, and legitimation of auditory perception.

As such, listening is subject to a veritable discipline of discursive regimes. Foucault says that discourse is a violence done to things; but the violence is also, and above all, done to the functions that identify those things. 'To make listening more acute, as a form of torture', as Duchamp wrote.[263]

What is at stake in the anchoring of sound is therefore not just a will to fix sound, but also the will to attest to and to affirm its essential nature. Discourses that have sound as their principal object, then, do not so much seek to qualify it as to essentialize it. In advocating and seeking to establish order and permanence, essentialist discourses reveal that they are above all affairs of authority and power. Listening, *conducted* by them, and becoming their instrument of heuristic verification, acts upon sound like an authoritarian and selective magnet, dispatching the sonorous back into limbo, into an absence from which only the *become-audible* will be spared. In this sense,

---

263. M. Duchamp, *Duchamp du signe. Écrits* (Paris: Flammarion, 1975), 156.

and in this sense only, we can make the following unexpected and paradoxical observation: *listening is a form of deafness.*[264]

When listening becomes nothing more than verification, decoding, reading, it loses its primal function of hearing everything that presents itself, everything that appears, and no longer captures anything except that which *speaks to it*. Subjected to discursive bombardments, to the extent that the discourses that make use of it are dogmatic, listening becomes a function of authority.

LISTENING, INSTRUMENT OF AUTHORITY AND POWER

In attesting to sound, in affirming its materiality, its essentiality or its permanence, discourse exerts an authority. It is because of this subservience to discourse that listening is a matter of interest to power and authority; control of listening (the listening of those upon whom one seeks to exert power) and control via listening (the surveillance of those whom one wishes to master) become decisive functions for anyone who seeks power.

Dumbfounded by Listening

As we have seen, sound sometimes takes on a sacred, magical character. All the more so when the cause of its appearing is uncertain, or cannot be rationalized. Control of such sound, of such sonorous apparitions, directly implies power over believers.

---

264. This proposition also resonates with that of Jean-Luc Guionnet, which follows from it: 'Constant alert renders the ear incapable of distinction, one might even say deaf.' 'Background Noise/Bruit de Fond', tr. O. Martell, <http://www.jeanlucguionnet.eu/IMG/pdf/background_pour_mattin.pdf>, 4.

In the city of Thebes stand the two Colossi of Memnon. One of these statues formerly had the reputation of producing a sound when the first rays of the sun reached it. Tacitus wrote that the statue, 'when struck by the sun's rays, [gave] out the sound of a human voice'.[265] Numerous authors of antiquity attested to the reality of this sound.[266] Not all of them saw it as a miracle, though. For example, when Strabo describes his experience of the 'voice' of the Colossus of Memnon, he sticks to the facts:

> It is believed that once each day a noise, as of a slight blow, emanates from the part of the latter that remains on the throne and its base; and I too, when I was present at the place [...] heard the noise at about the first hour, but whether it came from the base or from the colossus, or whether the noise was made on purpose by one of the men who were standing all round and near to the base, I am unable positively to assert; for on account of the uncertainty of the cause I am induced to believe anything rather than that the sound issued from stones thus fixed.[267]

In the *Description of Egypt*, a collective work written by a commission of scientists who accompanied Bonaparte on his expedition to Egypt, it is claimed that the stone produced no sound of itself:

> Whatever may have been the nature of the sound that came from the colossus, no doubt it was the result of some kind of

---

265. Tacitus, *Annals*, II, 61 (tr. A.J. Church).

266. Cf. Pliny the Elder, *Natural History* (XXXVI, 58); Pausanias, *Description of Greece* (1, 42), and also Strabo, *Geography* (XVII, 1).

267. Strabo, *Geography* (tr. H.L. Jones).

religious fraud. One might engage in any number of conjectures here, all equally probable, as to the mechanism used by the Egyptian priests to produce this sound. It seems to us very probable that the constructions surrounding it particularly favoured the emission of the miraculous sound: perhaps there was a subterranean passage that linked the pedestal of the colossus to the neighbouring edifices. We have often found such passageways running through the thick walls of temples, and especially sanctuaries. The matter from which the Memnon statue is carved is too hard to believe that it was hollowed out so as to link it with the subterranean passageway we suspect to exist.[268]

According to the scientists, then, the sound was produced by priests, for whom any miracle always has the ring of a blessing for their spiritual and material commerce. Another hypothesis has it that the stone may have produced the sound when expanded by the heat of the sun. Bernadin de Saint-Pierre synthesizes the two theories:

> In my opinion, however long one supposes the marvellous effect of the Memnon statue to have lasted, I conceive that it was produced by the dawn, and could easily be imitated without any need to renew the artifice until centuries later. We know that the Egyptian priests studied nature closely; that they had a science known by the name of magic, knowledge of which they kept to themselves. No doubt they must have been aware of the effect of the dilation of metals, including iron, which is contracted by cold and expanded by heat. They would have been able to place

---

268. *Description de l'Égypte ou Receuil des observations et recherches qui ont été faites en Égypte pendant l'expedition française, 1809–1828*, vol. II, second edition (Paris: Imprimerie de C.F.L. Panckoucke, 1821), 208–9.

in the large base of the statue a long spiral iron rod which, owing to its length, would tend to contract and expand with the least action of cold and heat. This technique would have sufficed to make some timbre resonate from the metal. Their colossal statues were sometimes hollowed out, as is the case with the Sphinx, near the pyramids of Cairo; and they may have had all kinds of machines at their disposal. The stone of the Memnon statue, which, according to Pliny, was a basalt with the density and the colour of iron, may itself very well contract and dilate like the metal of which it appears to be composed [...] thus having within itself a principle of movement—especially at dawn, when the contrast of the cold of night and the first rays of the sun would maximize its action. This effect would surely never fail under a sky like that of Upper Egypt, where it hardly ever rains. The sounds of the Memnon statue at the moment when the sun appeared on the Horizon of Thebes were therefore no more marvellous than the explosion of the Palais Royal cannon or the signal gun of the Jardin du Roi when the sun passes the Paris meridian.[269]

Be this as it may, the statue was to keep its secret. For, in the third century AD, Septimius Severus had the statue restored in homage to Memnon, putting an end to the phenomenon for good. What is important here is that this inexplicable noise made the Colossus of Memnon an important site of pilgrimage. People came from Greece and even from Rome, engraving 'audit memnonem' on the statue as testimony.

Whether or not the phenomenon was authentic or consisted in mere trickery ultimately does not change our interest

---

269. J.-H. Bernadin de Saint-Pierre, 'Notes de l'Arcadie' [1781], in *Études de la nature*, vol. II [1784] (Paris: Lefevre, 1836), 572.

in this story. For it shows how dumbfounding the listener can be a route to power, a way in which to exact power.

Another example of the manipulation of listening and the exercise of power through it is given by André Guillaume Contant d'Orville, in a work that aims to 'give a historical account of everything concerning the religion of each country, its dogmas, the changes it has undergone, the ceremonies to which it has given rise, the superstitious observations it has engendered, and the power it has obtained over the spirit of the people'.[270] This example concerns the Indians of Tierra-Firme and the way in which their priests managed to maintain their ascendancy over the people:

> The power that the priests claim of forcing the devil to respond to questions they pose to him, endows them with great authority over the whole nation, and their astuteness in performing the magical conjurations only in secret increases yet more the respect they are paid. They employ the most frightful contortions, cries, grimaces, and screams; and it is said that they can imitate the cries of ferocious beasts and the songs of all birds. To this horrible racket is added the sound of certain stones that they strike together rhythmically, and the lugubrious sound of tambourines, of cane flutes, and the sound that can be produced by certain animal bones joined together. By following a terrible noise with a dismal silence, they manage to impose their authority upon an imbecilic people.[271]

---

270. A.G. Contant d'Orville, *Histoire des différents peuples du monde, contenant les ceremonies religieuses et civiles, l'origine des religions*, vol. I (Paris: Herissant, 1770–1771), xiii.

271. Ibid., vol. 5, 251–2.

Of course, the phenomenon of authority can loop back into the very time of perception. Tyrannical power over listening is above all exerted, at every possible moment, upon listening itself. We ourselves are, by turns, our own cadre of charlatan priests and the dumbfounded 'imbecilic' people who venerate them. This dumbfounding of the listener reveals yet another aspect of the perpetual movement of listening, that twofold movement of the simultaneous production and reception of the audible.

We might evoke numerous additional examples where listeners are dumbfounded by what they hear, from local and intimate actions such as that of François Prelati, who maintained his ascendancy over Gilles de Rais through his invocations of the demon Barron, which invariably took place behind closed doors—Gilles, from behind the door, hearing only terrifying cries and the sound of blows 'as if someone were beating a feather bed'[272]—and which were crucial in determining the impious faith of the Marshal of France, to the most global and generalized action, such as the acoustic traditions of holy places which, by using reverberation, produce and carry magnified, augmented, haloed sounds that demand respect and call for the obedience of the faithful confronted with that which is greater than them. In this way, throughout history there have been many instances where, as in the Wizard of Oz, authority was founded on a strategy of the manipulation of the sensible so as to dumbfound the listener.

Indeed, this custom, this 'tradition', has not waned. It is sometimes displaced, transformed, conquering new territories—like that of the electromagnetic ether, for example.

---

272. G. Bataille, *The Trial of Gilles de Rais*, tr. R. Robertson (Los Angeles: Amok, 1991), 51.

For radio was and still is an important locus for the dumbfounding and control of the auditor. Indeed, Adorno and Horkheimer instruct us that radio is 'democratic' only in so far as 'it turns all participants into listeners and authoritatively subjects them to broadcast programs which are all exactly the same'.[273]

Adorno and Horkheimer attend to the new but always already present dimension of radio and the sound 'economy', connecting radio to commercial capitalism and its tyrannical tendencies. Adorno and Horkheimer doubtless belonged to the first generation to realize, and indeed to experience, the possibilities of mass manipulation harboured by radiophony. The Second World War, with its Nazi propaganda orchestrated by Joseph Goebbels, and indeed the war of the airwaves between Radio London and Radio Paris, marks a definitive turning point in the history of sound, where radio became an explicit stake of power.

In *The Electronic Revolution* William S. Burroughs imagines another exercise in the manipulation of crowds by way of listening and electroacoustic devices for sound diffusion. Here it is no longer a question of maintaining order or promoting ideologies; on the contrary, it is a question of disintegrating them and provoking disorder and confusion:

Here is a run of the mill, pre-riot situation. Protesters have been urged to demonstrate peacefully, police and guardsmen to exercise restraint. Ten tape recorders strapped under their coats, playback, and record controlled from lapel buttons. They have prerecorded riot sound effects from Chicago, Paris, Mexico City, Kent/Ohio. If they adjust sound levels of recordings to

---

273. T.W. Adorno and M. Horkheimer, *Dialectic of Enlightenment* [1944], tr. J. Cumming (New York: Continuum, 1989), 122.

surrounding sound levels, they will not be detected. Police scuffle with the demonstrators. The operators converge, turn on Chicago record, play back, move on to the next scuffles, record playback, keep moving. Things are hotting up, a cop is down groaning. Shrill chorus of recorded pig squeals and parody groans. [...] Just pointing out that cut/ups on the tape recorder can be used as a weapon.[274]

Whether it is a matter of supernatural sonorous evocations, mass-media marketing strategies, or the electroacoustic guerrilla tactics suggested by Burroughs, the control of listening remains fundamentally the same. By dumbfounding listeners, precipitating them into a situation of pure reception, he who 'sounds' establishes his dominance over he who listens.

The ear is the organ of the 'unproven', the unverifiable. What is heard is already no longer there. Listening, in the time of short-term auditory memory, seeks to consolidate sound for better or worse, to establish it within the regime of knowledge or that of affect, and to petrify it. Listening is doomed to form certainties on the basis of evanescent phenomena. Raudive strains his hearing to identify the voices of the dead in the desolate interstices of the radio frequency band. Whether or not the voices really are those of the dead or whether Raudive invents them does not matter. One way or the other, in order to make them out, Raudive will in a certain sense hallucinate

274. William S. Burroughs, *The Electronic Revolution* [1970] (Ubu editions), <http://www.ubu.com/historical/burroughs/electronic_revolution.pdf>. See also 'Invisible Generation', in C. Cox and D. Warner (eds.), *Audio Culture: Readings in Modern Music* (New York and London: Continuum, 2009), as well as his description, in *The Ticket That Exploded*, of the technique of the splice, a far more complex form of cut-up interlacing sounds from different sources.

them, unilaterally modifying the parlance of the dead (the speed of the torrent of words, the use of different languages within the same phrase). Whether or not we accept them, Raudive does draw out affirmations, *truths*, from a process of speculative listening. It is in this sense that listening must always be considered as a device of persuasion, of belief, and, in some cases, of submission. Listening is thus shaped into an authoritarian device by virtue of its propensity to construct something solid, to generate certainties, or the *expression* of certainties, from the ungraspable.

Authority via Listening

If it is possible to shore up power by capturing the listening of another, it is also possible to develop and practice strategies of power through the exercise of listening, precisely by virtue of this principle of solidification. Such practices can become a powerful instrument of power, or at the very least can bring about the ascendancy of he who listens over he who emits a sound, he who speaks. But once again, he who listens must be the sole depositary of that which has been expressed.

In the Catholic religion, the confession of sins was originally public and was practiced only rarely, for the most serious cases. It was only in 1215, at the Fourth Council of the Lateran, that confession became 'auricular', disclosed to the ears of the clergy alone. With the revelation of their sins transferred to priests rather than to God himself (through the collective), the faithful are finally brought to place the salvation of their souls into the hands of the man of the church. In arrogating to itself the right to pardon and absolve the faithful of their sins and (at the same council) abolishing the ordeal, the Church confiscates and institutionalizes a part of divine power, simultaneously rationalizing and systematizing it. Be that as it may, auricular confession only becomes an instrument of power in so far as, through listening, the confessor becomes the sole receiver of the supplicant's secrets.

Similarly, the ancient practice of espionage is only of value in so far as the secret is violated by a limited number of listeners, who agree to keep the information to themselves rather than revealing it, either for strategic advantage or to put pressure on the enemy. Through the ages acoustic espionage has developed a whole set of techniques employing a knowledge of architectural acoustics (those acoustic illusions imagined by the polymath Athanasius Kircher) and, later on, of electroacoustics (spy microphones, bugs, telephone taps, radio scanners, etc.).[275] Today, machinic, algorithmic audition is so acute that it can even extract meaningful information conveyed by sound that is inaccessible to the ear and to human intelligence. For example, researchers at the University of Berkeley have proved that it is possible to spy on someone typing on a keyboard simply by listening to and analyzing the sounds of the keystrokes.[276]

Wherever there is power, there is espionage: 'you can use espionage anywhere', as Sun Tzu told us in the sixth century BC.[277] In a book entitled *Listening: The Aesthetics of Espionage*, Peter Szendy emphasizes that 'all listening, to some extent, involves information-gathering, or a drive to

275. Cf. D. Zbikowski, 'The Listening Ear: Phenomena of Acoustic Surveillance', in T.Y. Levin, U. Frohne and P. Weibel (eds.), *CTRL [SPACE]: Rhetorics of Surveillance from Bentham to Big Brother* (Karlsruhe: ZKM/MIT Press, 2002).

276. L. Zhuang, F. Zhou, and J.D. Tygar, 'Case Study: Acoustic Keyboard Emanations', in M. Jakobsson and S. Myers (eds.), *Phishing and Countermeasures* (New York: Wiley-Interscience, 2007), 221–40.

277. Sun Tzu, *The Art of War*, tr. Hwang Chung-Mei (Selangor Darul Ehsan, Malaysia: Pelanduk, 1992), 53.

gather information'.[278] Thus indexical, primal listening, the primary type of listening, is always present, always working in the background—or rather differentiating itself, ramifying itself and adapting itself to the regimes of discourse that drive it. Espionage-listening is a particularly intriguing apparatus of power, since it continually extends the 'unproven' ever further. It is always possible to dismiss its deliverances, given that the information it yields usually relies only upon one sole listening—which can be manipulated in turn by counter-espionage practices, by divulging erroneous or false information delivered by 'condemned' spies, to take up Sun Tzu's typology.

Szendy is also right to liken spy listening to the primal indexical listening mentioned by Barthes and Nietzsche, the listening of fear, always on the alert, ready to identify traces of danger in the least whisper. Spy listening is a listening *under threat* which targets *indices* and *clues*. It is not a listening that embraces a place, a space, in order to enjoy it. It is not a listening that fans out, but one that projects itself *from a given place towards a point*. It is a listening that comprises just two terms: the point, the target at which it aims, and the trajectory. It is formed by way of a perceptual focalization, a veritable tunnel or wire stretched from the ear of the spy to the object of his listening.

Espionage-listening, then, is like a developing-bath for sound. It incarnates a tension in its concentration on one unique object, and exhibits a *perceptual will* to extract something tangible and verified from this object. Now, such a perceptual will brings with it the desire to firmly anchor an observation, to affirm it. But in affirming it, it affirms listening itself qua authoritarian phenomenon. Espionage-listening seeks to relieve itself

---

278. P. Szendy, *Sur écoute. Esthétique de l'espionnage* (Paris: Minuit, 2007), 23.

of the curse of listening, condemned to capture only fleeting and ephemeral objects: the spy concentrates only upon the information he will be able to extract from these fleeting objects, and has no aim other than to identify this information. But the spy, in his turn, can be revealed by listening; as, for example, in certain Japanese temples and palaces which feature *uguisubari*, 'nightingale floors' designed with the nails fixing down the floorboards arranged in such a way that the tiniest pressure creates a chirping noise, rendering it impossible to make even the most furtive movements without being discovered.

And yet the exercise of power through listening is not condemned to dissimulation alone; it can go beyond surreptitious espionage to become overt surveillance. When Jeremy Bentham developed the panopticon—a prison structure wherein every prisoner is at every moment *potentially* overlooked without knowing it—although he did not totally succeed in adapting the panoptical principle for sound,[279] did set out a strong principle for it: that discipline essentially resides not so much in active surveillance as in the *possibility* of such surveillance. Guided by this principle, surveillance-listening, manifest espionage, becomes an instrument of silence.

Moreover, listening as instrument of power does not just concern the expression of a given power, an empire. It is also a culturally-coded, determined, and functionalized practice of listening, as is the case in surveillance-listening.

---

279. Although Bentham did develop techniques to see without being seen, *even while being in view*, thus rendering surveillance potentially constant, he could not get around the bidirectional nature of sound. Thus, prisoners subject to acoustic surveillance could just as well spy on the conversations of their guards. Cf. Zbikowski, 'The Listening Ear', 42.

Authoritarian practices of listening generally establish a relation of domination between listener and listened-to; and such a power relation is often connected to some knowledge that gives one (the listener) a hold over the other (the listened-to). The most striking example of this is perhaps that of auscultation. Mediate auscultation (by means of the stethoscope) is a practice designed and developed by René Laënnec (his treatise was published in 1819). It enables the discovery of new, hitherto inaccessible audible clinical indications. Auscultation, over and above 'enacting and incarnating a new social and spatial relation between patient and doctor, [determines sound as] a possible field of data for medical perception and knowledge'.[280]

In apprehending the patient's condition through the internal noises and murmurs of the body, the doctor takes possession of a knowledge that is linked not only to medical expertise, but also to his very perception—that is to say, to his audition, which can now, with the aid of the stethoscopic prosthesis, breach the corporeal boundaries of his patient. The practitioner possesses a perceptual knowledge which he keeps for himself, collecting it in his ear. Auscultation implies a certain symbolic domination, the domination of he who hears in the other that which the latter, in himself, cannot hear and *does not know how to* hear.

Disciplined Listening

Not all of the various authoritarian practices of listening are solely a matter of instrumentalizing the latter or using it for the ends of power. Listening is not fated simply to be a function of authority; it can also be an *expression* of authority.

---

280. Sterne, *The Audible Past*, 103.

In which case it is no longer used to *exact* power, but only to illustrate it, to attest to it, to express it.

Listening has disciplined itself throughout the modern era. Scientific discoveries regarding audition and sound have permitted them to be objectivated. Following Cartesianism and the postulations of mechanism, as in La Mettrie, for instance, a new vision of the human body developed: a functionalist vision which, in particular, led to a discretized apprehension of the sensible, to a separation and an isolation of the senses, as formulated by the physiologist Johannes Müller, by Hermann von Helmholtz, and by Alexander Graham Bell. Helmholtz certainly contributed to a decomposition of sound itself, but also to that of the experience of sound at the level of listening—that is to say, the reception of sound. In fact, for Helmholtz these two stages represent two complementary sides of the same theory:

> We call *sensations* the impressions produced upon our senses in so far as they appear to us solely as particular states of our body (above all of our nervous system); on the contrary, we call them *perceptions* when they serve to form representations of external objects. When we recognise a certain vibratory movement as representing the sound of a violin, this is a perception; from it we infer the existence of a certain instrument that usually produces sounds of this type. When, on the contrary, we seek to decompose a complex sound into partial sounds, this is an act of pure sensation. For no determinate sonorous body corresponds to an isolated partial sound; separated from the other elements of the same sound, the harmonic is nothing but an element of our sensation.[281]

---

281. H. von Helmholtz, *Die Lehre von den Tonempfindungen als Physiologische Grundlage für die Theorie der Musik* [1863] (Braunschweig: Friedrich Vieweg and Son, 5th edition, 1896).

In distinguishing perceptions from sensations and by demonstrating (following Fourier) the harmonic properties of 'musical' sounds, Helmholtz does not just rationalize listening: through the correspondences he establishes between the decomposed nature of sound and the discretization of listening, he proposes and designs a regime of representation where every thing has its rightful place within auditory experience. Thus, in line with his theory of resonators, Helmholtz imagines a 'tuned' ear:

> Our ear can perceive both impressions, and we may well suppose that this owes to the existence of different terminal organs, so that the nervous activation of the vestibule and ampulla would serve for the perception of noises, Corti's fibres for the perception of sounds. What is more, it must be admitted that each of these fibres is tuned to a different tone, and that they form a regular series corresponding to the musical scale. According to Köliker, there are around 3000 Corti fibres in the cochlea of the human ear. Let us say there are 200 sounds situated beyond musical limits, and whose pitch is only imperfectly determined; there remain 2800 fibres for the seven octaves of musical instruments, that is to say 400 per octave, $33\frac{1}{3}$ for each semitone—in any case, enough to explain the ability to distinguish fractions of a semitone, to the extent that this is possible.[282]

In the harmonic order of the audible world discovered by Helmholtz, the ear is endowed with two distinct perceptual apparatuses. One is reserved for the vulgar, for noise; the other, more attuned, is dedicated to the regime of harmonic sounds. Helmholtz's theory is paradigmatic of the following

282. Ibid.

observation: in every case, the ordering, disciplining, and disciplinization of sound implies the disciplining of listening, and vice versa.

Techniques of listening therefore develop in lockstep with sound's becoming an object of knowledge. Sound is furnished with a timbre, an intensity, a duration; it is diffracted into parameters, into measurable data. Acoustics and electroacoustics show that these parameters can be identified and extracted, and that their abstraction into mathematical magnitudes is effective for certain ends. The phenomenon of resonance, which has always been known, is recognized and theorized, the wavelike nature of sound is discovered, its propensity toward periodicity is emphasized, the notions of cycles per second and then of frequency appear. All of these parameters are extracted and exploited in order to work out the principles of transduction, and to establish the foundations of modern acoustics. Sound becomes measurable: its imprint can be taken, it can be simulated. It is no longer fleeting and immaterial; it is tangible and quantifiable.

Thus listening comes 'naturally' under the influence of reason; and 'naturally', science will seek the proof of an acoustic order within the ear itself. At this point listening and the ear itself tend to become autonomous. The 'tympanic function' is isolated (in particular, let us recall, with Bell and Blake's phonautograph experiments); the receptive mechanisms of the ear are identified more and more precisely. Their functions are determined more and more fully. But listening does not become constituted as an object of knowledge purely by way of physiology, or at least only in its anatomical dimension; it also becomes the object and the stake of sociological and behavioural analyses.

Coming back to Helmholtz, it is certainly the case that a theory that tries to separate Corti's fibres into subgroups linked to the semitone scale, or to exhibit a supposed separation of the ear into two distinct perceptual mechanisms, today seems like a work of fantasy. Here science runs up against the animist obstacle, to use Bachelard's term: a moment when 'where this more or less certain knowledge answers questions that have not been put to it'.[283] In establishing a biological separation between the perception of noise and that of music, Helmholtz legitimates the supposed difference in nature between the two. What we see affirmed and affirming itself here through Helmholtz is the voice of reason, albeit a non-rational reason—let us not forget that beneath the expression of a discourse or in the formation of a regime of discourse there always lurks a regime of belief.

The relation to the sensible world is always subject to the influence of a *Weltanschauung*; now, 'to have a worldview [*Weltanschauung*] is to form for oneself an image of the world and of oneself, knowing what the world is and what one is oneself. [...] Every conception of the world has a singular tendency to consider itself as the last word on the universe, when it is only a name that we give to things'.[284]

If Jung is to be believed, the worldview is thus the pedestal upon which authority is erected, and on the basis of which an authoritarian discourse flourishes. In which case we need to understand precisely what the nature of the authoritarian consists in. It should be freed from its connotations of despotism, for authoritarianism is not identical with the authoritarian

---

283. G. Bachelard, *The Formation of the Scientific Mind*, tr. M. Mcallester Jones (Manchester: Clinamen, 2002), 154.

284. C.G. Jung, *L'Âme et la vie* (Paris: Le Livre de poche, 2008), 300.

as such. The former *imposes* its views upon a determinate object, whereas the latter, by *proposing* a certain view of an object, assumes or reinforces a vision of the world. To produce an authoritarian discourse is not to express a discourse that aims to engender authority, but to express the authority of that discourse, to claim the status of an authority through a discourse—which is something entirely different.

Now, in forming itself on the basis of a worldview, authoritarian discourse also draws on that which forms this worldview itself—namely, nothing other than the action of other discourses, articulated with beliefs. It is in this sense that we can say that behind each established discourse lies the expression of beliefs. In which case, disciplined listening is the fruit of a belief in the existence of an Order of the world, an order of which it would be just one modest expression among many others.

It is this belief in an order that generates and conditions a disciplinary development in the relation to listening. When Murray Schafer puts forward the concept of clairaudience, 'exceptional hearing ability', through this concept he communicates his own relation to sound, a relation which itself is determined by a worldview. But he does not stop there: in declaring that '[h]earing ability may be trained to the clairaudient state by means of EAR CLEANING exercises', he advocates and establishes a discipline of 'clear' listening that he claims to be able to pass on. Thus we confirm Jung's dictum according to which the worldview always has hegemonic aims, always dreams of a kingdom.

On the other hand, and to conclude on this point, one might wonder what, fundamentally, a disciplined listening is, or what an education of the ear might mean, and on what level discipline exerts its effects. One might also seek to determine whether an apprenticeship of listening must aim at an increase in auditory sensitivity, whether it is necessarily bound to the production of a better *reading* via listening, whether such an education targets perception itself, or whether it seeks to refine and to structure a discourse around what is perceived. For example, Alfred Tomatis's electronic ear supposedly serves to *re-educate* a 'faulty' listening, responsible for bad interfacing with the world at both the sensorial and the emotional level.[285] Here the objective is to re-equilibriate listening so as to re-establish a 'harmonious' auditory relation. In this way the Tomatis method claims to be able to intervene in illnesses such as autism. Thus the education of listening goes beyond listening.

Ultimately, listening and sound are not really what is at stake in discipline and education. In fact, through the control of sound and listening, the latter seek to control the discourses that govern them, that model them, and that culminate in the inauguration of a worldview that would preside over all circulation of the audible.

Listening Liquidated

The authoritarian investment in the sensible can only come about once the sensible itself is sufficiently ossified to become an object and a stake of power. For a reified sound is a formed sound, and the becoming of formed sound is governed by a discourse. The objectivation of sound, its reification, is a preliminary to its utilization by authority—that is to say, its placing into circulation within a discursive network of authority.

---

285. The electronic ear is an apparatus invented by Alfred Tomatis, designed to 'develop the function of hearing'. It consists of filters and latch circuits for amplification which, in particular, are supposed to act on the audio-vocal loop and on the ossicular chain.

Now, to the investment of the sonorous in the chain of discourse and power, its audibilizing, there seems to correspond, as a sort of counterweight, a dilution of sensation, which is as if anaesthetized under the influence of the discursive bombardment to which it is subjected. Adorno identified this phenomenon when he associated the figure of the 'commodity-form' in music with what he called the 'regression of listening'. But Adorno is principally concerned with the becoming of the work of art and its transformation into standardized 'cultural goods':

> Adorno considers the mass art emerging with the new techniques and technologies of reproduction as a degeneration of art. The market, which made the autonomy of bourgeois art possible in the first place, permits the emergence of a culture industry that penetrates into the pores of the work of art itself, and together with the commodity character of the work of art, forces the viewer into the attitudinal patterns of a consumer.[286]

The spectator, the auditor, thus develops a relation to art and to the sensible that Adorno regarded as perverted. By introducing the concept of a 'regression of listening' he shows how a discursive hegemony can exert an influence over perception to the point where it takes precedence over the latter. It has to be said that Adorno's notion of regression is very specific:

> This does not mean a relapse of the individual listener into an earlier phase of his own development, nor a decline in the collective

---

286. J. Habermas, 'Consciousness-Raising or Redemptive Criticism—The Contemporaneity of Walter Benjamin', tr. P. Brewster and C. H. Buchner, *New German Critique* 17 (Spring 1979), 30–59: 41.

general level, since the millions who are reached musically for the first time by today's mass communications cannot be compared with the audience of the past. Rather, it is contemporary listening which has regressed, arrested at the infantile stage.[287]

The process of the regression of listening, starting with a deficient listening, an attention deficit, then evolving into an 'atomized' stage where listening fixes only upon isolated objects, ignoring the interrelations that animate them, concludes with the disinvestment of listening itself and its withering away into a regime of anaesthesia.

Adorno depicts this liquidation of listening as the result of a sort of saturation of signifiance which engenders a perceptual refusal or indifference. This apathy of the sensible is the fruit of its reification. The final stage of a reified relation to the world corresponds, in fact, to an apathic regime. For Axel Honneth, the advent of such a regime parallels the subject's disinvestment in his relation to the world:

> [T]he subject is no longer empathetically engaged in interaction with his surroundings, but is instead placed in the perspective of a neutral observer, psychically and existentially untouched by his surroundings.[288]

Reification, as Honneth and Adorno define it—that is to say, in terms of its incursion into the sensible world—confirms the extent to which listening depends upon the discourses of which it is the stake and the object. Under the yoke of an alienating discourse, listening collapses or regresses into an apathic regime.

---

287. Adorno, 'The Fetish-Character in Music', 286.

288. Honneth, *Reification*, 24.

And yet the process of reification need not lead to such apathy. The complete subservience of listening to discourse can also be the source of an exaltation, a joy, and an aesthetic jouissance which, although one might dispute their authenticity, are nonetheless real. In his novel *Ferdydurke*, Witold Gombrowicz precisely questions the authenticity of the musical emotion aroused by a concert, giving one example of a listening caught in the nets of the discursive and focussed upon overdetermined sonorous objects:

> And so, when a pianist bangs out Chopin in a concert hall, you say that the magic of Chopin's music, masterfully rendered by this master pianist, has thrilled the audience. Yet it's possible that actually no one in the audience has been thrilled. Let's not exclude the possibility that, had they not known Chopin to be a great genius, and the pianist likewise, they would have listened to the music with less ardor. It's also possible that when some listeners, pale with emotion, applaud, scream, carry on, writhe in enthusiasm one should attribute this to the fact that others in the audience are also writhing, carrying on, shouting; because every one of them thinks that the others are experiencing an incredible ecstasy, a transcendent emotion, and therefore his emotions as well begin to rise on someone else's yeast; and thus it can easily happen that while no one in the concert hall has been directly enraptured, everyone expresses rapture—because everyone wants to conform to his neighbor. And it's not until all of them in a bunch have sufficiently excited each other, it is only then, I tell you, that these expressions of emotion arouse their emotion—*because we must adapt our feelings to what we express.*[289]

---

289. W. Gombrowicz, *Ferdydurke* [1937], tr. D. Borchardt (New Haven, CT: Yale University Press, 2012), 78 [emphasis added; translation modified].

Here Gombrowicz shows how the distribution of the sensible, to use Rancière's expression, can be activated like a contamination, making use of discursive and symbolic networks to fuel and excite the relation to the sensible, to enflame listening. But listening is also always the site of the unheard—the site of its denial, or rather its forgetting. To embrace the complexity of listening is to acknowledge and integrate its accursed share, its non-listening, its own liquidation—its capitulation, so to speak, in the face of the world of signs.

So listening is continually held in the balance between the time of sensation and the time of discourse, a time that induces it and a time that conducts it. This balance is also manifested in its orientation: now turned toward the subject, the seat of perception, now turned toward the world that produces the sensible and which must be communicated with in return. For authority can only establish itself when there is communication, and all discourse, upon which authority is based, implies such communication. Yet authority is not solely an expression of authority; it is also a formation, an ordering, and a structuring. Order supposes authority, and authority supposes order.

MODELIZATIONS

Taxonomies

It is by way of the burgeoning of knowledge linked to the act of listening, but also under the impulsion of the imperious need to impose a worldview upon the newly discovered (or rather rediscovered) sonorous territory, that it starts to become necessary to make ordinances, categories, and classifications that will allow the sonorous territory to be established qua *field of knowledge*, identified and integrated into the broader, vaster field of science.

According to Foucault, '[w]hen dealing with the ordering of complex natures (representations in general, as they are given in experience), one has to constitute a taxinomia, and to do that one has to establish a system of signs'.[290] The intent to classify is intrinsically linked to language and to discursive processes; it conditions them and is a result of them—so that the impulse to organize sound always corresponds to a discursification. Order, the ultimate object of all taxonomical enterprises, depends upon a placing-into-sign of the world.

The taxonomy of the sensible is not at all a purely abstract, irrelevant enterprise in the present day. On the contrary, it is very much alive, and harbours great ambitions for the renewal of the apprehension of the sensible. For example, the project SemanticHIFI initiated by IRCAM[291] shows clearly the role that taxonomy (which it calls 'indexing') can play in the creation of new stances of listening which, in fact, are only new avatars of the concept of a 'listening technique':

> Based on the diffusion of musical information that goes beyond simple sound recordings, and on the implementation of tools for indexing and personalized navigational interfaces, the project seeks a radical transformation in practices of access to music and augmented listening, to the point of blurring the traditional line between listening and playing. These high-fidelity systems are both listening stations and open instruments, capable of furnishing the technological vectors for a new understanding of music.[292]

---

290. Foucault, *The Order of Things*, 79–80.

291. Institut de Recherche et Coordination Acoustique/Musique.

292. <http://shf.ircam.fr/>.

The SemanticHIFI project consists in discretizing the elements that make up a musical programme: sound sources (instruments, voices), the acoustic characteristics of these sources (spatial locations, reverb levels, etc.), and the characteristics of the recording space are isolated during recording, so as to render them indexable, parametrizable, and modifiable by the listener. In developing the concept of 'active listening'—which is in fact *interactive* listening—SemanticHIFI operate their proposed extension of listening via a hypersegmentation of the audible, which is then made available for a practice which does nothing more than make sound available for a particular use. The individualization of listening enabled by SemanticHIFI brings to mind the disquiet of Adorno and Horkheimer at the becoming of an ever-regressing listening which appears in communities that industrially produce cultural goods, and where '[t]he peculiarity of the self is a monopoly commodity determined by society [...] falsely represented as natural'.[293] Addressing this very idea, Gérard Pelé, explaining the intended use of SemanticHIFI, clarifies that

> its domain of application is principally listening in the home where, today, socialization, sublimation and [...] the repression of individuals takes place through a global thinking of the whole aesthetic 'system' and through its industrial exploitation, from production to reception.[294]

The authoritarian virtue of classification resides in the fact that it organizes a space and that this space, qua organized, acquires a *reason* from which one can draw authority.

---

293. Adorno and Horkheimer, *Dialectic of Enlightenment*, 154.

294. Pelé, *Inesthétiques musicales au XXe siècle*, 213.

Thus the democratic enterprise of SemanticHIFI, given its recourse to the classification of the sensible, is fundamentally, albeit unconsciously, an authoritarian enterprise. Its paradox resides in the fact that it seeks to open up a freedom of listening, but it acts upon listening in a way that channels, atomizes, and reifies the audible into sensible objects that it then serves up to listening.

The ostensible purpose of the project is nothing less than to replace listening with a *practice* of listening. Bringing the principle of augmented reality into the domain of sound, SemanticHIFI adds another brick in the wall of the total codification of the sensible. The project is only one of the latest avatars of a long tradition of the modelization of sound, from its beginnings with the Pythagoreans, through modern acoustics, where it migrated at once toward a physiology and a sociology of listening only to spread out subsequently into a multitude of different enterprises drawing on formalist, phenomenological, and eventually cognitivist theories.

The whole issue here, the whole curse, if you like, constituted by the classification of the sensible, is the belief that the replacement of sound by its function leads to an emancipation of listening—when in fact it just constitutes one more sieve. When the object, an abstraction integrated into a structural system, takes the upper hand over the experience of listening and over the way in which one represents the given-to-be-heard, it must be observed that it is already no longer really a question of sound, but of a *model* of sound that has been determined and selected to take its place.

Of course we might, like Jean-Luc Nancy, protest that 'listening aims at—or is aroused by—the [tendency] where sound and sense mix together and resonate in each other, or through each other',[295] and that therefore any systematization of the object of listening is part and parcel of the process of listening itself. There is nothing to object against such an observation. Yet at the other extreme, the authoritarian representation of sound denies this same indissolubility of the audible by splintering it and reducing it to a meshwork of objects that are like syntagms, thereby denying the relations that already existed in sound, before it was filleted by the discretizing procedure.

On the other hand, we must also emphasize that the entanglement of sense and the sensible in listening never reaches a stable state, an immutable equilibrium. Meaning is always trying to achieve order, and classification is a basic tool to make the clearing of a frontier, a deciphering, into an immediate surveying.

Lévi-Strauss saw perfectly well that classification is not primarily of a practical order, but responds to 'intellectual requirements'.[296] Of course, the strategies of classification described in *The Savage Mind* are not the same as those mobilized by modern thought. Foucault succeeds in showing how the latter called into question one of the principal mainstays of these old strategies: resemblance.[297] On this subject he recalls an observation of philosopher Francis Bacon:

> The human Intellect, from its peculiar nature, easily supposes a greater order and equality in things than it actually finds; and, while there are many things in Nature unique, and quite irregular, still it feigns parallels, correspondents, and relations that have no

295. Nancy, *Listening*, 7.

296. Lévi-Strauss, *Savage Mind*, 9.

297. Foucault, *The Order of Things*; in particular ch. 3.2, 'Order', 55–64.

existence. Hence that fiction, 'that among the heavenly bodies all motion takes place by perfect circles'.[298]

231

MODELIZATIONS

Bacon's reflection still holds today: the principle of resemblance is still in effect, particularly in the sciences of perception. As in Schaeffer's work, this resemblance roots itself in an objectivity (either analytic, via acoustics, or descriptive, in phenomenology) in order to locate itself in the validated field of knowledge, while still remaining attached to the hazy world of beliefs. Hence the legitimation of the typo-morphology of sound, which, if not a savage thought, is certainly still articulated around similarities and differences, sketches out dividing lines, and *implies* hierarchies, assessments of appropriateness and good fit, and value judgments which the authority it has gained—or fabricated—entitles it to assume.

Scientific rationalism, a regime of discourse that is everpresent in questions of audition and in problematics relating to sound, has never entirely found its way out of savage thought. It tends to reach a certain *accommodation* with the unverified. The taxonomical tendency is a 'savage' drive to collect, a will to order.

This comes down to saying that listening, by way of this power of language and meaning that invests it through and through, tends, in its treatment of the sensible, to produce *models*—and, as Bacon's text suggests, models are approximations, instances where thought smooths out the apprehension of the world.

For example, the traditional acoustic description of sound, which decomposes it into three fundamental parameters—amplitude, frequency, and duration—comparable to the triad

298. F. Bacon, *Novum Organum* [1620]; cited in Foucault, *The Order of Things*, 57.

of musical sound—intensity, pitch, duration—implies a simple correspondence between perceived phenomenon and physical phenomenon. But such a reduction is impossible. We know very well, for example, that when rapid enough, amplitude modulation is heard as pitch; and that a change in frequency at a constant amplitude can bring about the sensation of an increase in energy similar to a rise in amplitude (the hyper-compressed music played on the radio shows this well enough: the dynamics that we hear are well beyond the dynamics of the actually emitted signal. The modification of the spectral balance of a piece can also suggest an increase in dynam-ics—as illustrated by 'loudness' treatment). The variables into which sound is decomposed thus exhibit an interdependence that is revealed in sound phenomena themselves as much as in their analytical representation.

Although the clarifications afforded by the acoustic model enable a better general comprehension of sound, at the same time this model, through the sieving that it carries out, and the grey areas that this operation produces, distances us from sound itself as, little by little, it is replaced by the triadic model.

The Plasticity of Sound

The modelization of sound is the agreement of a formation and a placing-into-sign of the sonorous. The model that emerges from this marries with and conforms to a regime of discourse, representing and marking out its perimeter. The same can be said of the musical model which long presided over our relation to the audible. Indeed, physical models initially had to grow up in the shadow of its entrenched determinations. But since the avant-gardes, the musical domain has undergone numerous transformations and has been taken to its utmost limits. It has been hybridized, and within it we have witnessed the birth of

practices that are entirely disconnected from musical traditions.
In parallel, the plastic arts have extended their field of investigation, always driven by the search for new modes of expression and new materials. Indeed, the notion of plasticity has developed to the point where it is now applied to sound itself.

Catherine Malabou, who has long worked on the notion of plasticity, sets it out it in mature form, affirming that 'all signs today point to the fact that *plasticity demands to accede to the concept*'.[299]

The notion of plasticity implies a new relation to sound. As material, sound becomes *manipulable*. For artists like Christian Marclay, this new plastic dimension of sound constitutes an unprecedented field of artistic investigation. Hence Marclay seeks a new materiality of sound, in particular through recording media:

> A scratch on a record [...] is even more valuable than a sound recorded in the groove, because that scratch or wound is going to make its material nature audible. The record is not just a sound rendered as an abstract entity, it is also an object, which is exactly what the scratch reveals.[300]

This materiality of sound is a materiality by proxy, contained in its imprints or its representations. And the artistic exploitation of a becoming-plastic of sound does not escape the derivative nature of its materiality. What is more, this becoming-plastic only exists through the materiality of its supports, or as a

---

299. C. Malabou, 'Ouverture: le voeu de la plasticité', in C. Malabou (ed), *Plasticité* (Paris: Léo Scheer, 2000).

300. C. Marclay, 'What You See Is What You Hear', *ArtPress* 309 (February 2005), 19.

symbolic evocation. This is the case for Christian Marclay's artworks, which are paradigmatic of contemporary plastic work that focuses on sound:

> Most of my plastic works are silent. It would not be worth noting this except that they are sculptures made from sonorous objects, or objects that are associated with sounds, like a record or a musical instrument, but presented in a silent state. [...] Sound transpires through its silence. The sense of hearing is thus put to the test—to fill up this silence, it has to yield to the imaginary, to memory.[301]

Marclay's work is articulated around the *symbolic* presence of sound, around its potentialities, its virtualities—in any case, not around the perception of sound itself. This is not at all to invalidate his approach; on the contrary, it shows that an a priori materialist approach to sound can very rapidly drift toward an abstraction of sound and its effacement in favour of *representations* of sound.

The materiality of sound invoked through the concept of plasticity is in fact more like a virtuality, an *imaginary* representation of materiality. In this sense, one cannot manipulate sound as one would manipulate clay; it is the *model* of sound that is manipulated, interrogated, reconfigured.

Furthermore, the confrontation of the sonorous model with sound itself in the plastic arts often serves to reveal their non-adequation. Let us look at two examples of sound installations, each of which illustrates in its own way the potential distortions that can take place between the modelization of sound and the sound that is actually produced.

---

301. C. Marclay, 'Le son en image', in Szendy (ed), *L'Écoute*, 86.

The first is a work by Bill Viola entitled *Hallway Nodes*. In

this installation, two partitions are used to form a corridor exactly 22 feet (around 6.7m) long. Two identical loudspeakers (positioned at the two ends of corridor) diffuse a sinusoidal wave of bass frequency (50 Hz). The interference of the two waves produces phenomena of acoustic nodes and antinodes (increase and decrease of acoustic intensity, according to the wave model). At each end, one encounters a peak, and there-fore a high amplitude: one *hears* the sound; whereas in the middle of the corridor, one progressively approaches a trough, a diminution of sound to the point of its complete extinction. But the problem that comes up in analyzing *Hallway Nodes* is that the experience of walking through the installation does not correspond to the model. What is actually perceived is something that would not be produced by the installation as described in its modelized form:

If, as Bill Viola says, there were two oscillators, their inevitable drift (in particular, temperature drift) would produce tiny shifts in frequency that would be manifested as pulsations. So the visitor would hear variations in sound level without changing position—which would not coincide with the artist's description. If he exploited the 'heterodyne' effect (his use of the expression 'heterodyning at 50 Hz' perhaps suggests a false interpretation), the frequencies of the sounds emitted by the two loudspeakers would be higher than the physical correlate and, consequently, would be perceptible in the neighbourhood of the sources, which also would not correspond to the picture he paints.[302]

302. G. Pelé, *Installations et soulagement esthétique*, forthcoming.

There is a gap, then, between the effect sought (and that obtaining in the installation itself) and the physical model of the setup that is supposed to produce this effect. We also find this inadequation between model and phenomenon in an installation by Takis entitled *Musical*:

> A magnet violently hits the sheet metal—an alternating direct current sets the metal in motion, this motion creating a sonic vibration.
> The metal is always hit at the same place—a pointer strikes a cord—always at the same place—an alternating direct current places the cord in oscillation.
> The cord and the metal sheet are hit at the same place and vibrate with the alternating direct current.
> Thus set in motion, the two elements create a powerful sound.
> A sound caused by a heavy blow.
> If the cord or sheet metal were hit at different places, there would be different sounds.
> The sounds should not be different: the magnet must hit the metal and the cord always at the same place.[303]

What is problematic about this description, written by Takis himself, is that it does not take into account the experience of the work itself, focusing only on what it *must*, or *should*, produce. Whereas if one were to encounter the work without any prior knowledge of the artist's intentions, one might well form an interpretation entirely opposed to these intentions. For the sounds are *always different*, and the magnet always strikes at a different place, given the simple fact that

303. Takis, May 1980. Text from *Écouter par les yeux, objets et environnements sonores* (Paris: ARC Musée d'Art Moderne de la Ville de Paris, 1980), 132.

it never comes back to the same initial position. In encountering the work, one therefore ends up anticipating the next blow, evaluating the difference between subsequent sounds, and contemplating the whole as a generator of difference. Where Takis seeks to exhibit permanence, regularity, order, what emerges is the startling impression of chance, chaos, difference and heterogeneity.

Not only is the artistic project repudiated by its realization, but the perceptual model that it proposes to put to work ends up producing a sensible experience that contradicts it. *Musical* is therefore an attempt to render sensible an ordered model of the sensible that simply does not exist. Here again, it is the vision of a determined, linear, and organized world that Takis seeks to communicate through his work. That this same work turns out to be a generator of chaos is an ironic reversal that illustrates, once more, the schizz between perceived experience and controlled experience subject to the authority of discourse.

In the case of Takis, the experience of sound is denied in favour of the model, the idea even. In Viola, the model legitimates the experience, through the expression of a technological sophistication, and fictionalizes its production by proposing an erroneous explanation for it. In both cases, sound is used as plastic element at the expense of a certain virtualization of sound which effaces sound in favour of the model that is supposed to reveal it.

The plastic approach to sound need not necessarily be developed only by way of models, though. It can effectively convoke sound as sensible raw material. This is the case in Joseph Beuys's work *PLIGHT*, an installation composed of 284 rolls of felt and wool lined up at double height to form two rooms arranged in an L-shape:

A grand concert piano is placed in the first room. The visitor discovers it to the right upon entering, with the keyboard facing him. The cover is shut and locked, in principle at least. An old blackboard, designed for teaching musical notation, is placed diagonally on the piano, making it impossible to open the cover. [...] The visitor coming into a room enters it physically, in a more resolute manner than he could do in imagination: the heat that his body produces, the air that he inhales and exhales, that he displaces in walking or talking, the sounds he might emit, seem to him to be immediately absorbed by the felt.[304]

The silencing here is not just symbolic. It is symbolized, of course, by the evocative nature of the closed piano, but there is also a real, pregnant silence—not a perfect silence, of course (we have already seen that *perfect silence* does not exist). *PLIGHT* evokes silence by subjecting the audience's listening to the acoustic damping of the space itself. The perception of sound and of the characteristics of sounds as they are deadened, muffled by the felt, is central here: perception itself *makes the work*. By means of the stifling materiality of the felt, *PLIGHT* becomes literally deafening. Beuys thus broaches the question of sound, sound as raw material, through its sensible properties:

The acoustic element and the sculptural quality of sound have always been essential for me in art; in terms of music, perhaps my past with the piano and cello led me in this direction. And then there was the use of sound as sculptural material in order to broaden the global understanding of sculpture from the point of view of the use of materials. All of them then become sculptural

---

304. *Joseph Beuys* (Paris: Éditions du Centre Pompidou, 1994), 244, 236.

materials—not only solid materials such as metal, clay, stone, but also sound, noises, a melody using language—and all of them acquire their form through thought; thus thought is adopted as a sculptural medium. This is an extreme position, the really transcendental position of production in general.[305]

With Beuys we have an illustration of the possibility of an authentically plastic thinking of sound—authentically plastic because it *materializes* sound, in a materiality that reveals itself not through a model that supposedly describes it, but through one's sensible experience of it in the work. And yet Beuys's approach is quite rare in the field of sound installations. More usually the plastic approach leads to a *reassignment* of the material and spatial field, in which sound develops in the direction of a symbolic or referential field; a reassignment that is permitted by the modelization of sound, by the adjunction to sound of *coordinates* that belong to a normalized referential system.

Precession of Listening

Modelization is an instrument of representation that produces an effect of the real, in so far as it proposes a certain reading of things and prepares for its simulation. Lucius Egroizard, a resident in Raymond Roussel's *Locus Solus*, toiling to reproduce, by means of esoteric procedures, the voice of his daughter who was trampled to death by assassins dancing the jig—that is to say, attempting to *model* his child's voice—in effect seeks to conjure away her death. He does so by simulating the vocal presence of his daughter, but also by *reducing*

---

305. Citing Joseph Beuys, J.-Y. Bosseur, *Le Sonore et le Visuel, Intersections musique/arts plastiques aujourd'hui* (Paris: Dis Voir, 1992), 80.

the experience of this presence to a set of parametrizable procedures, a little like Des Esseintes when he defuses his desire to travel by simulating the *presence* of England by wandering through the rain to a Paris 'pub'.

Through the different regimes of discourse that determine and govern it, listening tends to become an instrument of *simulation*; metaphorically speaking, it becomes the same procedure that Egroizard uses to determine that which he desires to hear, and will end up actually hearing. Now, simulation is not illusion: as Baudrillard writes, it is 'characterised by a *precession of the model*'.[306]

Schafer, whose idealism of sound we discussed above, crosses the Rubicon of listening by going so far as to affirm that 'we perceive only what we can name',[307] which amounts to saying that we can only apprehend that which we can model, and ultimately, only that which we can communicate. This, in a certain sense, is the difference that Antoine Fabre d'Olivet also establishes when he studies the recovery of a young boy whose hearing he has restored.[308] As the child discovers sound for the first time, he is initially overcome by torpor:

> At the moment when young Grivel enjoyed for the first time the auditive faculty, his intellectual faculties had, for fifteen years, been ignorant of its existence; so their agitation was strange to him, and they were a long time without producing the sentiment

---

306. J. Baudrillard, *Simulacra and Simulation*, tr. S. Faria Glaser (Ann Arbor, MA: University of Michigan Press, 1993), 16.

307. Schafer, *The Soundscape*, 34.

308. A. Fabre d'Olivet [1811], *The Healing of Rodolphe Grivel*, tr. N.L. Redfield (New York and London: Putnam's, 1927).

of hearing or the understanding of sounds. [...] [F]rom the 9th to the 12th of January, a sort of torpor, produced by fifteen years of immobility and non-exercise, had caused the effect of a deep sleep or lethargy in the intellectual faculties of young Grivel. The sound struck his ear without finding anything there that it could arouse; sensibility, vainly excited, was a sterile point without radius and without circumference. Thus the sound died out in a vacuum. So a sleeping animal has no feeling of a sting, although his quivering hide announces sensation.[309]

Fabre d'Olivet has no doubt that the young Grivel, although having recovered his *auditory faculty*, still does not hear, in so far as he is equipped with no facility for reading that which is captured by his ears:

This child, receiving the impression of all sounds without understanding any of them, that is to say, without grasping, classifying or judging them, found himself in a situation wholly new, strange, and undefinable even to us, but painful and fatiguing to him, and from which he made useless efforts to emerge. He was called; but did he know that he was called? One clapped near him; but what was it to clap? Who had taught him to distinguish its name? Could he recognise among thousands of noises, all unknown, a noise to which his attention had never been fixed, which his memory had never retained, of which he had not appreciated either the form or the value?[310]

And yet Rodolphe Grivel does indeed react to sounds: even if, at first, this reaction takes the form of a stupor, and even if

309. Ibid., 82, 86.
310. Ibid., 89.

he is not able to structure his listening in order to render the sonorous audible, he must nevertheless feel and express to himself the contradictory sentiments that the audition of an entire new, raw universe cannot fail to produce.

The distribution of the sensible passes by way of its mediation, and thus by way of representational conventions. And yet the simple fact of communicating does not *realize* sensation. Often—and here again is the omnipotence of discourse—the process is inverted, so that the model precedes experience, and representation outstrips sensation. Audition is then immediately subjected to the management of a discursive network that will almost instantaneously determine it.

Thus, at the very moment when the sensible is modelized, schematized, affirmed, and asserted, at the very moment when it is rendered communicable, it is belied. For to render the ineffable communicable, sayable, is also profoundly to deny it. Subjected listening moves within a global machinery of coding which, through discourse, modelizes all facets of sound. The great distribution of experience, the great community of listening, comes about via its coding.

TERRITORIAL LOGICS AND METAPHORS: THE ARCHIPELAGO

Cartographies, Phonographies

In that Empire, the Art of Cartography attained such Perfection that the map of a single Province occupied the entirety of a City, and the map of the Empire, the entirety of a Province. In time, those Unconscionable Maps no longer satisfied, and the Cartographers Guilds struck a Map of the Empire whose size was that of the Empire, and which coincided point for point with it. The following Generations, who were not so fond of the Study of Cartography as their Forebears had been, saw that that vast Map was Useless, and not without some Pitilessness was it, that they delivered it up to the Inclemencies of Sun and Winters. In the Deserts of the West, still today, there are Tattered Ruins of that Map, inhabited by Animals and Beggars; in all the Land there is no other Relic of the Disciplines of Geography.

—Suarez Miranda,Viajes devarones prudentes,

Libro IV, Cap. XLV, Lerida, 1658[311]

What Borges's short text recounts is the asymptotic nature of the model, its tendency to superimpose itself onto the real and to cover it over, without ever being able to complete this process, and at the cost of losing its very status as model and simply disappearing into a new reality, just as hopeless as the first, a new reality which once again calls for models in order to render it legible. This is why the map of the Empire at a 1:1 scale is abandoned, as it reinstates the real where the model was supposed to capture it, place it at a distance, and instrumentalize it.

As we have seen, the sonorous becomes audible via the intervention of a power of language. It is through the action of regimes of discourse and of modelizing tensions that sound *speaks* to listening, and becomes audible. The primary problem of listening is to identify and establish the traces in sound that will permit listening to grasp and appropriate it. But the trace 'exhibits the (voracious) property that the geographical system

311.   J. L. Borges, 'On Exactitude and Science', in *The Aleph and Other Stories*, tr. A. Hurley (London: Penguin Classics, 2004), 181.

has of being able to transform action into legibility, but in doing so it causes a way of being in the world to be forgotten'.[312]

In causing a 'way of being in the world' to be forgotten, though, it proposes another way, an aggregative vision, a vision of aggregation that structures and coordinates the position (and condition) of its being in the world. Tracing and marking are the instruments of possession, the premises of language and of the structured universe. Indeed, Fernand Deligny turned to tracing, to the traced (his famous 'errant lines') as a way to incarnate language in mute children:

> To trace is the proper action of man who has the use of the language that makes him what he is. [...] In Indian ink, the errant line inscribes, in its 'paths', what happens to a non-speaking child struggling with those things and ways of being that are our own. [...] To trace this errancy that afflicts them because they lack words, and to transcribe it....[313]

What the model or map delivers is the objectivation of experience via the representational operation provided by a system of language. Thus the tourist, gazing at his destination on a map of the world, seeks to validate the reality of his experience by subjecting it to the authority of the map. The sensible experience, the experience of the journey and the sensations associated with it, are intangible and ineffable. They are legitimated by the model, which, qua model, is but an abstraction.

---

312. M. de Certeau, *The Practice of Everyday Life*, tr. S. Rendall (Berkeley, Los Angeles and London: University of California Press, 1984), 97.

313. F. Deligny, 'Cahier de l'immuable 1. Recherches', 18 (April 1975), 3–4, reprinted in *Essais et copeaux* (Marseille: Le Mot et le reste, 2005), 11–12.

The logic of the model as instrument for the validation of experience, and thus of the object of experience, is particularly salient to the act of listening: it acts as a palliative to the fugacity and unpronounceability of sound. So modelization takes two complementary forms: the placing of sensation into words, so as to express and communicate them; and then their anchoring, their insertion into a worldview which is nothing but a territorial dream.

A whole current of work that exploits sonorous cartography has developed under the influence of Murray Schafer and the *World Soundscape Project*, taking in scientific (acoustic ecology and urbanism) as well as creative considerations. Numerous artists now propose systematic sonorous explorations of a specific place (a city, the course of a river) by linking together recordings through a map, often a virtual or interactive one, representing the precise location of each sound.

This practice is very often linked to a 'phonographic' approach. In a short text, Isaac Sterling defines phonographic practice as

> the capture of any event that can be reproduced and represented as sound. Auditory events are selected, framed by duration and method of capture, and presented in a particular format and context, all of which distinguishes a recording from the original event during which it was captured. In this respect, phonography is analogous to any other form of recording. It is distinct from recording in general only to the extent that the capture of sound is privileged over its production. This bias reflects an attempt to discover rather than invent.[314]

---

314. Yitchaz Dumiel (Isaac Sterling), 'What is Phonography?', <http://www.phonography.org/whatis.htm>.

The term 'phonography', along with the notion of writing that it supposes, explores and becomes entangled both with its 'symmetrical' stance, photography, with the ancestral support, the phonograph, and with the intention or tension of marking and tracing sound and one's experience of it within a determinate space, a determinate territory.

More generally, the will to write sound, to trace it, is a tendency writ large in twentieth-century art, from the evocation of music in Kandinsky's famous *improvisations* to the writing of sound onto optical film by Rudolf Pfenninger and Oskar Fischinger[315] or, later, by Norman McLaren, via various different attempts to establish synaesthetic correspondences between sound and light, colour, or image. Lázló Moholy-Nagy went so far as to imagine a sound synthesis via writing. In a 1922 text entitled 'Production-Reproduction' he proposes to use a vinyl disc not as a support for acoustic-mechanical transduction, the role that it plays in the process of phonographic reproduction, but as the support for a sound-writing, with the grooves engraved directly by 'human agency' thanks to techniques of enlargement and miniaturization.[316] According to Moholy-Nagy, in this way one could create a 'groove-script' alphabet that would enable a new writing of sound and a new method of composition which would no longer have need of any intermediary or player.

The phonographic/cartographic tendency is initially conceived as a cure, a remedy, in the struggle against the

---

315. Cf. T. Y. Levin, 'Des sons venus de nulle part', in *Sons & Lumières* (Paris: Éditions du Centre Pompidou, 2004), 51–60.

316. L. Moholy-Nagy, 'Production-Reproduction, Potentialities of the Phonograph' [1922–23], in K. Passuth, *Moholy-Nagy* (London: Thames and Hudson, 1985), 289–90: 289.

evaporation of sounds. It builds nets designed to capture them, to maintain them in a regime of permanence or, as in Moholy-Nagy, to manage their very generation. Perturbed by tensions, by drives, subject to a will to power, to control, this tendency may however exceed its mission, overstep its role. The experience of listening induced by the model can become an experience of listening *to a model of listening*. This is precisely what happens with the paradigm of augmented reality in the SemanticHIFI project.

Hence we arrive at 'technocratic (and scriptural) strategies that seek to create places in conformity with abstract models'.[317] The cartographic tendency breaks through the 1:1 relation, changing from a description of the real to a *prescription* for the real:

> Today abstraction is no longer that of the map, the double, the mirror, or the concept. Simulation is no longer that of a territory, a referential being, or a substance. It is the generation by models of a real without origin or reality: a hyperreal. The territory no longer precedes the map, nor does it survive it. It is nevertheless the map that precedes the territory—*precession of simulacra*.[318]

The territory becomes an alibi for the map, its *pretext*. The relation to sound, and to listening, that abstract sheaf that stretches out toward it, are driven ever more deliberately by a discursive movement that tends to sophisticate them. Listening has nothing to do with the sonorous that does not speak; it remains deaf to it. So listening tries to make it speak,

---

317.   de Certeau, *Practice of Everyday Life*, 29.

318.   Baudrillard, *Simulacra and Simulation*, 1.

even if that means making it say that which it does not say, or making it speak about that of which it has nothing to say. All of this is eminently territorial, for to speak is to stipulate authoritarian expressivity—that which, in affirming something else, affirms itself.

Sonorous cartography is at once materialized tendency and metaphor of the territorial logic that animates the sonorous world. The effects of the application of territory to sound appear at two levels: first of all literally, in the way in which all authoritarian approaches make of listening a stake of power or at least the expression of an ideology; and then metaphorically, in all enterprises of the tracing of sound, from the manifestation of the divine in thunder or the sound of church bells to the proliferation of metadata in the coding of flows of audio information—enterprises that make of the *supplement* of sound *its very reason*, procedures that instil expressive territorializing marks, setting up sound as the 'placeholder' of a symbolic territory. The audible is the sonorous that leaves a trace, that opens up a potential territorialization. An audible sound is nothing but a territory-sound, or at least a sound that is becoming-territory.

Discourses and Territories

Listening always tends to be indexical, to draw out, produce, or induce meaning in the object of its attention. This trace, this form, this power of language is the hook for all territorial subordination to a regime of discourse, whether topographical network, architecture, or structuring sieve. Object-sounds, territory-sounds, are linked to one another by the structuring power of these regimes, these frameworks of listening, these reading grids.

All the listenings of which we have spoken come together in one sole listening. Listening is indeed multiple; it is the point of confluence of different attentional dispositions, multiple perceptual expectations each of which, in its own way, seeks to establish a territory. Every *audibilis* is a refrain, in Deleuze and Guattari's sense, forming a territory with more or less clear contours, according to which the sound will be more or less expressive. Once again, it is sound which, in its appearing, will determine the becoming of the territory. For 'the territory is not primary in relation to the qualitative mark, it is the mark that makes the territory'.[319]

Above all, to define the audible as territory-sound is not to set up an abstraction, or to transmute sound into an idea of sound. On the contrary, it is to affirm and to assume that listening is a device for integration into a milieu and for the definition of plots within this milieu. But it is sound itself, via listening, that will define or produce this plot, its perimeter of identification. It is through its expressive qualities, or more exactly through the *identification* of these qualities, that sound becomes capable of marking. And, as Deleuze and Guattari say,

> [t]he expressive qualities we term aesthetic are certainly not 'pure' or symbolic qualities but proper qualities, in other words, appropriative qualities, passages from milieu components to territory components. The territory itself is a place of passage. The territory is the first assemblage, the first thing to constitute an assemblage; the assemblage is fundamentally territorial. The territory itself is a place of passage.[320]

---

319. Deleuze and Guattari, *A Thousand Plateaus*, 315.

320. Ibid., 322–3.

Michel de Certeau also indicates that the territorial approach cannot be reduced to a static approach, but must take on a dynamic, 'appropriative' dimension. He also shows how such an approach actually lies at the origin of territorial representation, of cartography:

> [I]f one takes the 'map' in its current geographical form, we can see that in the course of the period marked by the birth of modern scientific discourse (i.e., from the fifteenth to the seventeenth century) the map has slowly disengaged itself from the itineraries that were the condition of its possibility. The first medieval maps included only the rectilinear marking out of itineraries (performative indications chiefly concerning pilgrimages), along with the stops one was to make (cities which one was to pass through, spend the night in, pray at, etc.) and distances calculated in hours or in days, that is, in terms of the time it would take to cover them on foot. Each of these maps is a memorandum prescribing actions.[321]

Or more precisely, it is the spatial deployment of its expressivity. Now, it belongs to expressivity to be dynamic, mobile, to be continually changing. So sonorous territory is a territory by conquest, and, as Lyotard says,

> the conquest of a territory by the cavaliers immediately implies that they will have to abandon it, and thus delay its exhaustion. Things conquered in this way, looted, are already dead, and must be rejected as quickly as possible. It is in this sense that every conquest is a flight forward, towards other things not yet devalued and nevertheless already devalued.[322]

---

321. de Certeau, *Practice of Everyday Life*, 120.

322. Lyotard, *Libidinal Economy*, 235.

Carl von Clausewitz tells us that 'territory and the character of the ground bear a close and ever-present relation to warfare'.[323] So that, if discourse is a violence done to things, then equally, the territorial logic that it implies can see territory as the theatre of operations for a power struggle in which every *spokesman* for a discourse will seek to impose his will. And indeed such a logic is precisely a logic *of war*, responding perfectly to Clausewitz's definition: 'Force [is the] *means* of war; to impose our will on the enemy is its *object*.'[324] Once there is territory, there is contestation of territory, in which appropriation and the dream of domination are at stake.

The territory of the sonorous is the space that listening has at its disposal to evaluate, validate, and legitimate sound, the object of its attention. Like Lyotard's cavaliers, listening surveys sonorous territories, pillages them, and then abandons them, having made use of sound. But to make use of sound in order to reinvest it elsewhere is also to alter it; the instrumental use of sound is in a certain sense a using-up, an emptying-out.

Listening is territorializing. It proceeds via the identification of expressive marks, via the constitution of a territory in which it activates a discursive projection that accords with the establishment of a set of representational and discursive devices, procedures that allow it to make contact with a sound that it will know how to handle. Territory is the site where the refinement of the audible, the object of perception, into an object of discourse is operated and activated.

So territory is the site par excellence of transmutation:

---

323. C. von Clausewitz, *On War* [1832–34], tr. M. Howard and P. Paret (Princeton, NJ: Princeton University Press, 1984), 348 [translation modified].

324. Ibid., 75.

The territory is the site of a completed cycle of parentage and exchanges [...] there is no subject and everything is exchanged. The obligations are absolute therein—total reversibility—but no one knows death, since all is metamorphosed. Neither subject, nor death, nor unconscious, nor repression, since nothing stops the enchainment of forms.[325]

The enchainment of forms is the power of language, which reconfigures itself endlessly, the becoming-discourse that specifies itself. If territory is that magma wherein form and signs are forged, it is also the unitary space, the individuated locality on whose basis a superstructure, a territorial meta-structure, are fabricated. Sound territories are encapsulated one within the other, they supplement each other, contest each another, join with or cover over one another. A whole *territorial combinatorics*.

The expressive mark constitutes the territory, *makes* the territory as one *makes* an inkblot. Territory is isolated, subject to telluric movements, to the spasms of expressivity. What joins one territory to another is the map—the model and the structure that it presupposes. Borrowing terms from linguistics, we might suggest that the territory is to the *lemma* what the map is to *syntax*. The model enchains and articulates territorial units, audible sounds, according to its own reason, according to the discourses that modulate it, and according to the worldview that governs it.

Listening has always been a territorial question. Originally designed to map out an expansive space, as an instrument of alertness to capture distant or dissimulated dangers, but also to circumscribe and receive the principal modality of

---

325. Baudrillard, *Simulacra and Simulation*, 139.

communication (the voice), listening has always been exploited both by a spatial condition and by an indexical channelling. Listening is originally designed to trace the place, and to make it speak:

> So the sonorous place, space and place—and taking-place—as sonority, is not a place where the subject comes to make himself heard (like the concert hall or the studio into which the singer or instrumentalist enters); on the contrary, it is a place that becomes a subject insofar as sound resounds there.[326]

The sonorous place, the territory, must therefore double itself: it becomes at once physical space and the metaphorical space of audible sound, one fusing into the other, plunging acoustic marking and discursive marking into a regime of indistinction wherein one can stand in for the other: as with the echo that acoustically and metaphorically traces the becoming-audible of sound and charges it with physical qualities that are also symbolic attributes.

Like all territories, sonorous territories are subject to a superstructure, a network that aggregates them, groups them together, or opposes them to each other. Artistic, aesthetic, musical immersion in the depths of the sonorous world, and, in parallel, experimental and scientific immersion, have always been subject to a territorializing auditory atavism that aims to decode the information carried by sound rather than to listen to it *in* itself. Attempts to attend to the sounds themselves have revealed that form is always expressive, that a power of language and the beginnings of territorialization are always there. They have also shown that the presence of models or

---

326. Nancy, *Listening*, 17.

structures for the conduct of listening have in common, from the outset, the discursive placing into dependency of sound, its subjugation to discourse:

> [E]very region gives rise to regime and reign, to sign and mechanism, and if therefore all one's hopes were placed in it, one is certain to despair.[327]

Such a subjugation, as we have seen, can end up in a wholesale negation of sound, where the latter is reduced to being a utile pretext for the expression of an authority. Whether we take Raudive identifying the voices of the dead in radio frequencies, or the numerous phenomena of auditory auto-persuasion in musicians and audiophiles,[328] what is in operation is nothing but the imposition of a specific, contextualized belief upon a phenomena whose becoming was sufficiently 'twisted' to enter into the regime of the auditor's discourse and thereby to corroborate it:

> In the final instance, a sound, insofar as it is bound, has value not for its sonority but for the network of its actual and possible relations, just like the phoneme, a distinctive arbitrary unit.[329]

---

327. Lyotard, *Libidinal Economy*, 108.

328. Every musician or music-lover has at some time listened comparatively to several instruments or audio devices so as to identify qualitative differences, even if they are extremely subtle. Many also have had the experience, during such sessions, of *hearing* differences, thinking that they had changed from one to the other, when in fact they were listening to the same one. The objective parameters had not changed. But the anticipation of the switch, and the judgment that one sought to form, detect some discriminating characteristics.

329. J.-F. Lyotard, 'Several Silences', tr. J. Maier in *Driftworks* (New York: Semiotext(e), 1984), 91–110: 92.

The Archipelago

Sound is taken up in a fabric of signs and values that outflank it. 'To hear [an] event', writes Lyotard,

> is to transform it: into tears, gestures, laughter, dance, words, sounds, theorems, repainting your room, helping a friend move. [...] The intensity of noise-sound = an urge to produce something, circumstantially, in an endless return where nothing repeats itself.[330]

For Lyotard, the implication of signifiance and language in the perceptual act is an immediate one—from which he draws the necessary conclusions:

> [L]anguage already inhabits the sensory, and not only as what comes from elsewhere to immobilize, preserve, and remove it from the fluctuation of the instant, but rather as what, inside it—acting from within as its unconscious as it were, its rational unconscious—determines it through repeated negations applied to the elements of its spatial and temporal environment.[331]

Listening, that instrument for the capture of the sonorous sensible, is a process of *attachment*, a ligature running between a sensible, a language that articulates it, and a discourse that defines it. The territories of sound are aggregated, structured, by the intermediation of models and discourses that 'unconsciously' conduct listening. One sound calls for other sounds, one discursive channel implies others. Perceptual objects are dispersed, marshalled, compared, catalogued, recorded:

---

330. Ibid., 93.

331. Lyotard, *Discourse, Figure*, 39–40.

For the speaking animal, the most spontaneous treatment of perceptual space is inscription [*écriture*], that is to say, abstraction. Spontaneity leads to constructing the field as a system's fragment that 'speaks' through colors, lines, and values. The goal of attention is to recognize [...].[332]

Listening is thus an attachment In the sense that it is at once an instrument of perception and an instrument of the *writing* of this perception. It determines sonorous objects. And we must not forget that objects presuppose structures.

Beneath the sonorous islet there breathes the territorial machine, organizing discursive regimes. The sound that makes territory—a sound that is audible, expressive, and *recognized* by listening—is affirmed equally and simultaneously as individual, finite territory, and as a *stitch* in the fabric of a sonorous community. The insularity of sound is its twofold condition: to be alone *amidst* a multitude of others. Everywhere borders, networks of frontiers. Everywhere separations, regroupings, legitimations, contestations, and even exclusions. To this sonorous insularity there corresponds a becoming-archipelago of regimes of discourse. So that, just as objects presuppose structures, the islet presupposes the archipelago.

De Certeau identifies this insular nature in the realm of the text, in particular when he interrogates the origin of the individuation of the text qua work:

What is then the origin of the Great Wall of China that circumscribes a 'proper' in the text, isolates its semantic autonomy from everything else, and makes it the secret order of a 'work'?

---

332. Ibid., 155.

Who builds this barrier constituting the text as a sort of island that no reader can ever reach?[333]

Isolation also means distancing, and thus legitimacy. That which is not near, close to hand, though its ungraspability and its unchangeable nature quite quickly acquires an authority. The role of models, of representations, of cartographies in the broadest sense, is to enact a state of affairs according to a purely virtual procedure. What is important here is not whether or not the island really exists, but that it is inscribed on the map. Recourse to the map is recourse to an established state. A model rendered static, the map confers a pseudo-permanence upon that which is not permanent:

> The map, a totalizing stage on which elements of diverse origin are brought together to form the tableau of a 'state' of geographical knowledge, pushes away into its prehistory or into its posterity, as if into the wings, the operations of which it is the result or the necessary condition. It remains alone on the stage. The tour describers have disappeared.[334]

Sound can be constituted into an island and aggregated into an archipelago only in so far as it is dominated by discourses. Furthermore, it is these discourses and their empire over listening that isolate sounds into islets, only to then bring them together, endowing them with a coherence that takes the archipelago as its model; so that they themselves form an archipelago.

The sonorous archipelago forms interlacings of discursive regimes, whose influence over the sonorous islets is distributed

---

333. de Certeau, *Practice of Everyday Life*, 171.

334. Ibid., 121.

at the behest of the ideal currents that elect them or divest them. 'Archipelagos are abodes of the winds', writes Victor Hugo. 'Between the various islands there is a corridor that acts as a bellows—a law that is bad for the sea and good for the land. The wind carries away miasmas and brings about shipwrecks.'[335]

Each sonorous territory, lost in the immensity of the archipelago, can only be defined by the position it occupies and the expressive mark that constitutes it. But these can be redistributed according to the 'winds' of discourse. The expressive mark can be rewritten, reinterpreted: 'The place is a palimpsest.'[336] And thus sound can be projected into another regime of discourse and can take on other values, tell another story. Although the archipelago is made up of shifting islets, ready to disappear or move on at any moment, it nevertheless conserves and affirms a *certain* coherence, wagering on the inertia of discourses and on the very process of listening, which, in order to *hear*, must *recognize*. Even as the islet emerges, it is dependent upon those that already exist, always already dependent upon the archipelago-structure itself. It is never born in the middle, from nowhere. It is invariably unique, alone, *and* linked to others.

Structures, nets, and sieves, the archipelago and its avatars, appear at all stages of listening, always harbouring potentials of one sort or another.

---

335. V. Hugo, *Toilers of the Sea* [1883], tr. J. Hogarth (New York: Modern Library, 2002), 20.

336. de Certeau, *Practice of Everyday Life*, 202.

INSULARITY AND AUTHORITY

What is proper to an island is to be *isolated*,[337] and to be located only by way of its isolation. It is not integrated into a territory, but into a milieu (which is not territory, *in so far as it is not properly expressive*). Since it is isolated, it is naturally subject to univocal domination. *Every island has, at some time, known its tyrant*. Insularity thus supposes both conquests and the undoing of power: the island is the political site par excellence.

Listening, governed by discourses, engenders an insularity of the sonorous, creating objects and placing them in relation to one another (building an archipelago). The becoming-language of sound drives forward, is established, is affirmed. It isolates and structures, engendering a logic of recognition. And '[l]anguage is made not to be believed but to be obeyed, and to compel obedience'.[338]

The becoming-island of sounds, the becoming-archipelago of the sonorous world, is therefore also its disciplining, its subordination to regimes of discourse which are themselves a network, an archipelago. The archipelago of discourse shapes the sensible in its own image.

---

337. In Italian, 'island' is '*isola*'.

338. Deleuze and Guattari, *A Thousand Plateaus*, 7.

6

PHONOPHANIES

If every territory is the spatial manifestation of the expressive mark that constitutes it, then its frontiers emerge as sites of intermodulation between many such marks. What territory also reveals is that, while the expressive mark may presuppose identification and isolation (the conditions for its discrete existence), it also implies a structure or milieu that surpasses it and within which it is accreted. The spatial gridlines that emanate from a territory, its architected nature, resonate with the processing, management, and distribution of the sensible that coordinates it, maps out its landmarks, and administers it.

But this dependency on the expressive mark also means that it is proper to a territory to be in constant movement. Although such movement can sometimes engender, as a counter-reaction, the expression of an iron order, it can also shake the foundations of the milieu by dint of the changes it brings about; or challenge the integrity of the archipelago by altering its contours. To each matter its antimatter, to each territory its deterritorialization.

Phantom Islands: The Limits of Models

In his book *Lost Islands* Henri Stommel tells the stories of various lost islands which once figured on nautical charts, mappamundi, and terrestrial globes, and in some cases still do. Stommel takes the example of Ganges Island (also known as Nakanotorishima) supposedly located off the coast of Japan, the existence of which has been questioned since the beginning of the twentieth century (in 1911, a ship passing through the supposed position of the island reported that it was not there), although it still features on maritime charts. Stommel recounts how he somewhat mischievously asked a Lufthansa travel agent to plan a trip to Ganges Island for him, having noticed that it still figured on the airline company's map of the world.[339] This little anecdote reveals something important: that the model proceeds via inertia, or at least implies it; and that anything that features in the model *exists*, whatever might happen to it: if we can talk about Ganges Island it is because, in some sense, the island does indeed exist.

There can be many reasons for the appearance of a phantom island. It could be owing to a mistake in the calculation of position, or to the approximations of measuring instruments, giving rise to the discovery of a new island when in fact there is just a confusion with an already-identified existing island. It could equally be down to the forgetting of an island and its later rediscovery, creating de facto, through a second baptism, a doppelganger. Or else it might be instigated by the peddling of legends or counterfeit testimonies, as in the case of Rica de Oro and Rica de Plata, two islands supposed to harbour tremendous reserves of precious metals (of gold and silver respectively), or by perfectly deliberate mystifications such as those spread by Captain Morrell with his invention of Morrell and Byers Islands. Or, finally, it might be owing to the continuing existence upon maps of islands that did indeed once exist, but which have since disappeared, swallowed up by the waves—like Tuanahe, which is supposed to have sunk, along with its inhabitants, around the middle of the nineteenth century; or like New Moore Island, situated between India and Bangladesh, which recently fell victim to rising sea levels.

Whatever the reason for its existence, the phantom island exhibits the inevitable hiatus between the model and the real that it envisages. The real is unknowable; as for the model, it

---

339. H. Stommel, *Lost Islands: The Story of Islands That Have Vanished from Nautical Charts* (Vancouver: University of British Columbia Press, 1984).

is precisely an instrument of knowledge, seeking to attain the real heuristically. And yet the closer it comes to this real, the more it is distanced from it—just as the map of the Borgesian empire becomes increasingly useless the closer it gets to a 1:1 scale, ultimately merging with the empire itself.

On the authority of geographers, Deleuze identifies two classes of island: continental, accidental, derivative islands, and oceanic, originary, essential islands:

> Continental islands serve as a reminder that the sea is on top of the earth, taking advantage of the slightest sagging in the highest structures; oceanic islands, that the earth is still there, under the sea, gathering its strength to punch through to the surface.[340]

Whichever type they belong to, islands manifest and incarnate the same logic of separation:

> Dreaming of islands—whether with joy or in fear, it doesn't matter—is dreaming of pulling away, of being already separate, far from any continent, of being lost and alone—or it is dreaming of starting from scratch, recreating, beginning anew. Some islands drifted away from the continent, but the island is also that toward which one drifts; other islands originated in the ocean, but *the island is also the origin,* radical and absolute.[341]

The phantom island combines and merges these two becomings-island. It is always already there, its origin lost in the

---

340. G. Deleuze, 'Desert Islands', in *Desert Islands and Other Texts, 1953–1974* (New York and Los Angeles: Semiotext(e), 2004), 8.

341. Ibid., 10.

limbo of the past, and yet its existence can always be called into question; it is always potentially *no longer there*. It is isolated ground that eludes us, in so doing prompting the imperious need to grab hold of it, to prove its existence. But it is also a ground that can never be experienced, a shifting isle that ceaselessly drifts, impossibly subtracting itself from any possible exploration. To finally apply this metaphor to its object, it must be observed that sounds should be figured not just as islands, but as phantom islands, whose validity and cartographic existence within a model is disconnected from their physical integrity, and whose *reason* exceeds the space and time proper to models. Thus, in Washington Irving's novel, the Phantom Island is not discovered with the aid of a map, but *accidentally during a storm*.[342]

The authority of nautical charts, which causes islands to appear and disappear like golems extracted from and then returned to inert matter, is founded not on the *exposition* of facts but on the *expression* of convictions, of beliefs. The becoming-audible of sound is its inscription on a map. And like any inscription it is subject to approximations, and errors of assessment and interpretation.

An island can be surveyed, landed on, explored, but a sound is too versatile, too furtive for this. It is the island one glimpses fleetingly through the telescope, lost between two fogbanks, never to be seen again. Like the phantom island, it is an *impermanence* whose existence will be secured once and for all by inscribing it, representing it, often by integrating it into a larger structure, an archipelago. What is proper to the phantom island and to sound alike is that they contest fixed

---

342. W. Irving, 'The Phantom Island', in C. Neider (ed), *The Complete Tales of Washington Irving* (New York: Da Capo Press, 1998), 782–98.

territoriality by way of territoriality itself; they constitute a
territory all the better to cast it into doubt.

In response, the model fantasizes permanence or, if that
proves impossible, expels the devious island from its registers,
destroys it. So the archipelago of discourse is a dream archipelago in which every lost island is still present, in which every
audible is sedimented, reinforcing the reef so as to amass
further audibles in the future.

Archipelagic Listening
In *Ocean of Sound*, David Toop recounts some remarks of
Brian Eno's which reveal the two faces of an archipelagic
listening:

> I had taken a DAT recorder to Hyde Park and near Bayswater
> Road recorded a period of whatever sound was there: cars going
> by, dogs, people—I thought nothing much of it and I was sitting
> at home listening to it on my player. I suddenly had this idea.
> What about if I take a section of this—a 3-minute section, the
> length of a single—and I tried to learn it? [...] I started listening to
> this thing, over and over. Whenever I was sitting there working,
> I would have this thing on. I printed it on a DAT twenty times
> or something, so it just kept running over and over. I tried to
> learn it, exactly as one would a piece of music: oh yeah, that car,
> accelerates the engine, the revs in the engine go up and then
> that dog barks, and then you hear that pigeon off to the side
> there. This was an extremely interesting exercise to do, first of
> all because I found that you can learn it. *Something that is as*
> *completely arbitrary and disconnected as that, with sufficient*
> *listenings, becomes highly connected.* You can really imagine that
> this thing was constructed somehow: 'Right, then he puts this
> bit there and that pattern's just at the exact same moment as

this happening. Brilliant!' Since I've done that, I can listen to lots of things in quite a different way.[343]

Eno's may be an experiment in archipelagic listening, yet it is not an experiment in analytical listening. The analytical tradition of listening, which is principally a musical one, seeks to identify compositional structures and to show how they reveal the composer's intentions. It always aims to identify *pre-existing* structural arrangements. In Eno's case, there are no a priori structures to be found. It is repeated listening, an apprenticeship in the given-to-be-heard, that generates the structures, 'augments' the details, and renders audible sounds that had been ignored. Eno sets up both a sequencing and a cartography of his sound recording, under the auspices not of existing structures that he has discovered, but those of his own administration.

The archipelago does not aspire to become a legislative structure; it is already its own law. It is in this sense that Eno's approach is distinct from Murray Schafer's, for example. In Eno, listening framework and structure emerge from the given-to-be-heard, whereas with Schafer the given-to-be-heard will be recognized, segmented, and then validated or dropped on the basis of an ideology of sound and a pre-existing structure, a model. Although listening is always tempted by form, although it is always caught up in the meshwork of discourses, it is not doomed to be a mere instrument for the reading and verification of these discourses in the audible domain.

Although the archipelago may be a vector of authority or affirmation, then, it is not necessarily the seat of an authoritarianism. The other face of the archipelago is a site of multiplicity,

---

343. Toop, *Ocean of Sound*, 129 [emphasis mine].

comprising 'islands by their millions, studded with innumerable creeks, caves, and rocks stretching from sea to sea, and whose names respond and correspond to each other, from language to language, from dialect to dialect'.[344]

For Edouard Glissant, the archipelago leaves behind the representation of frontiers, the expression of limits, and is instead a promise of freedom:

> I believe in what I call archipelagic thought. Because it does not impose itself, it may be fragile, threatened, impermanent, but it is always an errant thinking, a thinking of displacement and not a thinking of imposition. It says that the place is not contradictory with its elsewhere, that our nature is not opposed to relation, just as poetics is not opposed to politics. And above all it is not a thinking of the system.[345]

And yet we must not fail to recognize that the archipelago designates first and foremost the sea itself (namely the Aegean sea, the principal sea, the 'arche-sea'), and that the multiplicity of the archipelago is only a *surface* multiplicity—as remarked by the curious Charles Fort, using the metaphor of the archipelago without naming it:

> White coral islands in a blue sea.
>
> Their seeming of distinctness: the seeming of individuality, or of positive difference one from another—but all are projections from the same sea bottom. The difference between sea and

---

344. M. Cacciari, 'L'Archipel', *Etudes* 384:3 (1996), 357.

345. E. Glissant, cited in D. Marron, 'Éléments pour une approche de l'archipel lyrique contemporain', talk given at a study day on 'Literature and Music', 31 March 2009, ENS, Paris.

land is not positive. In all water there is some earth; in all earth
there is some water.

So then that all seeming things are not things at all, if all are
inter-continuous [...].[346]

Similarly, sounds are never isolated. Since there is no absolute
silence, they are always mixed with other sounds, always
already linked, fusing into one gigantic, infinite, and immortal
sonorous continuum, gradually expanding throughout space
and time. At the limit, just as oceans are only arbitrarily separated, it can be said that sound is *one*, one vast oscillating
ocean from which emerge particularities, expressive locali-
ties. So that all of the noises on earth can be considered as
'decomposites', 'partials' of one great global sound, one single
complex vibration midway between the terrestrial electric
carrier wave of which Tesla dreamt[347] and the ocean of information that inspires Toop as he sets forth his own intuition of
an 'ocean of sound'.

The question we might ask, then—one that Deleuze
does not fail to pose—is that of how we are to confront the
undifferentiated:

Yet, what remains of souls once they are no longer attached
to particularities, what keeps them from melting into a whole?
What remains is precisely their 'originality,' that is, a sound that
each one produces, like a ritornello at the limit of language,
but that it produces only when it takes to the open road (or

---

346. C. Fort, *The Book of the Damned: The Collected Works of Charles Fort*
(London: Penguin, 2008), 6.

347. Cf. Tesla, 'The Problem of Increasing Human Energy'.

to the open sea) with its body, when it leads its life without seeking salvation.[348]

On one side we have architectures, power struggles, expressions of belief, all in the service of a great segmentation of the sensible and its administration, generating sounds, millions of sounds, all recognized, identified, utilized. And on the other we have the undifferentiated: one great unique terrestrial, cosmic sound. And yet

> [i]t would be false to contend that we are always immersed in the world as though in a bath of perceptions and meanings. Nor have we said the last word on the subject of our spatiotemporal experience by characterizing it as an enwrapped depth, an immanent transcendence, a chiasm. The world, too, is open to events: it is prey to slips, to surges of non-immersive zones, to crises of transcendence without counterpart.[349]

Even so, these two extremes do not present us with an exclusive alternative, they do not constitute a dilemma. Beyond regional authoritarianism and global integration, there is a third way, a third approach to territory via territory itself, in so far as it instigates a flight from its own constraints.

Deterritorialization

Deleuze and Guattari's dialectical approach is precisely that of phantom islands: territory calls for deterritorialization, and is its condition of possibility:

---

348. G. Deleuze, 'Bartleby; or the Formula', tr. D.W. Smith and M.A. Greco, in *Essays Critical and Clinical* (London and New York: Verso, 1998), 87.

349. Lyotard, *Discourse, Figure*, 130.

Territorializing marks simultaneously develop into motifs and counterpoints, and reorganize functions and regroup forces. But by virtue of this, the territory already unleashes something that will surpass it.[350]

It is expressive marks, *refrains*, that occasion such territorial shifts. Matters of expression have two faces and, like Janus, cast their doubled gaze in two different directions, one facing the constituted territory, the other already lost in the distance. But one cannot exist without the other:

[W]hat needs to be shown is that a musician requires a *first type* of refrain, a territorial or assemblage refrain, in order to transform it from within, deterritorialize it, producing a refrain of the *second type* as the final end of music: the cosmic refrain of a sound machine.[351]

What Deleuze and Guattari evoke here is the pendular movement of territorialization/deterritorialization whereby territory always presupposes its surpassing, and deterritorialization itself always implies an inevitable reterritorialization.

A sound that is deterritorialized frees itself from its host structure, from its milieu, its regime of discourse, its sonorous archipelago, no longer being accountable to them but becoming its own expressive regime. Yet nothing could be less certain than the *viability* of this autonomy. For the archipelago itself is constantly evolving, continually spreading out, capturing new sonorous spaces so as to territorialize them, render them audible. It is always a work in progress; and all progress is

---

350. Deleuze and Guattari, *A Thousand Plateaus*, 322.

351. Ibid., 349.

in time what, in the space of imperialism, the extension of frontiers is to the empire: displacement of a border (of an anteriority),
beyond which, it is agreed, there is nothing to hear. The lines are
hardly fixed than a freelancer, a black hunter, a solitary traveller,
returns and says: something can be heard, here's how.[352]

Autonomy never lasts forever, since its self-sufficiency is easy
prey for an operation of reification and reconquest. One must
therefore anticipate this, deterritorialize once more, activate
new territory-becomings. The concept of deterritorialization
implicates a veritable programme for exodus. Indeed deterritorialization supposes an *exoticism*, a *strangeness*; exoticism
is understood as a meta-territory that is always already there,
in waiting, reterritorializing the deterritorialized in a perpetual
elsewhere.

So the third way for sound—between its total audibilization, that is to say its complete submission to the structural
empire of discourses, and its absorption into a 'metasound', an
eternal and infinite sonorous continuum—is a way that leads
to exoticism, to foreignness or strangeness in its most literal
sense; it leads to the unheard-of or the unheard, to a sound
that is disruptive.

To understand that the archipelago is in constant movement, to admit that it is impossible to map, is first and foremost
to facilitate the circulation of sound, its redistribution; to permit
the emergence of the unheard. Certainly, the deterritorialized
is still caught up in a territorial problematic; and yet, having
forced the structure, or simply denied it, it is able once again to
be a territory *in becoming*. This is what happens with Deligny's
'errant lines': territories drawn with errant lines are striated with

---

352. Lyotard, *Libidinal Economy*, 252.

traces at the limit, traces that are scarcely traces and which presage nothing and end nowhere.

There must be some possibility of errant lines, of music as an errant line which marks out territories that do not *present* themselves but instead express their precariousness. Lines that always start from nothing, arriving nowhere, differing and soon disappearing. Errant lines mark out space into moving, heterogeneous, and anarchic territories, and in this sense it is utterly futile to try and speak *from* such a territory. Territories without legitimacy.

Impossible Territories

What might it be, this becoming-territory of sound (a becoming which is, so to speak, connatural with it) that does not call up 'regime and sign, sign and mechanism'? Can there be territories that are not subject to the grip of discourses, territories that challenge the empire, islands that imperil the integrity of the archipelago?

To seek the unheard-of is to seek the unknown territory, the one that disrupts the territorial chain, the chain of language. To seek the unheard is not so much to seek to make new sounds emerge as to set out to encounter impossible territories. Questions such as these have already been posed; in particular by Foucault, with his concept of heterotopia:

> There are also, probably in every culture, in every civilization, real places—places that do exist and that are formed in the very founding of society—which are something like counter-sites, a kind of effectively enacted utopia in which the real sites, all the other real sites that can be found within the culture, are simultaneously represented, contested, and inverted. Places of this kind are outside of all places, even though it

may be possible to indicate their location in reality. Because these places are absolutely different from all the sites that they reflect and speak about, I shall call them, by way of contrast to utopias, heterotopias.[353]

The principle of the other place, the heterotopic principle, applies primarily to social spaces. It is the place where that which is prohibited elsewhere is allowed, or at least the place whose function is to bracket out the global system of conventions. This having been said, external, effective space and internal, perceptual, or affective space are not hermetically sealed from each other, and any critique of the administration of internal spaces is also a social critique. Pushing the concept of heterotopia as far as it will go, Bruno Guiganti invents the concept of atopianism, which he defines 'in its fully-developed form' as 'an aesthetic critique of the sites of discourse'.[354]

Guiganti observes a *de facto* deterritorialization of modes of expression owing to the emergence of digital and information technologies:

Telematic networks finally take the destructuring of sites of discourse to an unprecedented degree of completion. They deterritorialize the more or less stabilized complex structures of symbolic mediation within groups of individuals and specialized domains of knowledge, without our being able to predict or assess the ambiguous forms of reterritorialization that may emerge from such a process.[355]

353. M. Foucault, 'Of Other Spaces' [lecture at the *Cercle d'études architecturales*, 14 March 1967], tr. J. Miskowiec, *Diacritics* 16:1 (Spring 1986), 22–7: 25.

354. B. Guiganti, 'Qu'est-ce que l'atopisme?', *Atopie* 0 (1999).

355. Ibid.

In a world surrounded by satellites, the reconquering or reformation of territory becomes more than hazardous: it can only even be attempted through the authoritarist prism of the arbitrary. Guiganti continues:

> No point, then in dreaming of a hypothetical restoration of traditional values, or of some absolute knowledge that would finally resolve the contradictions of individual and social existence. There seems to be only one practicable way forward: that of thinking and of realizing our life precisely on the basis of the non-place that is the very condition of all possibility.[356]

There is a third type of space, after the 'absolutely other' heterotopic place and the atopic 'no-place', that can incarnate deterritorialized space. It is neither the alternative space of redistribution nor the negative space of reconfiguration, but the multiple space of recombination, the Interzone. In Burroughs, the Interzone is a state without state, the international zone, properly heterogeneous, a sort of buffer zone into which everything marginal to the normalized zones is expelled. The Interzone is to territory what the cut-up is to the text: a ruinous reassemblage of the system of signs. Neither other space nor no space, the Interzone is the intermediate space, the space of diaspora, constituted only by the movements of flux that traverse it, and upon which it imposes no circulation routes or paths. The Interzone is an excessive space that cannot crystallize because it is perpetually overflowing.

To see what corresponds to these territories in the becoming-territorial of sound—or more exactly its becoming-audible, becoming territory-sound par excellence—one must therefore

356. Ibid.

determine how sound can come into accord with contradictory tensions, with that sheaf of opposed territorializing, deterritorializing, and reterritorializing forces that will direct it and constrain it, always according to the same schema of loss and reconquest. Thus it remains to define how an expressive mark, a sound that makes territory, can incarnate an 'absolutely other' space, a non-place or a multiple place, beyond the twofold principle of integration into and recognition by a regime of audibility and a normative screening—that is to say, beyond the archipelago and its cartography.

What is the necessary condition in order for the archipelago, at once structure and multitude, no longer to become the place of order and legitimation? What must be in place in order for it no longer to be the 'henchman' of the expression of a *Weltaanschauung*, an authoritarian network constituted by listening in which all the sound-objects collected by the latter will be aggregated and sedimented? How do we refer the archipelago back to its multitude, its Interzone nature?

The condition is as follows: Listening must be rendered *aphonic*, it must no longer *speak*, no longer *pronounce* sound, no longer *write* sound. It must be submitted to silence, to muteness. It must be confronted with different sonorous protocols, with *inaudible* sounds. Listening must be disarmed.

'OBLIQUE STRATEGIES' I: THE SHIFTING SANDS OF THE GIVEN-TO-BE-HEARD

In 1975, Brian Eno and Peter Schmidt produced a card game called *Oblique Strategies*, the subtitle of which was '*Over one hundred worthwhile dilemmas*'. The purpose of this 'game' is to help resolve problems that crop up in the creative process, by seeing them in a different light. More concretely, the game consists in drawing a card from the pack when a problem occurs, and following what it suggests 'even if its appropriateness is quite unclear'[357]—the cards contain phrases such as 'Cluster analysis' or 'Remove specifics and convert to ambiguities'.[358]

The stimulating introduction of chance, of reformulation, the effacing of the decision-maker and the transfer of his power to an arbitrary combinatorics—these all seem like points at which an authoritarian creative approach and a structuring management of the sensible disintegrate. On the other hand, when he develops the concept of ambient music, Eno returns to Satie's furniture music, which Muzak Inc. had already revisited only to sterilize it with the procedures of commodity logic. Eno instead seeks to use ambient music—which must be 'as ignorable as it is interesting'[359]—to deepen listening. With the concept of ambient music he therefore formalizes something that others before him had already approached. He defines a new function for music or sonorous creation which is not the expression of an intention, nor the exposition or affirmation of a musical discourse, but instead an 'ecological' device, an environmental expressive apparatus. In a certain sense, in doing so he reaffirms the multitude of sound in its oceanic continuity.

Sound is not a prisoner of the archipelagic structure, then; it is not doomed to be a vector of order and authority for this structure. It can take many paths, many channels, can elaborate many strategies, oblique strategies. And through them, it can reclaim its rights.

---

357. Introductory card in *Oblique Strategies*, 1975.

358. *Oblique Strategies*.

359. B. Eno, 'Ambient Music' [1978], in Cox and Warner (eds.), *Audio Culture*, 97.

We will not attempt to be exhaustive or even to detail the genesis or the economy of such strategies. Each of them is a world unto itself, and we must only evoke them, open the door that leads to them. We will simply present some of these agents of the disaggregation of sound, agents which echo, oppose, and interpenetrate with all the strategies for the aggregation and structuring of listening. Sound, also, must recognise its accursed share.

The *Informe* and the Heterogeneous

In 1929, in the journal *Documents*, Georges Bataille, as a part of his critical dictionary, gives his milestone definition of the notion of the *informe*:

> [*I*]*nforme* is not only an adjective having a given meaning, but a term that serves to bring things down in the world, generally requiring that each thing have its form. What it designates has no rights in any sense and gets itself squashed everywhere, like a spider or an earthworm. In fact, for academic men to be happy, the universe would have to take shape. All of philosophy has no other goal: it is a matter of giving a frock coat to what is, a mathematical frock coat. On the other hand, affirming that the universe resembles nothing and is only *informe* amounts to saying that the universe is something like a spider or spit.[360]

We must keep in mind that the *informe* is never an absence of form, but rather the *bringing down* of form. But this is already a reflexive understanding of the term. What can be

---

360. G. Bataille, 'Informe', in *Documents* 7 (1929), tr. A. Stoekl with C.R. Lovitt and D.M. Leslie Jr. in *Visions of Excess: Selected Writings 1927–1939* (Minneapolis, MN: University of Minnesota Press, 1985), 31.

made out in Bataille's lines already are the critical promises of the *informe*. It is, to so speak, a dialectical approach, playing on resemblances, dissemblances, on the disgusting, on the heterogeneous, and on deviations.

Indeed, the relation to the *informe* can also be an immediate relation, which is not a bringing down of form but a dilution of formal outlines, a perceptual blur or fluctuation. This is the case, for example, when young Hans Castorp, the hero of Thomas Mann's great novel *The Magic Mountain*, confronts the peaks of Davos:

> Around ten o'clock the sun would appear like a wisp of softly illumined vapour above its mountain, a pale spook spreading a faint shimmer of reality over the vague, indiscernible landscape. But it all melted into a ghostly delicate pallor, with no definite lines, nothing the eye could follow with certainty. The contours of the peaks merged, were lost in fog and mist. Expanses of snow suffused with soft light rose in layers, one behind another, leading your gaze into formlessness.[361]

Such a perception of the formless, the *informe*, a perception adrift *in the absence of graspable objects*, or a bleached-out perception of a world without outlines, may be designated a 'henidic' perception, to take up Otto Weininger's term:

> If one approaches any object from a long distance, initially one always discerns only quite vague outlines, but one has very vivid feelings, which recede in the same measure as one approaches more closely and becomes more sharply aware of the details.

---

361. T. Mann, *The Magic Mountain* [1924], tr. J.E. Woods (New York: Vintage, 1996), 263 [translation modified].

(This, as should be stated expressly, is not a matter of any 'feelings of expectancy.') Imagine, for example, the first sight of a human sphenoid detached from its sutures; or of many pictures and paintings as soon as they are seen from a position half a meter this side or that side of the right distance. I remember in particular the impression made on me by some passages of demisemiquavers in Beethoven piano excerpts and by a treatise full of triple integrals before I could read music or had any conception of integration. This is what Avenarius and Petzold *overlooked*: that whenever the *elements stand out in greater relief* the *characterization* (emotional emphasis) is to some extent *removed* from them.[362]

It is the object of this perception prior to the 'removal of characterization' that Weininger calls the 'henid':

It is integral to the concept of the henid that it can only be described as one hazy whole. *As certain as it is that in due course the henid will be identified with a fully articulated content, it is equally certain that it is not yet that articulated content itself*, from which it differs somehow, by the degree of consciousness, the lack of relief, the fusion of background and principal object, the absence of a 'focal point' within the 'field of vision'.

Thus, one can neither observe nor describe any individual henids: *one can only take note of their having been there*.

Similarly, perhaps Hans Castorp will subsequently figure his view of the alpine landscape in a clearer, more segmented way; perhaps he will succeed in describing it to himself, *narrating it to himself*. Perhaps he will never manage to do so. As Weininger emphasizes—and this seems fundamental—perception is not *immediately* objectivating; it has need of an extra step, which he calls 'clarification'.

The *informe* is the agent of uncertainty in perception. It is that which casts doubt, a sort of anti-identification. It is a dis-identified given. It is perception deprived of its faculty of recognition, it is the perception of that which is absolutely unknown. One is reminded of Plotinus's phrase: 'Form is the trace of the formless [*to gar ikhnos tou amorphous morphè*]'.[363] The formless, the *informe*, is that which has left no trace; and it is precisely through the trace that the demarcation between the audible and the sonorous, between that which is heard and that which is not, operates.

Hence the *informe* is not heard. This is what Fabre d'Olivet's young patient Rodolphe Grivel experiences as he emerges from his state of deafness. He is struck by sounds, but does not recognize them, perceives no trace in them that would allow him to integrate them into a regime of discourse and value, to objectivate them. They remain nothing but spectres that whirl around him senselessly and unpredictably. Only later on, firstly by identifying their cause, and then by associating them with other known sounds, will he tame them, domesticate them, render them audible.

There is no absolute *informe*, for there is always *some* form to be brought down. The task is never complete. Moreover, the *informe* is eminently contextual. It depends upon the history and knowledge of he or she who perceives it (Grivel perceives the *informe* where everyone else *hears* sounds), but also on his or her spatial position relative to the sensible object. To borrow an example from the register of the visible, this is the case with the famous anamorphic skull in Holbein's *Ambassadors*. At a 'normal', respectable distance, we perceive a strange ovoid disc at the feet of the ambassadors, recalling the form of a cuttlefish. It is only when we look from the level of the surface of the painting itself that we perceive the baneful death's head, a strange *memento mori* only 'hinted at'—as if, for Holbein, the revelation of death went hand in hand with the revelation of the facture of the painting (touches, brushstrokes, pigments) in a *distanceless* relation, in the establishing of an intimacy; as if such a relation could only be felt *from up close*, vanishing the instant one steps away, returning to the *informe* when one resumes one's distance.

Such observations have already been made and 'worked through'; for example in Adorno, when he describes a becoming-*informe* of music. *Musique informelle*, he says, rejects 'the hostile extremes of faith in the material and absolute organisation'.[364] Here Adorno expresses a certain intuition envisaging a process of the reification of the sensible operative not only during the reception of 'cultural goods', but also at the stage of production. The two extremes he designates contribute both to the reification of sensation in sound objects ('faith in the material') and to the structuring of sensible experience ('absolute organisation').

Adorno uses the term *informelle* as a strategy designed to counteract the hegemony of the couplet object-structure (the archipelagic relation) in musical creation. But Adorno is

---

364. T.W. Adorno, 'Vers une musique informelle', in *Quasi Una Fantasia: Essays on Modern Music*, tr. R. Livingstone (London: Verso, 1998), 269–321: 296.

still Adorno, and the use of the term 'informelle' designates not so much the musical form as the compositional stance:

> What is meant is a type of music which has discarded all forms which are external or abstract or which confront it in an inflexible way. At the same time, although such music should be completely free of anything irreducibly alien to itself or superimposed on it, it should nevertheless constitute itself in an objectively compelling way, in the musical substance itself, and not in terms of external laws.[365]

It would have to wait for composers like John Cage before musics were found that could respond 'formally' to the name of the *informelle*, musics in which formal saliencies would fade away. As an enlightened observer, David Toop bears witness to these metamorphoses of music, which 'once structured like an armadillo now took the shape of a jellyfish'.[366]

As we have said, the *informe* is not the total absence of form; it is form at its limits, on the verge of disintegration. The *informe* is the cutting edge separating form from the aformal. It is ready at any moment to topple into one or the other. In fact, it oscillates constantly between them.

Never pure, the *informe* is a highly heterogeneous 'substance'. Therefore—and this is implied in the definition given by Bataille, who thereby further nuances that of Plotinus—the *informe* is not necessarily bound to become form; it is not a form in-becoming. The *informe* is disarmed, confounded form that can be neither described nor fixed. It is *formal indecision*, a transgression and a contestation of form, working constantly at its dissolution. Faced with the *informe*, the attitude of

---

365. Ibid., 272.

366. Toop, *Ocean of Sound*, 100.

perception can only be that of disarray. In the following passage Augustine describes his own experience of the *informe*:

> [M]y mind tossed up and down foul and horrible 'forms' out of all order, but yet 'forms' and I called it without form not that it wanted all form, but because it had such as my mind would, if presented to it, turn from, as unwonted and jarring, and human frailness would be troubled at. And still that which I conceived, was without form, not as being deprived of all form, but in comparison of more beautiful forms; and true reason did persuade me, that I must utterly uncase it of all remnants of form whatsoever, if I would conceive matter absolutely without form; and I could not; for sooner could I imagine that not to be at all, which should be deprived of all form, than conceive a thing betwixt form and nothing, neither formed, nor nothing, a formless almost nothing.[367]

Everyone has experienced this at some time or other: being at a loss, perceiving something that awakens nothing in oneself, apart perhaps from fear. The *informe* awakens something indistinct, unclassifiable, radically strange, exotic. It manifests itself—proceeding via resemblance, by contrast—not in any positive way, but precisely through its impossibility. The *informe* is identified as unidentifiable, recognized as unrecognizable. Its resemblance-by-contrast says *nothing could be like this*; it is 'agonizing'.[368] One might therefore say that the *informe* is 'heterologically' dissimilar.[369]

---

367. Augustine, *Confessions*, XVII, VI, 6 (tr. E.B. Pusey). Cited in Didi-Huberman, *La Ressemblance informe*, 5.

368. Didi-Huberman, *La Ressemblance informe*, 23.

369. In 'The Use Value of D.A.F. de Sade' [1930], Bataille defines heterology as being 'the science of what is completely other', adding that it is opposed to any homogeneous representation of the world'. *Visions of Excess*, 91–102: 97.

This means that to evoke a formless approach to sound is to rely on a heterological dimension of 'sounding'—that is, to suppose an unrecognizable expressive approach that maximally hinders all attempts at signifiant reinvestment and integration into a preexisting discursive system. An '*informe* music' must in effect say nothing, or at least must affirm nothing. Its signifiance, kept to an absolute minimum, must never go beyond the evocative.

The Imperceptible and Decentring

We don't know who or what inhabits the burrow and speaks through Kafka's pen. We know only that he, or *it*, thinks. The inhabitant of the burrow is the territorial being par excellence. It continually auscultates, shapes, modifies, repairs the tunnels of its burrow, exulting in the architectural and strategic perfection of its dwelling, savouring the quietude of its hearth. One day, though, it is troubled by a strange, impalpable sound of which it can determine neither the cause nor the provenance. This sound rapidly comes to monopolize its attention:

> I don't seem to be getting any nearer to the place where the noise is, it goes on always on the same thin note, with regular pauses, now a sort of whistling, but again like a kind of piping. [...] It is really nothing to worry about; sometimes I think that nobody but myself would hear it; it is true, I hear it now more and more distinctly, for my ear has grown keener through practice; though in reality it is exactly the same noise wherever I may hear it, as I have convinced myself by comparing my impressions. Nor is it growing louder; I recognize this when I listen in the middle of the passage instead of pressing my ear against the wall. Then it is

only with an effort, indeed with great intentness, that I can more guess at than hear the merest breath of sound now and then.[370]

The inhabitant of the burrow experiences the limits of the perceptible, or rather undergoes a limit-experience of the perceptible. The imperceptible is not that which goes unperceived, but that which one cannot quite manage to perceive, while perceiving that this is the case. The imperceptible 'is also the *percipiendum*'.[371] This sensible limit, this effacement of the marks that sign a sound, this noise at the frontier of the audible, has a twofold effect. First of all it leaves the inhabitant's listening in suspense, as he is obliged to regularly verify whether the sound is still ongoing, and in order to do so must cease all activity and be silent. It is constraining. Neither coming closer nor getting further away, this 'breath of sound' also sets up a regime of pseudo-permanence that will ultimately jeopardize the territorial integrity of the burrow and the proprietorial status of its inhabitant. This imperceptible sensible appearance does not mark; it effaces other marks. It hollows out the other as the process of caseous necrosis hollows out caverns in the tubercular patient.

As well as being acousmatic, listening to the noise in the burrow therefore becomes *phantomatic*: it casts doubt on itself, incapable of grasping this ungraspable sound that emerges and disappears, coming *ever so slightly* nearer, or rather giving the impression of coming nearer as one focuses on it. Thus the inhabitant of the burrow ends up persuading himself that the sound is indeed *approaching*.

---

370. F. Kafka, 'The Burrow', in *The Complete Stories*, 354–86: 371–2 [translation modified].

371. Deleuze and Guattari, *A Thousand Plateaus*, 281.

The imperceptible, as we said above, is not so much that which absolutely cannot be perceived as that which resists perception, that which is positioned at the very limits of our perception: 'impregnable sites of an imperceptible territory that is constantly overflowing'.[372] To get out of the clutches of determinations and rationalizations—such seems to be the promise of the imperceptible, in the sense that it is non-recuperable. Sound work with the imperceptible can therefore only be a work on thresholds, between thresholds, fragile interstices short of which nothing is any longer perceptible and beyond which all is cognizable, recognizable. Such work is the temptation of the *almost nothing*, of sound that fails to present itself, evaporating before it has appeared.

The imperceptible participates in a form of deterritorialization in so far as it *operates* within the becoming of sound, modulating its appearing to the point of disappearance. Indeed, the imperceptible supposes a setting in motion:

> Movement has an essential relation to the imperceptible; it is by nature imperceptible. Perception can grasp movement only as the displacement of a moving body or the development of a form. Movements, becomings, in other words, pure relations of speed and slowness, pure affects, are below and above the threshold of perception. Doubtless, thresholds of perception are relative; there is always a threshold capable of grasping what eludes another: the eagle's eye... But the adequate threshold can in turn operate only as a function of a perceptible form and a perceived, discerned subject. So that movement in itself continues to occur elsewhere: if we serialize perception, the movement always takes place above the maximum threshold

---

372. P. Criton, 'Territoires imperceptibles', *Chimères* 30 (Spring 1997), 65.

and below the minimum threshold, in expanding or contracting intervals (microintervals).[373]

This temptation of the imperceptible as motif of microvariation has been expressed in music before: from the spectral approach to microtonal music, passing through 'microsound', to certain fringe ambient or 'onkyo' currents, we find the same will to play with the thresholds of perception, to solicit hearing at its limits, at its breaking points, thereby seeking to free oneself from 'proper form' and its identifiability. Such musical currents linked to the imperceptible were in fact foreseen many years previously, by Ludwig Wittgenstein:

> I should not be surprised if the music of the future would be monophonic [*einstimmig*]. Or is this just because I cannot clearly imagine several voices? In any case, I cannot imagine that the old large forms (string quartet, symphony, oratorio, etc) could play any role at all. If something like this comes, it will have to be— I believe—simple, *transparent*.[374]

Attention has increasingly been paid, then, to the emergence and disappearance of the sonorous within sound itself. The imperceptible, qua sonorous transparency, does not simply resist the enterprises of determination, the weaving of the signifiant; it submits the listener to the law of the void. And indeed, when he thinks of such sounds, Wittgenstein anticipates his possible future deafness, his inability to clearly discriminate them. Just as the sound of the digger alerts the

---

373. Deleuze and Guattari, *A Thousand Plateaus*, 280–81.

374. L. Wittgenstein, in I. Somavilla (ed), *Denkbewegungen: Tagebücher 1930–1932, 1936–1937* (Frankfurt am Main: Fischer, 1999), 31 [emphasis mine].

inhabitant of the burrow, jeopardizing the frontiers of his dwelling, casting doubt on the very existence of the burrow as a territorial unit (which is, so to speak, violated), the imperceptible contests the auditor through his very listening. The auditor is invaded by doubt, then forced to listen to his own listening, to scrutinize it, questioning its acuity, its correctness, its *pertinence*. It is in this sense that the listening of the imperceptible may swiftly become vertiginous. It places in peril the integrity of the auditor him or herself.

The experience of the imperceptible is a differential, continually shifting experience. The sound of the digger *seems* to approach and then to fade away, only to finally remain the same. Imperceptible permanence *quavers*; it always seems to be about to disappear or to become explicit, and thus *decentres* the auditor to the degree that the given-to-be-heard dwindles away or becomes stronger in the course of its microvariations.

This activation of a decentring via the modulations of the imperceptible can be grasped through Maurice Blanchot's description of Thomas's experience in the sea.[375] As he swims, Thomas gradually melts into and fuses with the water. The experience of decentring for which Blanchot uses Thomas's adventure as a metaphor is at once an *infra-sensible* experience and the experience of a self-metamorphosis.

In his study on *Thomas the Obscure*, Jean Starobinski writes that

> the new resource that Thomas discovers consists in a mode of
> existence which, at the price not only of an attenuation of the
> self but of its radical metamorphosis, renders the asphyxiating
> depths of the water habitable. An unexpected aptitude permits

---

375. Blanchot, *Thomas the Obscure*, 7–9.

him to survive in the deadly medium, not by losing his identity but by passing into another form, into a *being-other*.[376]

The experience of decentring is suggested by the becoming-molecular of imperceptible sensibles, agitated by incessant variations, limit oscillations which even and above all imperil themselves. Thomas does not drown because he himself no longer knows which world surrounds him—he is already that world. It is only once he is totally lost, no longer distinct from the sea, that he is saved. The imperceptible breaks the subject-object dialectic: there is no longer any object to be grasped, but only differentials of amplitude, of pitch, which attract to them the *ideal* auditor—an auditor which itself also *differentiates*.

The imperceptible opens onto an extraterritorial horizon, rendering the perceiving subject incapable of any longer perceiving himself as a territorialized entity. Unlike the sound-object, the imperceptible constrains the sensible relation to remain within a non-authoritarian modality. No structure, no fixed distribution between subject, object, and structure, can be convoked. The perceiving subject is deprived of his nodal principle, of his role as the great collector of the sensible. He is fleeting, already departing. The perception of the imperceptible is located in an other space, then: simultaneously a most intimate space and one that is utterly impersonal.

During his swim Thomas observes someone in the distance. Already, in a sort of postlude to his *becoming-ocean*, he abandons himself to this fleeting appearance, impossible to fix, properly imperceptible:

---

376. J. Starobinski, 'Thomas l'obscur, chapitre 1er', *Critique* 229 (June 1966), 507.

Peering out, he discovered a man who was swimming far off, nearly lost below the horizon. At such a distance, the swimmer was always escaping him. He would see him, then lose sight of him, though he had the feeling that he was following his every move: not only perceiving him clearly all the time, but being brought near him in a completely intimate way, such that no other sort of contact could have brought him closer. He stayed a long time, watching and waiting. There was in this contemplation something painful which resembled the manifestation of an excessive freedom, a freedom obtained by breaking every bond. His face clouded over and took on an unusual expression.[377]

The imperceptible, qua extraterritorial, qua territory without mark, a sound that makes no trace within the predefined space of sound, is a territory of non-division. Within the archipelago the imperceptible cannot be. It does not *trade*, it celebrates no encounters. It is a desert in which those belonging to the 'community of those without community', the 'inoperative community', lose themselves.[378] A desert that the likes of Jacques Rigaut and Jacques Vaché have paced silently, an outpost that precedes complete erasure, the silent desert of the late Duchamp.

We have said that total silence does not exist. *Perceptually*, Cage's experiment in the anechoic chamber traces out the limit of silence, still and always full of noise. *Symbolically*, silence implies withdrawal, retreat. It is the unsaid. And finally in its *idealized*—that is to say modelized—form, silence imposes or supposes order: 'When Leriche says that health is the silence

---

377. Blanchot, *Thomas the Obscure*, 9.

378. J.-L. Nancy, *The Inoperative Community*, tr. P. Connor, L. Garbus, M. Holland and S. Sawhney (Minneapolis, MN and Oxford: Minnesota University Press, 1991).

of the organs, he shows that he does not have an ear, that he has the classic European policed-policing ear.'[379]

Thus the silences of Vaché and Duchamp are no longer absolute silences: they are imperceptibles. The imperceptible opens up a dialogue between that which is unarticulated and that which is molecularized. The transmitter fails to transmit, or transmits only reluctantly. The auditor fails to hear, and himself vanishes when he meets with the evanescent. Like the *informe*, the imperceptible breaks from perceptual certainties by leading listening into free, mute zones, beyond or falling short of the empire of discourses.

The Indeterminate, The Indistinct

Midway between the imperceptible and the *informe* we can make out another concept, one that is perhaps more vague, doubtless more trivial, but which listening constantly comes up against: the indistinct. A sound is indistinct when it is too far away, when it is masked, when it is drowned in reverberation, etc. An isolated sound is rarely indistinct, unless it is imperceptible or *informe*. Yet even if the indistinct is located at the junction of the *informe* and the imperceptible, it is something else entirely. The indistinct is to the audible what blurriness is to the visible. In its degradation the indistinct sound loses some of the formal and/or semantic information it contains, and reaches the ear only imperfectly.

The indistinct should not however be considered only as a failure in the transmission of the sensible; it is not purely negative. For not only does it attenuate sensible effects; it also *produces* them, and therefore indistinction can be a creative procedure. The art of sound can play on the indistinct, using

---

379. Lyotard, 'Several Silences', 8.

sensible ambiguity to trace out a deviant expressivity, working more through suggestion and evocation than through the exposition of a *formal development*.

The music of Giacinto Scelsi, for example, is a music of the indistinct. It is not purely indistinct in itself, but it proceeds via the indistinct on at least two different levels. Firstly, at the level of its form it cannot be apprehended according to any structural saliencies or schemas. Scelsi's works are above all masses, melting fluids, in which the sonorities of instruments amalgamate in a fantastical manner, with acoustic phenomena taking precedence over note-by-note organization.

Other musicians such as Phill Niblock and Charlemagne Palestine, and the whole movement of drone music,[380] of which they are tutelary members, have carried on this work, in sound-musics that only reveal themselves through the subtle modulations that animate them, emerging from the carrier that is the drone itself. Scelsi's music prefigures the possibility of a unique use of the drone as musical paradigm. He creates a mass from which emergent sonorities emerge, always working together, forming a sound at once unique and multiple, simple and complex, their apprehension depending upon the auditor's degree of concentration and immersion.

In Scelsi, as in drone music, music is conceived far more as a fluid matter, an energy, than as the manifestation of a discourse that develops over time. It is in this sense that it is indistinct: in the sense that it produces an indistinct discourse, sometimes an ineffable one, continuity being the opposite of segmentation and segmentation being the very principle of distinction.

---

380. A music composed of sonorous drones and sound fields slowly evolving continuously and arhythmically. See Caux, *Le Silence, les couleurs du prisme*, 83 and 142–3.

It might therefore come as a surprise that Scelsi himself speaks of identification, since, as we have seen, identification is the principal tool for the segmentation of the sonorous continuum into objects, into basic cells, so as to bring about a syntagmatic construction of audible sound:

> Without [the faculty of identification], all external and internal experiences […] remain within vague and indefinite consciousness: those states we sometimes experience, which are difficult to define and which we find it hard to imagine carrying on for too long—for, as soon as possible, the faculty of identification intervenes. […] The very nature of the faculty of identification means that the experiences and images that result from it are in large part 'cognition', and therefore signification or sensible content. This is why we might speak of poetry, or art, as means for knowledge.[381]

Even if we subscribe to this analysis of Scelsi's, showing how the pre-identificatory, 'henid' state is a state of fuzziness or indistinction, subsequently structured in a process of identification which then allows what is felt to be made into an object of knowledge, it does not seem to be applicable to Scelsi's own music (which, indeed, he does not use as an example) in so far as the latter mobilizes hearing in a completely different register, that of energetic immersion and transmutation, a term which he doubtless would not refuse. Michel Guiomar, in his *Principles of an Aesthetic of Death*, outlines a similarly clear distinction between what he calls the 'reic', that is to say the 'representational' identification of an object, and

---

381. G. Scelsi, *Art et Connaissance*, cited by J.-B. Riffaut, 'La poésie de Giacinto Scelsi', in P.-A. Castanet (ed), *Giacinto Scelsi aujourd'hui* (Paris: CDMC, 2008), 25–6.

'phenomenal investigation', an immersion in the sensible that is impeded, or even obstructed, by the reic.[382]

In this way, Scelsi's music can be considered to be a music of phenomenal investigation, rather than a music of identification. It is an indistinct breath that opens up to the experience of the sonorous—it is more than a metaphor for some structural or harmonic order. Scelsi, Scelsi the mystic, creates a music that is a power of evocation: the energy of sound.[383] In Scelsi the indistinct is manifest in its resistance to exhibiting a structure and to being *legible*. What is more, this is a music of *disidentification*, and indeed it is because sonority takes precedence and because the music implies a phenomenal investigation that the work can only result from a certain empiricism.

For Scelsi's music also proceeds via indistinction at the level of composition itself, in the generation of pieces which are not written beforehand, but experimentally composed, *discovered* by Scelsi and a few faithful musicians. Indeed, this indistinction in composition was such that a futile controversy broke out upon the composer's death, as his transcriber (who was certainly more than just a transcriber) claimed authorship of some of Scelsi's works. Futile, because Scelsi himself had never made any claim to the status of composer, preferring to call his practice 'a state of passive lucidity'[384] or to describe his 'messaging' activity as that of a 'postman'.

For Scelsi, music is a medium to intensify the sonorous energetic flux, rather than one that expresses an architecture

---

382. M. Guiomar, *Principes d'une esthétique de la mort* (Paris: José Corti, 1967), 47–9.

383. 'Sound can be considered as the cosmic force that is at the basis of everything', he claims. G. Scelsi, 'Son et musique' [1953–4], in *Les anges sont ailleurs...* (Arles: Actes Sud, 2006), 128.

384. G. Scelsi, 'Autoquestionnaire', in *Les anges sont ailleurs...*, 142.

of the sensible. Moreover, in his work, sound unquestionably takes precedence over music:

> Music cannot exist without sound, but sound can very well exist without music. So it seems that sound is more important. [...] All we can say is that rather than music, we must perhaps speak of organized sounds.[385]

This *laisser-aller* attitude to music and the primacy of sound over music is also found, in a certain way, in John Cage—albeit less intuitively and more experimentally, more *practically*. Cage's non-intentionality and the indeterminacy that flows from it are above all procedural. He brings them in not as musical finalities, but as compositional means. Indeterminacy qua procedural form also necessarily comes through in the performance of the music: Cage's music bears traces of a non-intentionality which manifest themselves in his pieces as a polymorphy (with formal choices deferred to the performer, thus increasing the possibilities of the sonorous rendition of a piece) or in the transparency of a writing that is processual rather than articulated into objects.

Indeterminacy in Cage operates at three different levels of the musical process: Firstly, and above all, in the process of the development of the compositional approach and that of composition itself (as for example in *Variations III*);[386] subsequently in the performance and interpretation; and finally, as

---

385. G. Scelsi, 'Son et musique', 125, 130.

386. Kostelanetz, *Conversing with Cage*, 69–70. The score of *Variations III* (1962–3), 'for any number of people performing any actions', is a set of 42 circles made from transparent plastic, which are thrown onto a surface: 'so what you have in the end is a complex of overlapping circles'. This complex will determine the whole process of the performance of the work.

the logical corollary, in what is given to be heard. At this last stage there is a risk of thinking that Cage is indifferent to the sonorous rendition of the score. In fact there is indifference, but not in the sense that Cage's music can do without its sonorous form (even—and we might say above all—his silent piece *4'33"*). Cage's indifference is an absence of any preference vis-à-vis the sonorous material and sounds in general. Since he has 'never heard any sound [he] didn't love', Cage chooses to circumvent an arbitrary and authoritarian choice that he is subjectively unable to make. For example, when he prepares his piano for the *Sonatas and Interludes* 'as one chooses shells while walking along a beach',[387] Cage expresses a will to operate that abolishes the criteria of taste as compositional motor, but does not scorn sonorous rendition.

Moreover, Cage sees this *indifference*, this a priori sonorous indistinction, as the only possible salvation for music:

> One need not fear about the future of music.
> But this fearlessness only follows if, at the parting of the ways, where it is realized that sounds occur whether intended or not, one turns in the direction of those he does not intend. This turning is psychological and seems at first to be a giving up of everything that belongs to humanity—for a musician, the giving up of music. This psychological turning leads to the world of nature, where, gradually or suddenly, one sees that humanity and nature, not separate, are in this world together; that nothing was lost when everything was given away. In fact, everything is gained. In musical terms, any sounds may occur in any combination and in any continuity.[388]

---

387. Cage, *Silence*, 19.

388. Ibid., 8.

Here once again, as for the imperceptible, Deleuze and Guattari see in Cage's music an important attempt at the deterritorialization of the musical, not so much in regard to his will to extend the possibilities of music to all sounds, as in the application of a processual approach:

> It is undoubtedly John Cage who first and most perfectly deployed this fixed sound plane, which affirms a process against all structure and genesis, a floating time against pulsed time or tempo, experimentation against any kind of interpretation, and in which silence as sonorous rest also marks the absolute state of movement.[389]

Cage himself opposes a process music, fluid and anti-authoritarian, to an object-music:

> We could say this of all music objects. They bend sounds to what composers want. But for the sounds to obey, they have to already exist. They do exist. I am interested in the fact that they are there, rather than in the will of the composer. 'Meaning' does not interest me. With a process-based music, there is no meaning 'anywhere'. And therefore 'meaninglessness' everywhere. So, object-based musics are, in themselves, 'meaningless'. Sounds don't worry about whether they make sense or whether they're heading in the right direction. They don't need that direction or misdirection to be themselves. They *are*, and that's enough for them. And for me too.[390]

---

389.   Deleuze and Guattari, *A Thousand Plateaus*, 267.

390.   Cage and Charles, *For the Birds*, 50.

If in Cage's attitude we detect a refusal to take risks, a fear of misdirection, this is a critique that might be addressed to Zen impassivity in general, since it consists in neutralizing one's idiosyncracies and therefore one's own errors. Nonetheless, the combined efforts of Cage in favour of process (whose importance and implications he sums up in the phrase of a great Japanese potter, 'it is not the pot that interests me, but the making of it...'), indeterminacy, and non-intentionality, engender new musical possibilities and a new territory, made up of anarchized (rather than hierarchized) elements. Cage gives the example of stars which may be considered to be in a constellation (through the establishment of an arbitrary relationship between them)—that is to say, a celestial archipelago:

> What makes the constellation into an object is the relationship I impose on its components. But I can refrain from positing that relationship. I can consider the stars as separate yet close, *nearly* united in a single constellation. Then I simply have a group of stars.[391]

Cage's stance on music, which grew and evolved over more than fifty years, is vast and complex, and we do not intend to give a panoramic view or a detailed analysis of it here. But although it is true that Cage's approach always remains inscribed within a modern western tradition of music, and although he does not question the status of composition,[392]

---

391. Cage and Charles, *For the Birds*, 79.

392. Ibid. In a piece called *Atlas Eclipticalis*, Cage also uses a map of the stars to create his score. Indeed one might compare Cage's attitude to the stars to the celebrated stance of Stockhausen, the great figure of musical authoritarianism: 'Sounds are like the stars at night. We think that they are just chaos, but when we begin to study them, we perceive that this is a fantastic composition which is coherent, with its constellations, its planets'.

he did considerably extend the possibilities of music—even going so far as to provocatively imagine music being rendered obsolete by a liberated listening capable of enjoying each and every sound.

Taking up a resolutely anti-Cagean position, Francisco Lopez denounces Cage's 'panacoustics' where anything goes, with no criteria of preference.[393] In this stance Lopez sees an absolutism and a continuation of traditional musical authoritarianism postulating *in abstracto* which sound is or is not musical (with Cage going to the extreme by integrating *all* sounds). It is precisely on this subject, however, that Lopez wrongly accuses Cage. With Cage, for the first time music finds itself on the verge of implosion, of collapse *from the inside*. To suggest that Cage continues a musical history and, by virtue of this, is a part of it and consolidated it, is to deny the possibility of any contestation, even the most revolutionary, of a pre-existing field.

By opposing a process-music to an object-music, Cage challenges a whole culture of listening to music at the same time as he critiques a certain conception of musical composition, giving rise to a veritable social critique:

> Bach's music suggests order and glorifies for those who hear it their regard for order, which in their lives is expressed by daily jobs nine to five and the appliances with which they surround themselves and which, when plugged in, God willing, work.[394]

---

393. See Francisco Lopez, 'Cagean Philosophy: A Devious Version of the Classical Procedural Paradigm', 1996, <www.franciscolopez.net/essays.html>. For Lopez, in Cage '[c]oncepts of indeterminacy and non-intervention, rhetorically connected to Zen philosophy, are used as mere adornments of an attitude that, not having the awareness or the courage to be fully consistent with them, still keeps firmly in place the academic version of the figure of the composer'.

394. Cage, *Silence*, 262–3.

It is no exaggeration, then, to see in Cage's work the expression of a sonorous anarchy that persists in being musical, and to see 'a tendency in [his] compositional means away from ideas of order towards no ideas of order'.[395]

Whatever Lopez might say, Cage's musical activity and the legacy he left behind have functioned to erode twentieth-century western musical convictions, on the level of compositional problematics as well as that of stances of listening and the discourses that govern them.

Cagean indistinction is above all an indistinction of taste. What is expressed through composition as process, through recourse to operations of chance to 'write' music, and finally through the freedom he gives to his performers to follow or disregard his instructions, is a quest for an approach that neither places the composer's ego centre stage nor solicits the ego of the listener.

In fact, Cage calls for a detached listening where it is no longer a matter of using audition to form views or discover truths, but of simply listening, as a pure expenditure. Here it is indeed listening that is indetermining, since it postpones, so to speak, the reason of the sound. This is a limit-listening in which the audible is effaced in favour of the sonorous—not, as in Schaeffer, via desemanticization and formal objectivation, but simply through the suspension of the stakes that depend on listening. The significance of Zen for Cage's work therefore lies in its furnishing a contemplative approach to sound that is opposed to a traditional musical paradigm which consists less in contemplating music than in decoding it, reading it.

Like the *informe* and the imperceptible, the indistinct, whether it is a given-to-be-heard or a stance of reception,

---

395. Ibid., 20.

involves a veritable strategy of the disidentification of sound, engendering a loss of audibility, of legibility, which can reactivate the possibility of a less mediated relation to sound, and can effectively reduce the interventions of discourse into the process of listening.

The relation to the sensible is never pure. The abandonment of identification, which cannot be avoided if one chooses to work with limit-forms (the *informe*, the imperceptible, the indistinct) does however allow for a re-establishing of access to the sonorous, where before it had been obstructed by the substitution of the audible for sound, that is to say a substitution of the textual for the sensible, or again, an enslavement of listening to behaviours and regimes of discourse that determined sound and listening.

'OBLIQUE STRATEGIES' II: EXPLOSION OF THE SIGN-SOUND

Sound always involves the entanglement of two roots which are of different natures: that of the sensible and that of sense. It is only by setting up a hierarchy between these two levels whereby one interprets the other, that a relation to sound can be established that is dependent on the discourse that administers it. Listening then becomes the site of expression, of challenges and conflicts between desires, beliefs, and powers. Very often sound has been little more than a pretext for and a legitimation of such expression: an alibi for the affirmation or denunciation of these desires, beliefs, and powers.

And yet there is unquestionably an *autonomic idea* of sound, a concept that both designates and exceeds it; a conception that implies that sound can be a symbolic object, or at least an object of representation, independent of any actual acoustic manifestation. This is what David Toop postulates in his book *Sinister*

Resonance,[396] in which he studies the metaphorical presence and utilization of sound in 'the silent arts', and particularly in the novel and in painting.

No doubt one could address various critiques to this approach, especially in regard to the risk of perpetuating a confusionism whereby the conceptual approach to sound would become autonomous to the point of forsaking the ear altogether. Such an autonomization of sound beyond the sensible can already be found in the strictest forms of physicalism, which, as we have seen, consider sound to be above all else a vibratory event. We also find it in mysticism—for example in the theosopher Rudolf Steiner, for whom listening is primarily a spiritual listening, oriented toward sounds that appear to the spirit but have no physical properties, and which constitute a veritable 'ocean of sounds and tonalities'.[397] This spiritual listening is also illustrated by the 'mystical sounds' described by Mircea Eliade, sounds that one can only hear 'internally'.

Yet this conception of sound also suggests that sound and listening can reclaim their rights over discourse by reconfiguring the discursive regime in place; that is to say, by resorting to a conceptual dimension of the sonorous and to a 'discursive', rather than purely sensible, production of sound. The stakes here are twofold: to modify the lineaments of power by establishing discursive alternatives, and to demonstrate the relative and arbitrary nature of the dominant regimes of discourse.

---

396. D. Toop, *Sinister Resonance: The Mediumship of the Listener* (London and New York: Continuum, 2010).

397. R. Steiner, *Theosophy: An Introduction to the Spiritual Processes in Human Life and in the Cosmos* [1904] (Hudson, NY: Anthroposophic Press, 1994), 125.

Here, sound, sound as concept, is expressed as *separate* from sensible sound, rather than *integrated* with it. In a certain sense, sound becomes an intermediary material, distinct in itself in so far as it is not conceived solely as an object of commentary.

If the imperceptible, the *informe*, the indistinct, and the indeterminate cast a veil of insecurity over the form of sound (which always presents a temptation to abide by proper form), if they constrain the development of discourses by refusing them their objects, if they drown the archipelagic structure in a sensible mist, sound qua signifiant element can also be an instrument for the disruption of discourses, altering them by the same means by which they intend to alter it. The formal and discursive peril that the audible risks in extreme manifestations of the sonorous can also be activated within discursive production itself, through the use of sound as separate concept.

Such an axis is central, for instance, to Seth Kim-Cohen's analysis in the book *In the Blink of an Ear*, where he is inspired by Marcel Duchamp and his will to develop a 'non-retinal' painting.[398] Following Duchamp, Kim-Cohen adopts the term 'non-cochlear' to designate a sonic art that would not have to resign itself to being an affair of the ear alone (although he specifies that, even so, the aim here is not 'an eradication of phenomena'), but would enter back into 'conversation with

---

398. 'The idea for me was [...] to bring in gray matter in opposition to the retinal. For me the retinal is a thing that has lasted since Courbet. After Romanticism, with Courbet, every series for a hundred years of painting or plastic art was based on the retinal impression.' M. Duchamp, 'To Change Names, Simply', interview with Guy Viau on Canadian Radio Television, 17 July 1960, tr. S. Skinner Kilborne in *Tout Fait: The Marcel Duchamp Studies Online Journal*, 2:4 (2002), <http://www.toutfait.com/issues/volume2/issue_4/interviews/md_guy/md_guy.html>.

the cross talk of the world', thus exiting from the logic of 'sound-in-itself'.[399]

Ritual and the Blasphemous

In a startling short text entitled 'Primal Sound', Rainer Maria Rilke recounts his first encounter with a phonograph, when he was still a schoolboy. His teacher, a technology enthusiast, had showed his pupils how to make this newly-invented machine from quite simple parts. Years later, having retained the memory of this lesson on the respective roles of each element of the phonograph, Rilke imagines running the needle over a completely different medium than the traditional wax cylinder. Having in his possession a human skull, he cannot help but wonder what sounds might be produced were the needle drawn along the coronal suture of this human remnant.

Rilke is extremely troubled as he reveals his idea, which he never put into practice, since he sensed its blasphemous nature. The blasphemy fundamentally resides not so much in the instrumentalization of human remains (as practiced by Michael de Witt under the name of *Zero Kama*)[400] as in the *ex nihilo* production of a sound by means of an apparatus of *reproduction*. It is this, in fact, that is the true sin, in Arthur Machen's sense—it lies in the disruption, the perversion of the order of things.[401]

---

399. S. Kim-Cohen, *In the Blink of an Ear: Towards a Non-Cochlear Sonic Art* (New York and London: Continuum, 2009), xxii–xxiii.

400. De Witt's album *The Secret Eye of L.A.Y.L.A.H.* (Nekrophile Rekords, 1984) was supposedly composed entirely from sounds produced by human bones.

401. 'What would your feelings be, seriously, if your cat or your dog began to talk to you, and to dispute with you in human accents? You would be overwhelmed with horror. I am sure of it. And if the roses in your garden sang a weird song, you would go mad. And suppose the stones in the road began to

According to Kim-Cohen, to carry out such an action 'is meaningless. As sound, it no longer maintains any connection to the conditions that produced it. As sound, it is contextless data, pure noise'.[402] Rilke himself recognizes the impossible nature of this idea, 'too limited, too explicit',[403] yet incommunicable. What makes Rilke shy away from his notion is the totally arbitrary nature of the enterprise, which would create a sort of monster, machined and engendered solely by one man's fantasy. We might note the existence, almost a hundred years later, of artists such as Project Dark, who continue the creation of monstrous connections with phonographs by making records out of objects as varied as biscuits and sawblades, and 'playing' them.

Although Kim-Cohen's reservations reveal *moral reasons* that are akin to those of Rilke, he poses the problem in an entirely different way. Sceptical of the idea of 'sound-in-itself', Kim-Cohen develops an approach to sound considered as a thematic material with referential properties, as the bearer of a history—a conception which he opposes to a formalism of sound.

And yet what Kim-Cohen neglects, and what Schaeffer had neglected before him, is the fact that the power of discourse that inhabits listening is also a power of fiction. In disregarding this, Kim-Cohen makes a twofold error in his assessment: firstly by considering that a sound whose origin and context

---

swell and grow before your eyes [...] these examples may give you some notion of what sin really is.' A. Machen, 'The White People', in *The White People and Other Weird Stories* (London: Penguin Classics, 2011), 113.

402. Kim-Cohen, *Blink of an Ear*, 100.

403. R. M. Rilke, *Selected Works, vol. I, Prose*, tr. G. C. Houston (New York: New Directions, 1961), 56.

of appearance cannot be determined is null and void, which amounts to denying the validity of acousmatic listening; and secondly by overlooking the fact that the appearing of sound (the needle in the coronal suture), even if it is arbitrary and senseless, when *listened* to will produce sense and narrative. Through listening, sound is constantly reinvested by sense.

One anti-authoritarian approach to the expression of sound, then, consists in playing on this production of sense which, because of its arbitrary, blasphemous nature, goes against established order and structures, undoing a priori stances of listening by scrambling the codes of reception, by generating unease.

In doing so, a whole gamut of the given-to-be-heard is revealed on its periphery, that is to say in the context of its appearance or presentation. And the context is never neutral. It can therefore play the role of a supplement, a *parergon*[404] which, while peripheral to the work, and to sound, contributes to its determination.

Now, the context of presentation of an expressive production of sound, from the tolling of bells on the hour to thunderstorms to concerts, is almost always ritual in nature.

Every ritual action, moreover, has a corresponding phrase, since there is always a minimal representation through which the nature and object of the ritual is expressed, even if this is achieved only through an interior language. It is for this reason that there is no such thing as a wordless ritual; an apparent

---

404. 'A *parergon* comes against, beside, and in addition to the *ergon*, the work done [*fait*], the fact [*le fait*], the work, but it does not fall to one side, it touches and cooperates within the operation, from a certain outside. Neither simply outside nor simply inside.' J. Derrida, *The Truth in Painting*, tr. G. Bennington and I. McLeod (Chicago and London: The University of Chicago Press, 1987), 54.

silence does not mean that inaudible incantations expressing the magician's will are not being made.[405]

In fact, if the ritual 'bears within it a phrase', this is because it is always the *parergon* of an expressive appearing; it always frames a sensible manifestation, conferring upon it the supplement of sense that can determine it. The ritual is always a means, never an end. Sensible manifestations are always ends, substitutes for sacred ends, 'placeholders'.

The ritual, qua sonorous *parergon*, is of considerable importance. Those who would eventually become the situationists understood this well, as they located the work of revolution less at the level of the intrinsic quality of the 'work of art' than in the creation of a situation of appearance excluded from the logic of the spectacle:

> The development will assume the acquisition of unheard-of SOUNDS. There will be a faculty of listening, because attention must no longer be fixed for comprehension, but to grasp the beauty that has heretofore remained hermetic. Customary musical entities will be succeeded by syncopated sequences emphasizing vibrations chosen for their cadence, their intensity, or their timbre. Harmonic coherence and easy synchronism are so many parasitical factors that must be abolished. But is this music? That is the question that will be asked, since novelty always brings with it the feeling of violation, of sacrilege—that which is dead is sacred, but that which is new, that is to say different—this is what is pernicious.
>
> No, it is no longer music. The reign of the cornet came to an end at the same time as that of the stonemason. The difference

---

405. Mauss, *General Theory of Magic*, 70–71.

between the arts augments the confusion. Thus one will no longer distinguish between the strong arts, but a master art will absorb them: the art of concrete, for example. In the same way, the new architecture will determine a sonic plasticity (through the use of molecular waves) which will be identified with décor. We will then see the discovery of astonishing new climates.[406]

What Jacques Fillon calls for here is the departitioning of the arts and their reassembly around architecture,[407] the opening up of contexts of presentation (sites of micro-power) with the aim of engendering unheard-of 'climates' and disruptive sonorous situations that are no longer separate from everyday life but integrated into it in the hope of transfiguring it or, as Bataille would say, of dramatizing it, thus freeing the subjective relation to the sensible from the yoke of a transcendent reason.

The Artificial and the Overcoded

The aesthetic criteria linked to sound reproduction have from the outset been governed by a concern for realism, or in any case by a *naturalist* spirit, with protocols of reproduction aiming to be as 'transparent' as possible and to render the most 'natural' sound possible. To this day, these remain the

---

406. J. Fillon, 'De l'ambiance sonore dans une construction plus étendue', *Potlach* 21 (30 June 1955).

407. According to the painter Asger Jorn, close to the lettrists and a participant in the founding of CoBrA and the Situationist International, 'Architecture is always the end result of a mental and artistic evolution [...] Architecture is the culmination of every artistic venture because creating an architecture means creating an ambience and determining a mode of life.' A. Jorn, 'Image and Form' [*Potlatch* 15 (December 1954)], tr. K. Knabb, in *Fraternité Avant Tout: Asger Jorn's Writings on Art and Architecture, 1938–1958* (Rotterdam: 010, 2011).

dominant criteria for all practices of listening that take as a qualitative gauge the notion of *fidelity*. But we know the limits of such protocols, especially as far as their postulation of an 'ideal' pseudo-objective auditor is concerned.[408]

Opposed to this approach we find stances that generate an aesthetic jouissance not from the verisimilitude of the given-to-be-heard but, on the contrary, from its factitious or unverisimilar character, its artificiality. The artificial is the inversion of the model or its perversion, where the model is no longer a testimony or simulacra of the real, but becomes a fictional and poetic instrument. 'In this alternate vision,' writes Céleste Olalquiaga, 'appearances (whether as allegories, artifices, copies or simulacra) are not divorced from, but rather deeply constitutive of meaning, to which they add a material dimension that, instead of reducing it, multiplies its potential.'[409]

And indeed, when Des Esseintes artificially creates the *impression* of the sea, he is thereby able not only to enjoy a sensible illusion, but also to savour his own power as a creator or constructor of artifice. Such pleasure comes of the hiatus, the distancing of the sensible image (the sea) from reality (the sea is not there, there is no sea).

The artificial presupposes modelization, a mastery of the language of codes. But rather than constituting them as truth-speaking, as *parrhesia* as Foucault would say, it establishes them as factitious refinement, postulating that 'false-speaking' can also offer a certain authenticity. To immerse oneself in

---

408. In simple multichannel devices for phonographic capture/diffusion, we find again the notion of the 'sweet spot', which implicitly considers the only true position for listening to be the central position, something that *in reality* is hardly ever achieved, in the situation of a concert.

409. C. Olalquiaga, *The Artificial Kingdom: A Treasury of the Kitsch Experience* (New York: Pantheon, 1998), 272.

the artificial is to seek an authentic relation to the world not through 'forms of veridiction', to take up another Foucauldian term, but rather through *modes of falsification*—with the truth, the unique and perfect truth, remaining unknowable, unreachable, and even inconceivable.

Taking leave of the aesthetic complacency characteristic of the decadent spirit, but precisely acknowledging a certain bankruptcy of the search for a unique truth, the postmodern epoch, in which, according to Jean-François Lyotard, all grand narratives of legitimation are lacking,[410] returns to and reinvests outmoded discourses, which it now endows with a critical and aesthetic distance, in an enterprise that is one of overcoding.

Within the vast domain of sonorous creation as elsewhere in the plastic arts, this postmodern reinvestment, this testimony to the dilapidation of discourses, has manifested itself in an increasing recourse to techniques of citation, reappropriation, and rereading of existing works. From the simple borrowing of a musical motif in the form of a citation or homage, all the way to 'plunderphonics', the reinvestment of sound is always less a search for the reconfiguration of existing sonorous material than the expression of a critical discourse, or at least a commentary, on the ideological and discursive field of which the original sound was the object.

For instance when John Oswald, originator of the concept of plunderphonics, produces a piece entitled *Dab*, based on

---

410. Cf. J.-F. Lyotard, *The Postmodern Condition: A Report on Knowledge*, tr. G. Bennington and B. Massumi (Manchester: Manchester University Press, 1984). See also *The Postmodern Explained: Correspondence, 1982–1985* (Minneapolis, MN: Minnesota University Press, 1992). According to Lyotard, '[s]implifying to the extreme, I define *postmodern* as incredulity toward meta-narratives. [...] Where, after the metanarratives, can legitimacy reside?' *The Postmodern Condition*, xxiv–xxv.

Michael Jackson's famous *Bad*, his choice is oriented less by the intrinsic musical quality of the sound material than by that which it evokes, that towards which it signs. However, there is more artistically at stake in this practice than the construction of an expressive object that is a mere commentary on the original. This object is itself an original form, as Oswald emphasizes in the preamble to his plunderphonics manifesto, entitled 'Plunderphonics, or Audio Piracy as a Compositional Prerogative':

> Musical instruments produce sounds. Composers produce music. Musical instruments reproduce music. Tape recorders, radios, disc players, etc., reproduce sound. A device such as a wind-up music box produces sound and reproduces music. A phonograph in the hands of a hip hop/scratch artist [...] produces sounds which are unique and not reproduced—the record player becomes a musical instrument. A sampler, in essence a recording, transforming instrument, is simultaneously a documenting device and a creative device, in effect reducing a distinction manifested by copyright.[411]

Adopting the cut-up technique developed by William Burroughs and Brion Gysin in the 50s, Oswald obtains in sound what the writers of the Beat Generation had previously sought in their texts: original productions that operate on pre-existing complex materials.

In fact, the motif of the postmodern spirit is not just a matter of taking up a position of perpetual commentary. It is more a reinjection of expressive codes, aiming at the creation

---

411.   J. Oswald, 'Plunderphonics, or Audio Piracy as a Compositional Prerogative', <http://www.plunderphonics.com/xhtml/xplunder.html>.`

of new originals through the overcoding of existing entities. In an album entitled *Eisotrophobia*, the American artist Akira Rabelais uses performances of piano works by Erik Satie and Béla Bartók filtered and treated by various software applications, of which one in particular, *Argeïphontes Lyre*, derives from a set of cryptic treatments developed by Rabelais himself. The end result is quite undefinable: the *music* of the original pieces is still there, but seems distanced, while being endowed with an abrasive presence. Rabelais highlights the question of interpretation, and therefore of creation through reinvestment, with a galaxy of digital audio techniques and virtual musical prostheses such as his *Argeïphontes Lyre*. The title of the software designates the lyre of Hermes by the nickname that consecrates Hermes as the assassin of Argus Panoptes, the hundred-eyed giant. We must also remember that eisotrophobia is a fear of mirrors, and more precisely of seeing oneself in a mirror—the fear of a replication that is necessarily different, the fear of a loss of integrity.

By mutating known and renowned musics, Rabelais assumes his place within a musical tradition even as he signals a break with it, as much in terms of the invention of a new protocol of interpretation (spectral transformation) as in his conception of the musical, a conception that is now concerned as much with the reading of music (and its corollary, instrumental interpretation) as with the sonorous outcome, the given-to-be-heard in its most evanescent aspect.

By transfiguring the musical ideas of Satie or Bartók by way of spectral alterations, Rabelais pursues a path that will therefore lead more to an erosion of the given-to-be-heard than to a formal deconstruction of musical discourse (as operated by the sound cut-up or by plunderphonics).

And yet he still participates, in his own way, in a postmodernity which faces both future and past, taking a critical distance from the postmodern current and instead redistributing, or calling into question and putting back into play, concepts and works. Responding to the bankruptcy of discourses, the postmodern spirit plunges into the sensible past with the twofold aim of producing something unheard-of and casting a critical gaze over the traditional schemas that administered the expressive production of sound—but does so through the re-exploitation of these very same schemas.

Chaos and Critique

The critical approach to the expressive use of sound explodes the *positive* framework of audition, on the discursive and cultural planes as well as the perceptual plane. One of the most significant examples of work in this destructive economy is that of noise music. As we have seen, noise has been elucidated in different ways and has taken on various social functions depending on the epoch and culture in question. Within the framework of functional relations and information theory, noise responds to the definition of a 'signal the sender does not want to transmit'.[412] In general, noise is considered as a negative sound, and to qualify music as noise has traditionally been a way of dismissing it.

Contemporary noise culture takes its cue from this dismissal, this deceptive aesthetic conception. Ultimately it has little to do with the approach advocated by Russolo, which sees noises as harbouring the promise of unprecedented musical pleasures. Instead it is often an expressive and artistic

---

412. A. Moles, *Information Theory and Aesthetic Perception* (Illinois: University of Illinois Press, 1968); cited in Cox and Warner (eds.) *Audio Culture*, 48.

manifestation of a contestation of the social, political, and aesthetic order. Indeed, noise music originated in 'industrial' music (thus baptized after Industrial Records, the label of the English group Throbbing Gristle),[413] which materialized at the convergence of avant-garde electronic music and punk culture.

More than any other movement, industrial music from Throbbing Gristle on assumed that extreme music is an form intrinsically appropriate for conveying a socio-political critique. The logo of Industrial Records, which seems to represent a factory, turns out to be a photograph of the building that housed the ovens of Auschwitz. As described by Drew Daniel, this reference is explained by the fact that the extermination camp represents for them less 'a historical memorial to a forty-year-old war [than] the secret truth of everyday life: the camps had shown that the factory model can be applied to anything, including life and death'.[414]

Combining machine rhythms, glacial synths, a maelstrom of lo-fi noise, and disillusioned lyrics, Throbbing Gristle's music is the perfect expression of a nihilist sensibility striving to extract itself from general contemporary cynicism. Their musical sub-version crystallizes an ideological battle between the defenders of social order or cultural conservatism and the promoters of artistic, political, and social alternatives. In being exposed to its own limits, music becomes an outpost of contestation.

In the same way, the expressive employment of noise tends to explode the categories defined by a structured approach

---

413. The label's slogan, 'industrial music for industrial people', itself exposes the critical and political dimensions of Throbbing Gristle's music.

414. D. Daniel, *20 Jazz Funk Greats* (London: Bloomsbury, 2008), 16. See also *Re/Search #6/7: Industrial Culture Handbook* (1983).

to listening, music, and sound. At once *informe*, perceptible beyond tolerable levels, and indistinct, the expressive use of noise is of a critical, referential order. Noise music thus summons up formal chaos with sonic outbursts that express, sometimes with great ferocity, its refusal of an established order, taking as its first target the musical order itself and the modes of listening associated with it. In this way noise challenges the very possibility of its being an object of listening. When during her concerts the Japanese artist Sachiko Matsubara, aka Sachiko M., generates sinusoids at an almost unbearable volume, she subverts the ostensible aim of a concert, which is supposed to give pleasure and satisfaction, and offers the auditor nothing that might arouse any pleasure or any desire to listen. 'The people who always come to listen could stop coming, it doesn't matter to me', she declares.[415] Noise music is the final stage in an expressive deconstruction of the musical paradigm and of the art of sound as language. In parallel it also reveals, in a savage, primal, gesture, the expressive and critical power of rumblings and screams and the evocative power of the inarticulate. To the ideology of origins which insists that 'in the beginning was the Word', it opposes the affirmation that in the beginning *was the scream*.

Noise music also courts an *acephalic* sound, where the physical dimension takes precedence. This acephalic relation to the noise-form of sound is often pursued through the potential reversal between production and audition of noise. The American artist Randy H.Y. Yau, for example, fully realizes

---

415. 'The Queen of the Sinewave Kingdom Explains Herself', interview with Sachiko Matsubara by Takashi Azuyama, in *Improvised Music from Japan, 2002–2003* (CD box set, IMJ, cat. 10CD, 2001), 15.

this confrontation. Screaming into a loudspeaker that amplifies his voice, which of course unfailingly generates thunderous feedback, Yau makes himself the first auditor and first victim of the sonic devastation he himself produces. He thus positions himself at a pivotal point, incarnating the struggle and the clashing of two desiring-tensions: one that aims to produce the most vociferous sound possible, and another that prays for it to stop.

The expressive use of noise is a 'telluric' vector for the contestation of a structured and ordered governance of the audible. It is the radical contestation of this order. We might apply the following phrase of Lyotard's to those artists who use noise as their material of expression and contestation:

> They do not reduce the unknown to the known, they make everything one thought one knew unstable in proportion to what one used to know [...].[416]

SONOROUS RESISTANCE

There is a whole world in which sound is not reduced to a function of legitimation, nor convoked as mere commentary in order to assert a worldview. If sound is a sensible element that is eminently territorial, it is before anything else an element that unfolds over time, rendering it versatile, variable, and fleeting. There is a whole world that deals with sound in its evanescence, in its precariousness, revealing it and working it through experimentation, loosening the bonds of discourse. In the end, it is the story of the domination of discourse over sound and listening that is itself dominated

---

416.   Lyotard, *Libidinal Economy*, 253.

by fear and by the refusal of precariousness, the uncertain, and the vague.

The Persistence of the Sonorous

In his text *Listening*, Jean-Luc Nancy writes that

> [t]he sonorous [...] outweighs form. It does not dissolve it, but rather enlarges it; it gives it an amplitude, a density, and a vibration or an undulation whose outline never does anything but approach.[417]

Ultimately, in light of what has been revealed above, it seems that Nancy's proposition should be turned the other way around: it is form that, through listening, outweighs the sonorous, drawing it toward the audible, but does not dissolve it. Form, as 'power of language', articulates the sensible, conditions it. The audible, as we have seen, is sound that is listened to, that is read, that is communicated. In this sense listening is a writing of the audible onto sound, like a sort of palimpsest. By virtue of this, listening itself can be communicated—as Peter Szendy has shown,[418] in particular through the example of the musical arrangement, or that of DJs who express and *give to be heard* their experience and their practice as listeners—that is to say, their own listening.

But the audible is not all of sound. The sonorous—savage, ineffable—is not wholly dissolved into the audible. It persists. If the sonorous is unheard, it is unheard in so far as it cannot be reinvested in a discursive production.

---

417. Nancy, *Listening*, 2.

418. See Szendy, *Écoute*.

In a short text dating from 1894 and entitled *The End of Books*, Octave Uzanne predicts the disappearance of books and of printing, 'threatened with death by the various devices for registering sound which have lately been invented, and which little by little will go on to perfection'.[419] Through the character in his story, Uzanne goes on to explain that under the impulsion of the discovery of the phonograph, and given the human predilection for comfort and ease ('for every means of sparing himself the play and the waste of the organs'), it will in future become easier to listen to a recorded text rather than read it; and that this will also rebalance the uneven burden on our ears and our eyes, 'too long abused'. Uzanne pursues his fantasy further, describing the whole 'economical' transfer of literature as it passes from an exclusive practice (the reading of a book) into a sort of emancipatory leisure activity accessible to all (thus he imagines the installation of 'phonographotecks' and phonographic devices in all 'public carriages, the waiting rooms, the state-rooms of steamers, the halls and chambers of hotels').

If this prophecy never came to pass (and probably never will) it is because a book can never be replaced by a *reading*. The book, as support for a text, cannot be reinstated in sound form, for the sonorous medium is always more than a text, always conveys more than what the author described, since it conveys that which the reader adds to it. It bears, so to speak, an echo of the text, a second voice that expresses itself through superimposition; that of the *interpreter* of the text. The text, qua imprint of a thought, qua fossil, cannot be replaced by its oralization. So there is no equivalence between this support and its interpretation, even when the reader, the *narrator*, is the author himself.

419.   O. Uzanne, 'The End of Books', *Scribner's Magazine* 16 (1894), 221–31: 224.

Conversely, sound is not reducible to a text. Uzanne's approach implicitly reveals the conception—the dream—of the domination of the text and of discourse over the sensible. For him, the only future for phonography lies in its replacing of the book—as if sound could only serve speech and, through it, language and discourses.

Although he anticipates the invention of the Walkman (which he baptizes the pocket 'phono-operagraph'), Uzanne does not intuit what its principal application will be: listening to music. It seems that, for Uzanne, everything has to be related to the textual. Lyotard has remarked on this tendency to subordinate the sensible to the textual, particularly in the visual domain. As he emphasizes,

> That the world remains to be read basically means that an Other, on the other side, transcribes the given objects, and that with the appropriate point of view I could theoretically decipher it.[420]

Faced with this reduction of the sensible world to a text to be deciphered, Lyotard protests, insisting that

> the given is not a text, it possesses an inherent thickness, or rather a difference, which is not to be read, but rather seen; and this difference, and the immobile mobility that reveals it, are what continually fall into oblivion in the process of signification.[421]

This thickness, this gap, is what Lyotard calls the *figural*. The figural is what is proper to that which is seen but cannot be reduced to a discourse. It is the informulable, silent, and yet fecund part of sensible experience. Taking the example of

---

420. Lyotard, *Discourse, Figure*, 4.

421. Ibid., 3.

Cézanne, Henry Maldiney grasps perfectly well what the figural implies, and the extent to which this implication cannot be replaced by a text, a tissue of signs:

> When Cézanne, sitting in the cart with his coachman, falls prey to a sort of ecstasy which even begins to descend on his companion, and cries: 'Look! Those blues! Those blues over there under the pines!', these blues are the organs of his communication with the world, the pathic moment of his total presence to their appearing.[422]

The sonorous is to sound what the figural is to the image. Sound is not doomed to be exclusively a medium of discourse, whatever Uzanne might think. The sonorous is a modality that *persists* in all sound and perdures even in the audible. Like Lyotard's figural, the sonorous resists a total textualization of the acoustic sensible. The sonorous prevails, inaudible, in the preconscious strata. It is immediate, immanent to listening, and cannot be extracted from it, cannot be the object of any commentary, cannot be objectivated. Although it is ineffable and incommunicable from one auditor to another, the sonorous is nonetheless present in sensible experience and, like the blue of the pines for Cézanne, plays the role of an 'organ of communication with the world'.

And yet the sonorous is not the figural. It is fleeting, ungraspable, precarious. It is not like a landscape that we can view at our leisure. The sonorous cannot be observed. In fact the sonorous is precisely that precariousness that places the

---

422. H. Maldiney, *Regard, Parole, Espace*, cited by Jean Oury in *Création et Schizophrénie*, 82.

audible in peril of disappearance. The sonorous is uncertainty,
the unproved, the unverifiable.

If we nonetheless persist in objectivating the entanglement of the sonorous and the audible that is 'sound', we should not consider it as an object, but rather as an *objectile*—that which, for Deleuze, takes the place of the object where 'fluctuation of the norm replaces the permanence of a law; where the object assumes a place in a continuum in variation'.[423]

If the deep nature of an object lies in its permanence, then that of the objectile resides in its modulations. The sonorous is without mark, it makes no territory but twists territory, contests it, refuses to condone its perenniality. Sound is a modulated, fugitive instance which is destined to disappear. It is the theatre of operations wherein the sonorous, that fleeting and mute entity, resists, persists, and contaminates all permanence, all audible certainty, continually precipitating it into a precarious state from which listening in turn, in the grip of discourse, seeks to escape.

Against an Ontology of Sound

Listening and the relation to sound in general are fundamentally impure, then. The entanglement of sense and the sensible that is determining for the object of listening is precisely the proof that there is no direct access to the nature of sound, but only a labyrinthine network, an archipelago of discursive apparatuses which will integrate and interpret that which is given to be heard, generating models for the apprehension of the sensible world and strategies that predetermine it.

---

423. G. Deleuze, *The Fold: Leibniz and the Baroque*, tr. T. Conley (London: Athlone, 1993), 19.

We must therefore draw two conclusions from these observations: that sound is fundamentally a *disparate*, that its very nature is disseminated. And that It is ubiquitous, at once present in sound's appearing and in its appearance, pulverized in and through devices for the presentation, reception, and interpretation of sonorous phenomena, separated and braided between the sonorous and the audible. As it undergoes all of this, the heterogeneous and divided nature of sound manifests an absence of any homogeneous, circumscribed nature.

Sound is situated in an intermediate space, a narrow crest line upon which, in the very time of perception, the reception, projection, and representation of the sensible interface with each other. A sound that no one hears, that no one perceives or can manage to apprehend, is not really a sound. What is lacking is its appearing. For in order to be perceived a sound must leave a trace, thereby becoming something more than a sound, already endowed with a set of ideal mechanisms that are plugged into a wider network of signifiance.

There is no nature of sound. It is the artifices of belief and discursive devices that fabricate a nature adequate to it. Sound, qua disparate, thus proves to have an impossible, unattainable nature. All discourses of authority that base themselves on the postulation of a nature of sound, an *essence* of sound, therefore seem doomed to reproduce to infinity an accursed routine whereby, in seeking to grasp sound, to fix it and to identify it according to a nature that would be proper to it, one does nothing but *denature* it, propelling it further yet into ideality, rendering it yet more unattainable.

There is no essence of sound and *therefore there is no ontology of sound to be discovered or established*. There is no hidden order harbouring a pure and homogeneous nature of sound, no place from which its sensation could be made to speak.

To speak from the place of a listening (whether reduced or not), from an audible—that is to say from a *sound-object-sign* complex—is always to speak according to a discourse, and not directly from the prehension of the sensible.

To no longer try to speak from to this unattainable place, to no longer seek strategies to approach it, is to mark a pause in the legitimative cycle of listening where the appearing of sound and sound's appearance find themselves ceaselessly solicited to justify themselves and to legitimate each other. We then glimpse a new horizon, the opening up of a listening that is no longer compelled to verify or validate a discourse, but instead confronts the ungraspable, the imperceptible, and the *informe*, thus becoming the auxiliary of an experience of uncertainty rather than that of a function of legitimation.

To no longer invest in the search for an essence of sound, to devalue it as a question, is also to leave behind the image of a territory-sound so as to rediscover sound as a temporal modality. To the fixed governance of territory-sound is opposed the dynamic economy of sonorous situations, different in every case. The abandonment of the essentialist project of sound seems to be the condition sine qua non of a reappropriation of listening, which has too often been reduced to a function of heuristic verification for the regime of discourse that controls it.

Of course everything speaks according to a regime of discourse, and nothing savage and immediate can be directly communicated or shared. Thus, to renounce the essentialist project, to accept sound as a disparate, is also to accept that sound is multiplied as a function of its 'applications', and that the sound of which we *speak* is never anything but the representation we make of a sound that has been heard and is *already gone*.

Sound has no nature, sound is a becoming. There is therefore no essence to be sought, but only interstices within which sound is unmarked or evades its mark. It is and always will be unattainable. In the end, if 'everything that is attained is destroyed' then sound, qua always-other, promises to remain indestructible—and the listening that targets it, inexhaustible.

PHONOPHANY VS. APOPHENIA

From pure auditory stimulus to pure conceptual referent, the spectrum of sound spreads out in multiple directions. The pneumatic theory ultimately has the merit of bringing to light the investigation of sense within the sensible and through the sensible. The *pneuma* is, par excellence, matter that penetrates the immaterial, spirit. Sound, breath, and soul are fused in a hybrid fluid; and breath, the vital principle, also harbours *a spectral entity*.

Even when dematerialized by being represented as a wave, sound is never deprived of this faculty of 'immaterial' penetration. It is not reducible to its pure physical manifestation, nor can it be equated with a pure ideality.

The appearance of sound, phonophany, is the face offered to subjectivity of a necessarily lacunar reality. The bridging of this gap, its exploitation, is precisely the function of discourses of authority. Authority acts as a discursive sticking-plaster over a reality that is continually breached. It makes the sensible speak, makes it into a signal.

The real object of the desire of listening is an apophenic object,[424] an object that addresses itself and makes the world

---

424. Apophenia, in its strictly psychiatric sense, is a condition leading an individual to consider certain of his sensations or certain perceived objects as being *coded messages* that are meant for him. In more general terms, any

speak to it, affirming an order of things and ensuring the legitimacy of the place of the perceiver, who is also a moving part in this order of things. The real object of the desire of listening is not sound but that which, through sound, serves as a *revelation*.

---

arbitrary or unmotivated link posited between the object of a perception and a discursive elaboration, between a perceived object and a represented object, has an apophenic dimension.

EPILOGUE

A sonorous archipelago: territories emerge, zones of legitimacy, authoritarian constructions, the first elements of a strategy and a combinatorics that will structure the archipelago. Islands take shape only to disappear a moment later, drawn under the surface of the waves by the immersive attraction of each sound.

The sonorous archipelago is not a cartography of the discursive network that enables the apprehension of the audible, but a territorial and dynamic metaphor for all of its legitimative setups. There is no map, no architecture. There is no place of sound, no territory of sound. There is no essence of sound, there are only setups of apprehension.

Phantom islands, sonorous islands, are *informe* territories where many a 'given-to-be-heard' takes shape and is then deposed, as afforded by the transience of a moment of appearing. The sonorous territory, together with its temporal precariousness, its proper extraterritoriality past or yet to come, then starts to fall apart, being far more a sonorous *situation* than a pre-established territorial regime 'seating' its authority in the belief that it will last forever.

Listening must no longer exclusively reassure, read, and decode. As Barthes writes, 'there is a disintegration of the Law which prescribes direct, unique listening; by definition, listening was *applied*; today we ask listening to *release*'.[425] Now, to 'release' is precisely to open up to *panic*. If loss of control and the admission of the precariousness of becomings is terrifying, it is also the occasion for multiple experiences which, like a Wild Hunt, catch short and lay low the authoritarian poles that administer a sensible now become too tumultuous, too dangerous. John Cage says that he has no ear for music: 'I simply

---

425. Barthes, 'Listening', 258.

keep my ears open'.[426] To have no 'ear' is to refuse to cede the decision of one's hearing to the established regimes. To have open ears is to open oneself up to experiences and experiments, to uncertainties. It is to resist when faced with 'the diverse invitations to suspend artistic experimentation'—invitations which, as Lyotard reminds us, are also 'a call for order, a desire for unity, for identity, for security, or popularity'.[427]

There can be no doubt: the listening that understands, reads, *hears*, the listening that explains itself and explains the world, has had its day. The ear must come back to what it is: the privileged organ of fear. It must leave behind the metaphysical certainties of the harmony of the spheres, the esoteric alphabet of the twelve-tone system, the authoritarian approach to demiurgic composition, etc. Listening is the experience of sound appearing; of its appearing and its diaphaneity. It is not an anticipation of signs that will come to confirm a world view and to draw jouissance, order, and authority from it.

But neither does this *other listening* aim at a pure nature of the sonorous or at sound in itself. It *releases* the interstices within which sound is unmarked, where it goes off the map, assumes its character as a phantom island, advocates for a territorial limit-existence, a veritable *temporary autonomous zone.*[428]

The archipelago, then, is lost: it returns to its milieu, to the vast ocean of sound, an interminable continuum or ungraspable heterogeneity, unknowable, itself *informe*. But to try to extract some kind of metastructure from the archipelago is still to bow

---

426. Cage, Kostelanetz, *Conversing with Cage*, 232.

427. Lyotard, *Postmodern Condition*, 73.

428. See H. Bey, *TAZ: The Temporary Autonomous Zone* (New York: Semiotext(e), 1991).

to a structuring listening. Like language, the archipelago is
always already-there, always inscribed within a double movement of aggregation and disaggregation. Filled with phantom
islands, vulnerable to the shifting of the terrain, shrouded in
a fog that clings to its contours, the sonorous archipelago,
stretching out into the far distance, is an archipelago-world.

BIBLIOGRAPHY

Description de l'Égypte ou Receuil des observations et recherches qui ont été faites en Égypte pendant l'expedition française, 1809–1828, vol. II, second edition. Paris: Imprimerie de C.F.L. Panckoucke, 1821.

Adorno, T.W. 'On the Fetish-Character in Music and the Regression of Listening', in A. Arato and E. Gebhardt (eds.), *The Essential Frankfurt School Reader* (New York: Continuum, 1985), 270.

———, 'Vers une musique informelle', in *Quasi Una Fantasia: Essays on Modern Music*, tr. R. Livingstone. London: Verso, 1998, 269–321.

———, and M. Horkheimer, *Dialectic of Enlightenment* [1944], tr. J. Cumming. New York: Continuum, 1989.

———, and W. Benjamin, *The Complete Correspondence 1928–1940*, tr. N. Walker. Cambridge, MA: Harvard University Press, 1999.

Agamben, G, *Language and Death: The Place of Negativity*, tr. K. E. Pinkus with M. Hardt. Minneapolis: University of Minnesota Press, 2006.

Alvarado, A. 'An Interview with Gregory Whitehead'. <http://archive.free103point9.org/2007/07/13.alvaradowhitehead.pdf>.

Apollonius Rhodius, *The Argonautica*, tr. R.C. Seaton. < http://www.gutenberg.org/files/830/830-h/830-h.htm>.

Aristotle, *De Motu Animalium*, tr. M.C. Nussbaum. Princeton, NJ: Princeton University Press, 1978.

———, 'De Anima', tr. J.A. Smith, in *The Basic Works of Aristotle* (New York: Modern Library, 2001), 535–603.

Arnheim, R. *Radio*, tr. M. Ludwig and H. Read. London: Faber, 1936.

Assoun, P.-L. *Le Fétichisme*. Paris: PUF, 1994.

Augustine (Saint). *The Confessions of Saint Augustine*, tr. E.B. Pusey. <http://www.ccel.org/ccel/augustine/confess>.

Bachelard, G. *The Formation of the Scientific Mind*, tr. M. Mcallester Jones (Manchester: Clinamen, 2002).

Barthes, R. 'The Grain of the Voice', in *Image–Music–Text*, tr. S. Heath. London: Fontana, 1977.

———, 'Listening', in *The Responsibility of Forms*, tr. R. Howard. New York: Hill and Wang, 1985.

Bataille, G. 'Informe', in *Visions of Excess: Selected Writings 1927–1939*, tr. A. Stoekl with C.R. Lovitt and D.M. Leslie Jr. Minneapolis, MN: University of Minnesota Press, 1985.

———, 'The Modern Spirit and the Play of Transpositions', in D. Ades and S. Baker (eds.), *Undercover Surrealism*. Cambridge, MA: MIT Press, 2006.

———, *Story of the Eye, tr.* J. Neugroschal. London: Penguin Classics, 2001.

———, *The Trial of Gilles de Rais*, tr. R. Robertson. Los Angeles: Amok, 1991.

———, 'The Use Value of D.A.F. de Sade (An Open Letter to My Current Comrades)', in *Visions of Excess*.

Baudelaire, C. 'The Salon of 1859', in *The Mirror of Art: Critical Studies by Baudelaire*, tr. J. Mayne. New York: Doubleday Anchor, 1956.

Baudrillard, J. *Simulacra and Simulation*, tr. S. Faria Glaser. Ann Arbor, MA: University of Michigan Press, 1993.

———, *The System of Objects*, tr. J. Benedict. London and New York: Verso, 1996.

Benjamin, W., *Gessammelte Schriften*, vol. VI., ed. R. Tiedemann and H. Schweppenhauser. Frankfurt am Main: Suhrkamp, 1987.

———, *Fragments*. Paris: PUF, 2001.

————, 'Little History of Photography', in *Selected Writings, Volume 2 1927–1934*, tr. R. Livingstone et al. Cambridge, MA and London: Belknap Press of Harvard University Press, 1999.

————, 'On some Motifs in Baudelaire', in *Illuminations*, tr. H. Zohn. New York: Schocken Books, 2007.

————, 'The Work of Art in the Age of Mechanical Reproduction', in H. Arendt (ed), *Illuminations*, tr. H. Zohn. New York: Schocken, 2007.

Bernadin de Saint-Pierre, J.-H. 'Notes de l'Arcadie' [1781], in *Études de la nature*, vol. II. Paris: Lefevre, 1836.

Bernard of Clairvaux. *Commentary on the Song of Songs*, tr. D. Wright. <http://archive.org/details/St.BernardOnTheSongOfSongs>.

Bey, H. *TAZ: The Temporary Autonomous Zone*. New York: Semiotext(e), 1991.

Blanchot, M. *The Book to Come*, tr. C. Mandell. Stanford, CA: Stanford University Press, 2003.

————, *Thomas the Obscure*, tr. R. Lamberton. New York: Station Hill Press, 1988.

Blesser, B. and Salter L.-R., eds. *Spaces Speak, Are You Listening? Experiencing Aural Architecture*. Cambridge, MA: MIT Press, 2007.

Borges, J. L. 'On Exactitude and Science', in *The Aleph and Other Stories*, tr. A. Hurley. London: Penguin Classics, 2004.

Bosseur, K.-Y. *Le Sonore et le Visuel, Intersections musique/arts plastiques aujourd'hui. Paris*: Dis Voir, 1992.

Büchner, G. *Lenz*, tr. R. Sieburth. New York: Archipelago Books, 2004.

Burroughs, *The Electronic Revolution*. Ubu editions. <http://www.ubu.com/historical/burroughs/electronicrevolution.pdf>.

Cacciari, B. 'L'Archipel', *Etudes* 384:3 (1996).

Cage, J. *Silence*. Middletown, CT: Wesleyan University Press, 1961.

Casati, R. and J. Dokic. *La Philosophie du son*. Nîmes: Chambon, 1994.

————, *Philosophy of Sound*. <http://jeannicod.ccsd.cnrs.fr/ijn_00420036>.

338

Caux, D. *Le Silence, les couleurs du prisme et la mécanique du temps qui passe*. Paris: L'éclat, 2009.

Chaignet, A.-E. 'le pneuma', in *Histoire de la psychologie des Grecs*. Paris: Hachette, 1887.

Charles, D. *Gloses sur John Cage*. Paris: UGE, 1978.

Chion, M. *Guide des objets sonores*. Paris: INA-GRM-Buchet/Chastel, 1983.

———, *Guide to Sound Objects*, tr. J. Dack and C. North. <http://www.academia.edu/2574473/Guide_to_Sound_Objects._Pierre_Schaeffer_and_Musical_Research_trans._John_Dack_and_Christine_North>.

———, 'Comment tourner autour d'un objet sonore', in P. Szendy (ed), *L'Écoute*. Paris: L'Harmattan/Ircam-Centre Pompidou, 2000.

Chraïbi, S. 'Fétichisation de la pulsion invocante en pulsion audio-phonatoire', in *Psychologie Clinique 19: La voix dans la rencontre clinique*. Paris: L'Harmattan, 2005.

Chrétien, J.-L. 'Plotin en mouvement', *Archives de Philosophie* 64 (2001–2), 243–58.

Clausewitz, K. von. *On War*, tr. M. Howard and P. Paret. Princeton, NJ: Princeton University Press, 1984.

Cleomedes, *De motu circulari corporum caelestium*, tr. H.R. Ziegler. <https://archive.org/details/kykliktheriasmoozieggoog>.

Combarieu, J. *Music: Its Laws and Evolution*. New York: D. Appleton and Company, 1910.

Contant d'Orville, A.G. *Histoire des différents peuples du monde, contenant les ceremonies religieuses et civiles, l'origine des religions*, vol. I. Paris: Herissant, 1770–1771.

Cox, C. and D. Warner, eds. *Audio Culture: Readings in Modern Music*. New York and London: Continuum, 2009.

Criton, P. 'Territoires imperceptibles', *Chimères* 30 (Spring 1997).

Daniel, D. *20 Jazz Funk Greats*. London: Bloomsbury, 2008.

de Certeau, M. *The Practice of Everyday Life*, tr. S. Rendall. Berkeley, Los Angeles and London: University of California Press, 1984.

Deleuze, G. 'Bartleby; or the Formula', tr. D.W. Smith and M.A. Greco, in *Essays Critical and Clinical*. London and New York: Verso, 1998.

——, 'Desert Islands', in *Desert Islands and Other Texts 1953–1974*. New York and Los Angeles: Semiotext(e), 2004.

——, *Difference and Repetition*, tr. P. Patton. London and New York: Continuum, 2004.

——, *The Fold: Leibniz and the Baroque*, tr. T. Conley. London: Athlone, 1993.

——, and Guattari, F. *A Thousand Plateaus*, tr. B. Massumi. Minneapolis and London: Minnesota University Press, 1987.

Deligny, F. 'Cahier de l'immuable 1. Recherches', in *Essais et copeaux*. Marseille: Le Mot et le reste, 2005.

Derrida, J. *Of Grammatology*, tr. G. C. Spivak. Baltimore, MY: Johns Hopkins University Press, 1997.

——, *The Truth in Painting*, tr. G. Bennington and I. McLeod. Chicago and London: The University of Chicago Press, 1987.

——, *Voice and Phenomenon*, tr. L. Lawlor. Evanston, IL: Northwestern University Press, 2011.

——, *Writing and Difference*, tr. A. Bass. Chicago: University of Chicago Press, 1993.

Didi-Huberman G., *La Ressemblance informe*. Paris: Macula, 2003.

Didi-Huberman G., ed. *L'Empreinte*. Paris: Editions du Centre Pompidou, 1997.

Diederichsen, D. 'Entendre la couleur—Le *big band* de Matthew Herbert', in *Argument son—De Britney Spears à Helmut Lachenmann: critique* électroacoustique *de la société et autres essais sur la musique*. Dijon: Les Presses du Réel, 2007.

Duchamp, M. *Duchamp du signe. Écrits*. Paris: Flammarion, 1975.

——, *Notes*. Paris: Champs-Flammarion, 1999.

340

——, 'To Change Names, Simply', tr. S. Skinner Kilborne. *Tout Fait: The Marcel Duchamp Studies Online Journal* 2:4 (2002). <http://www.toutfait.com/issues/volume2/issue4/interviews/ mdguy/mdguy.html>.

Eliot, T. S. *The Use of Poetry and the Use of Criticism.* Cambridge, MA: Harvard University Press, 1933.

Eno, B. 'Ambient Music', in C. Cox and D. Warner (eds.), *Audio Culture.*

Eliade, M. *Shamanism: Archaic Techniques of Ecstasy,* tr. W. R. Trask. Princeton, NJ: Princeton University Press, 2004.

Fabre d'Olivet, A. *The Healing of Rodolphe Grivel,* tr. N.L. Redfield. New York and London: Putnam's, 1927.

Fillon, J. 'De l'ambiance sonore dans une construction plus étendue', *Potlach* 21 (30 June 1955).

Floriot, R. *Contribution à l'étude des vases acoustiques du Moyen Âge.* Paris: Gap, 1965.

Fort, C. *The Book of the Damned: The Collected Works of Charles Fort.* London: Penguin, 2008.

Foucault, M. *Archaeology of Knowledge,* tr. A.M. Sheridan Smith. London: Routledge, 1989.

——, 'L'arrière-fable', in *Dits et écrits, 1: 1954–1975.* Paris: Gallimard, 2001.

——, 'Of Other Spaces', tr. J. Miskowiec. *Diacritics* 16:1 (Spring 1986).

——, 'The Order of Discourse', in R. Young (ed), *Untying the Text: A Post-Structuralist Reader.* Boston, London and Henley: Routledge and Kegan Paul, 1981.

Freud, S., 'Three Essays on Sexuality', in J. Strachey (ed), *The Standard Edition of the Complete Psychological Works of Sigmund Freud,* vol. VII. London: The Hogarth Press, 1953.

Fumaroli, M. 'Introduction' in J.K. Huysmans, *À Rebours.* Paris: Gallimard, 1977.

Garelli, J. 'Introduction à la problématique de Gilbert Simondon', in G. Simondon, *L'Individu et sa genèse physico-biologique*. Grenoble: Editions Jérôme Millon, 1995.

Garnault, P. 'Les théories paléo-égyptiennes de la circulation, de la respiration, de la phonation et de l'audition, dans leur rapports avec la théorie du *pneuma*'. *Bulletins de la Société d'anthropologie de Paris*, 2:1, 1901.

Gombrowicz, *Ferdydurke*, tr. D. Borchardt. New Haven, CT: Yale University Press, 2012.

Gosselin, S. 'Le fétichisme, de Michel de Certeau à Karl Marx'. *Atelier philosophique* 5 (29 October 2003). <www.apo33.org>.

Guiganti, B. 'Qu'est-ce que l'atopisme?'. *Atopie* 0 (1999).

Guiomar, M. *Principes d'une esthétique de la mort*. Paris: José Corti, 1967.

Guionnet, J.-L. 'Background Noise/Bruit de Fond', tr. O. Martell. <http://www.jeanlucguionnet.eu/IMG/pdf/background_pour_mattin.pdf>.

Habermas, J. 'Consciousness-Raising or Redemptive Criticism—The Contemporaneity of Walter Benjamin', tr. P. Brewster and C. H. Buchner. *New German Critique* 17 (Spring 1979), 30–59.

Helmholtz, H. von. *Die Lehre von den Tonempfindungen als Physiologische Grundlage für die Theorie der Musik*. Braunschweig: Friedrich Vieweg and Son, 1896.

Hervey de Saint-Denys, L. de. *Dreams and How to Guide Them*, tr. N. Fry. London: Duckworth, 1982.

Hesse, H. *Peter Camenzind: A Novel*, tr. M. Roloff. New York: Picador, 2003.

Hugo, V. *Toilers of the Sea,* tr. J. Hogarth. New York: Modern Library, 2002.

Husserl, E. *Ideas Pertaining to a Pure Phenomenology and to a Phenomenological Philosophy, First Book*, tr. F. Kersten. Dordrecht: Kluwer, 1983.

Huysmans, J.-K. *Against Nature*, tr. M. Mauldon. Oxford: Oxford University Press, 1998.

Ingold, T. 'Against Soundscape', in A. Carlyle (ed), *Autumn Leaves*. London and Paris: CRiSAP/Double Entendre, 2007.

Irving, W. 'The Phantom Island', in C. Neider (ed), *The Complete Tales of Washington Irving*. New York: Da Capo Press, 1998.

Itard, J.-M.-G. *Traité des maladies de l'oreille et de l'audition*. Paris: Méquignon-Marvis Libraire, 1821.

James, W. *Essays in Radical Empiricism*. Cambridge, MA: Harvard University Press, 1976.

Jorn, A. 'Image and Form', tr. K. Knabb, in *Fraternité Avant Tout: Asger Jorn's Writings on Art and Architecture, 1938–1958*. Rotterdam: 010 Publishers, 2011.

Jung, C.G. *L'Âme et la vie*. Paris: Le Livre de poche, 2008.

Kafka, F. *The Complete Stories*, tr. W. and E. Muir. New York: Schocken Books, 1995.

Kierkegaard, S. 'Diapsalmata'. In *Either/Or, Part 1*, tr. H.V. Vong and E.H. Hong. Princeton, NJ: Princeton University Press, 1987.

Kim-Cohen, S. *In the Blink of an Ear: Towards a Non-Cochlear Sonic Art*. New York and London: Continuum, 2009.

Klossowski, P. *Living Currency*, tr. J. Levinson. <http://anticoncept. phpnet.us/Livingcurrency.htm>.

Kostelanetz, R. *Conversing with Cage*. New York and London: Routledge, 2005.

Lamarck, J,-B. de. *Mémoires de physique et d'histoire naturelle*. Paris, 1797.

———, 'Mémoire sur la matière du son', in *Journal de physique, de chimie et d'histoires naturelles*. Paris, 1799.

Larcher, H. *L'Acoustique cistercienne et l'unité sonore*. Paris: Labergerie, 1971.

Lautréamont, Comte de [Isidore-Lucien Ducasse]. *Maldoror*, tr. P. Knight. London: Penguin Classics, 1978.

Lévi-Strauss, C. *From Honey to Ashes: Introduction to a Science of Mythology: 2*, tr. J. and D. Weightman. London: Cape, 1973.

———, *The Raw and the Cooked: Introduction to a Science of Mythology: I*, tr. J. and D. Weightman. London: Cape, 1970.

———, *The Savage Mind*. London: Weidenfeld and Nicolson, 1966.

Levin, T.Y. 'Des sons venus de nulle part', in *Sons & Lumières*. Paris: Éditions du Centre Pompidou, 2004.

Loos, A. 'The Mystery of Acoustics', in *On Architecture*. Riverside, CA: Ariadne Press, 2002.

Lopez, F. 'Cagean Philosophy: A Devious Version of the Classical Procedural Paradigm'. <www.franciscolopez.net/essays.html>.

Lucretius, *On the Nature of Things*, tr. W. E. Leonard. New York: Dover, 2004.

Lyotard, J.-F. *Discourse, Figure*, tr. A. Hudek and M. Lydon. Minneapolis, MN and London: University of Minnesota Press, 2011.

———, *Libidinal Economy*, tr. I.H. Grant. Bloomington, IN: Indiana University Press, 1993.

———, *La Phénoménologie*. Paris: PUF, 1954.

———, *Rudiments païens*. Paris: UGE, 1977.

———, *The Postmodern Condition: A Report on Knowledge*, tr. G. Bennington and B. Massumi. Manchester: Manchester University Press, 1984.

———, *The Postmodern Explained: Correspondence, 1982–1985*. Minneapolis, MN: Minnesota University Press, 1992.

———, 'Several Silences', tr. J. Maier in *Driftworks*. New York: Semiotext(e), 1984.

Maldiney, H. *Regard, Parole, Espace*. Paris: Cerf, 2012.

Mann, T. *The Magic Mountain*, tr. J.E. Woods. New York: Vintage, 1996.

Marx, K. *Capital Volume I*, tr. B. Fowkes. London: Penguin Classics, 1990.

Matsubara, S. 'The Queen of the Sinewave Kingdom Explains Herself', in *Improvised Music from Japan, 2002–2003*. CD box set, IMJ, cat. 10CD, 2001.

Mauss, M. 'Art and Myth According to Wilhelm Wundt', in A. Riley, S. Daynes, C. Isnart (eds.), *Saints, Heroes, Myths and Rites: Classic Durkheimian Studies of Religion and Society*. London and New York: Routledge, 2016, 17–38.

———, *A General Theory of Magic*, tr. R. Brain. London and New York: Routledge, 2001.

Machen, A. 'The White People', in *The White People and Other Weird Stories*. London: Penguin Classics, 2011.

Malabou, 'Ouverture: le voeu de la plasticité', in C. Malabou (ed), *Plasticité*. Paris: Léo Scheer, 2000.

Mattin and A. Iles, eds. *Noise and Capitalism*. Donostia and San Sebastian: Arteleku Audiolab, 2009.

Marclay, 'Le son en image', in Szendy (ed), *L'Écoute*, 86.

———, 'What You See Is What You Hear'. *ArtPress* 309 (February 2005).

Merleau-Ponty, M. *Phenomenology of Perception*, tr. D. A. Landes. London and New York: Routledge, 2012.

Michelstaedter, C. *Persuasion and Rhetoric*, tr. R. S. Valentino. Cambridge, MA: Harvard University Press, 2004.

Moholy-Nagy, L. 'Production-Reproduction, Potentialities of the Phonograph', in K. Passuth, *Moholy-Nagy*. London: Thames and Hudson, 1985.

Moles, A. *Information Theory and Aesthetic Perception*. Illinois: University of Illinois Press, 1968.

Nancy, J.-L. *Corpus*, tr. R. A. Rand. New York: Fordham University Press, 2008.

———, *The Inoperative Community*, tr. P. Connor, L. Garbus, M. Holland and S. Sawhney. Minneapolis, MN and Oxford: Minnesota University Press, 1991.

———, *Listening*, tr. C. Mandell. New York: Fordham University Press, 2007.

Nietzsche, F. *Daybreak: Thoughts on the Prejudices of Morality,* tr. M. Clark and B. Leiter. Cambridge: Cambridge University Press, 1997.

Olalquiaga, C. *The Artificial Kingdom: On the Kitsch Experience.* New York: Pantheon Books, 1998.

Oswald, J. 'Plunderphonics, or Audio Piracy as a Compositional Prerogative'. <http://www.plunderphonics.com/xhtml/xplunder.html>.

Oury, J. *Création et schizophrénie*. Paris: Galilée, 1989.

———, 'L'objet chez Lacan'. <www.revue-institutions.com/articles/oury_objetlacan.pdf>.

Ovid, *The Metamorphoses*, tr. A.S. Kline. <http://ovid.lib.virginia.edu/trans/Ovhome.htm>.

Pausanias, *Description of Greece*, tr. W.H.S. Jones and H.A. Ormerod. <http://www.perseus.tufts.edu/hopper/text?doc=Perseus:text:1999.01.0160>.

Pelé, G. *Inesthétiques musicales au XXe siècle*. Paris: IDEAT-CNRS/Université Paris 1/L'Harmattan, 2007.

———, *Installations et soulagement esthétique*, forthcoming.

Plato, *The Collected Dialogues of Plato,* ed. E. Hamilton and H. Cairns. Princeton, NJ: Princeton University Press, 1989.

Pliny the Elder, *The Natural History*, tr. J. Bostock. <http://www.perseus.tufts.edu/hopper/text?doc=Plin.+Nat.+toc>.

Poe, E.A. 'The Tell-Tale Heart', in *Tales of Mystery and Imagination*. Ware: Wordsworth Classics, 1993.

Proust, M. *Correspondance, vols 10–12 (1910–1913)*. Paris: Plon, 1983–84.

Rancière, J. *Le Spectateur émancipé*. Paris: La Fabrique, 2008.

Raudive, K. *Breakthrough: An Amazing Experiment in Electronic Communication with the Dead*. Gerrards Cross: Colin Smythe, 1971.

Ribettes, J.-M. *Fétiches & Fétichismes*. Paris: Passage de Retz/Éditions Blanche, 1999.

Riffaut, J.-B. 'La poésie de Giacinto Scelsi', in P.-A. Castanet (ed), *Giacinto Scelsi aujourd'hui*. Paris: CDMC, 2008.

Rilke, R.M. 'Primal Sound', in *Selected Works, vol. I, Prose*, tr. G. C. Houston. New York: New Directions, 1961.

Rouget, G. *Music and Trance: A Theory of the Relations between Music and Possession*. Chicago: University of Chicago Press, 1985.

Sade, D.A.F. de. *The 120 Days of Sodom*, tr. A. Wainhouse and R. Seaver. New York: Grove Weidenfeld, 1966.

Satie, E. 'Memoirs of an Amnesiac', tr. N. Wilkins in N. Wilkins (ed), *The Writings of Erik Satie*. London: Eulenburg Books, 1980.

Saussure, F. de. *Course in General Linguistics*, tr. W. Baskin. New York, Toronto and London: McGraw-Hill, 1966.

———, *Writings in General Linguistics*, ed., tr. S. Bouquet, R. Engler, C. Sanders and M. Pires. Oxford: Oxford University Press, 2006.

Scelsi, G. 'Son et musique', in *Les anges sont ailleurs....* Arles: Actes Sud, 2006.

Schaeffer, P. *Traité des objets musicaux. Paris*: Seuil, 1966.

———, *Treatise on Musical Objects*, tr. C. North and J. Dack. Oakland, CA: University of California Press, forthcoming.

Schafer, R. Murray. *The Soundscape: Our Sonic Environment and the Tuning of the World*. Rochester, VM: Destiny Books, 1994.

Schopenhauer, A. *The World as Will and Representation*, vol I, tr. E.F.J. Payne. New York: Dover, 1969.

Segalen, V. *Dans un monde sonore*. Paris: Fata Morgana, 1985.

Sey, J. 'Sounds like...The cult of the imaginary wavelength', in E. G. Jensen and B. Labelle (eds.) *Radio Territories*. Los Angeles and Copenhagen: Errant Bodies Press, 2007.

Simondon, G. *L'Individu et sa genèse physico-biologique*. Grenoble: Éditions Jérôme Millon, 1995.

Starobinski, J. 'Thomas l'obscur, chapitre 1er'. *Critique* 229 (June 1966).

Steiner, R. *Theosophy: An Introduction to the Spiritual Processes in Human Life and in the Cosmos*. Hudson, NY: Anthroposophic Press, 1994.

Sterling, I. 'What is Phonography?'. <http://www. phonography.org/ whatis.htm>.

Sterne, J. *The Audible Past*. Durham, NC: Duke University Press, 2003.

Stommel, H. *Lost Islands: The Story of Islands That Have Vanished from Nautical Charts*. Vancouver: University of British Columbia Press, 1984.

Strabo, *Geography*, tr. H.C. Hamilton and W. Falconer. <http://www. perseus.tufts.edu/hopper/text?doc=Perseus:text:1999.01.0239>.

Szendy, P, ed. *Écoute. Une histoire de nos oreilles*. Paris: Minuit, 2001.

Szendy, P. *Sur écoute, Esthétique de l'espionnage*. Paris: Minuit, 2007.

Tacitus, *The Annals*, tr. A.J. Church. <http://www.perseus.tufts.edu/ hopper/text?doc=Tac.+Ann.>.

Takis [P. Vasillakis]. 'Musical', in Écouter *par les yeux, objets et environnements sonores*. Paris: ARC Musée d'Art Moderne de la Ville de Paris, 1980.

Tesla, N. 'The Problem of Increasing Human Energy'. *Century Illustrated Magazine*, June 1900.

Thévoz, M. *Le Miroir infidèle*. Paris: Minuit, 1996.

Tisdall, C. *Joseph Beuys*. New York: Guggenheim, 1979.

Toop, D. *Ocean of Sound: Aether Talk, Ambient Sound and Imaginary Worlds*. London: Serpent's Tail, 1995.

———, 'Notes toward a History of Listening'. *Art Press* 2:15 (November 2009–January 2010).

———, *Sinister Resonance: The Mediumship of the Listener*. London and New York: Continuum, 2010.

Tzu, Sun. *The Art of War*, tr. Hwang Chung-Mei. Selangor Darul Ehsan, Malaysia: Pelanduk, 1992.

Uzanne, O. 'The End of Books'. *Scribner's Magazine* 16 (1894), 221–31.

Valéry, P. *Cahiers/Notebooks 2*, tr. P. Gifford, S. Miles, R. Pickering and B. Stimpson. Frankfurt am Main: Peter Lang, 2000.

Van Den Broeck, E. 'Un phénomène mystérieux de la physique du globe'. *Ciel & Terre* 17 (1897).

Villiers de l'Isle-Adam, A. de. *Tomorrow's Eve*, tr. R. M. Adams. Chicago: University of Illinois Press, 2001.

Walser, R. 'Snowwhite', in *Robert Walser Rediscovered*, tr. W. Arndt. Hanover and London: University Press of New England, 1985.

Weininger, O. *Sex and Character*. London: William Heinemann, 1906.

Wittgenstein, L. *Denkbewegungen: Tagebücher 1930–1932, 1936–1937*. Frankfurt am Main: Fischer, 1999.

Zbikowski, D. 'The Listening Ear: Phenomena of Acoustic Surveillance', in T.Y. Levin, U. Frohne and P. Weibel (eds.), *CTRL [SPACE]: Rhetorics of Surveillance from Bentham to Big Brother*. Karlsruhe: ZKM/MIT Press, 2002.

Zhuang, L., F. Zhou, and J.D. Tygar. 'Case Study: Acoustic Keyboard Emanations', in M. Jakobsson and S. Myers (eds.), *Phishing and Countermeasures*. New York: Wiley-Interscience, 2007, 221–40.

INDEX OF NAMES

A

Adorno, Theodor W. xi, 153–155, 210, 223–224, 228, 283–284
Agamben, Giorgio 114
Alcmaeon of Croton 10, 79
Alvarado, Allie 50
Appollonius Rhodius 144
Aquinas, Thomas 11
Aristotle 9, 10–12, 101–103
Arnheim, Rudolf 46, 47
Assoun, Paul-Laurent 154
Augustine (Saint) 82, 163–164, 285

B

Bachelard, Gaston 220
Bacon, Francis 230
Barthes, Roland 13, 71–73, 78, 135, 148, 166
Bataille, Georges 148, 161, 209, 279–280
Baudelaire, Charles 159–160
Baudrillard, Jean 137, 240, 247, 252
Bell, Alexander Graham 36, 66, 79, 217
Benjamin, Walter 39–40, 43, 48, 122–123, 131, 159–160, 202
Bentham, Jeremy 215
Bernadin de Saint-Pierre, Jacques-Henri 207
Bernard of Clairvaux 29
Beuys, Joseph 237–239
Blake, Clarence 36, 66

Blanchot, Maurice 19, 95–97, 290–292
Bohr, Niels 111
Borges, Jorge-Luis 242–243
Bosseur, Jean-Yves 239
Bourseul, Charles 45
Brosses, Charles de 149
Büchner, Georg 169
Burroughs, William S. xi, 210–211, 276, 313

C

Cacciari, Massimo 269
Cage, John 53–54, 56, 284, 297–302
Casati, Roberto 83–87, 89–90, 97, 130
Caux, Daniel 294
Cézanne, Paul 322
Chaignet, Albert-Edouard 63
Charcot, Jean-Martin 151
Charles, Daniel 54
Chion, Michel 103–104, 107, 108, 109, 125
Chladni, Ernst Florens Friedrich 35
Chraïbi, Sofia 143
Chrétien, Jean-Louis 282
Clausewitz, Carl von 251
Cleomedes 12
Combarieu, Jules 184–185
Comte, Auguste 168, 176
Contant d'Orville, André Guillaume 208
Criton, Pascale 288

D

Daniel, Drew 316
de Certeau, Michel 244, 247, 250,
    256–257, 258
de Lauris, Georges 46
Deleuze, Gilles 51, 52, 115, 126–128,
    172, 249, 259, 265, 270–272,
    287, 288–289, 299, 323
Deligny, Fernand 244, 273
de Martinville, Edouard-Léon Scott
    36
Democritus 10
Derrida, Jacques 13, 31, 115, 117–118,
    119, 308
de Sade, Donatien Alphonse Fran-
    çois 141–142
de Witt, Michael 306
Didi-Huberman, Georges 33, 34, 39,
    45, 121
Diederichsen, Diedrich 186, 188
Dokic, Jérôme 83–87, 89–90, 97,
    130
Duchamp, Marcel 31–33, 46, 203,
    292, 305

E

Edison, Thomas Alva x, 40–42
Eliade, Mircea 17
Eliot, T.S. 61
Eno, Brian 267–268, 277–278
Epicurus 10

F

Fabre d'Olivet, Antoine 240–242,
    282
Fallopio, Gabriele 10, 79
Fillon, Jacques 309
Fischinger, Oskar 246
Floriot, René 28
Fort, Charles 269
Foucault, Michel 58, 129, 197–199,
    200, 201, 203, 227, 230, 274, 311
Freud, Sigmund 162, 178

Fumaroli, Marc 165

G

Garelli, Jacques 111
Garnault, Paul 10, 13
Glissant, Edouard 269
Goebbels, Joseph 210
Gombrowicz, Witold 225–226
Gosselin, Sophie 149
Guattari, Félix 51, 52, 126–128,
    172, 249, 259, 271–272, 287,
    288–289, 299
Guiganti, Bruno 275–276
Guiomar, Michel 295–6
Guionnet, Jean-Luc 204
Gysin, Brion 313

H

Habermas, Jürgen 223
Heisenberg, Werner 111
Helmholtz, Hermann von 217–218,
    220
Hervey de Saint-Denys, Léon d'
    173–176
Hesse, Hermann 139–140
Holbein, Hans 283
Honneth, Axel 121, 224
Horkheimer, Max 210, 228
Hugo, Victor 258
Husserl, Edmund 106
Huxley, Aldous 22
Huysmans, Joris-Karl 159–160, 165,
    167–168

I

Ingold, Tim 182
Irving, Washington 266
Itard, Jean Marc Gaspard 10

J

James, William 92
Jorn, Asger 310

Joyce, James x
Jung, Carl Gustav 220
Jürgenson, Friedrich 20

K

Kafka, Franz 144–145, 286–288
Kandinsky, Wassily 246
Kierkegaard, Søren 41
Kim-Cohen, Seth 305–307
Kircher, Athanasius 28, 213
Klossowksi, Pierre 136, 161

L

Lacan, Jacques 143, 157
Laënnec, Rene Theophile Hyacinthe x, 216
Lamarck, Jean-Baptiste de 62–63
La Mettrie, Julien Offray de 217
Larcher, Hubert 29
Lautréamont, Comte de [Isidore-Lucien Ducasse] 146–147
Leibniz, Gottfried Wilhelm 190
Levin, Thomas Y. 246
Lévi-Strauss, Claude 14, 16, 55, 64, 230
Loos, Adolf 63–64
Lopez, Francisco 301–302
Lucretius 24–25
Lyotard, Jean-François 56, 81, 82, 106, 158, 162, 191, 200, 250, 254, 255, 271, 273, 293, 312, 318, 321–322

M

Machen, Arthur 306–307
Malabou, Catherine 233
Maldiney, Henri 322
Mann, Thomas 280
Marclay, Christian 233
Marx, Karl 150, 154
Matsubara, Sachiko 317
Mauss, Marcel 15, 155–156, 309
McLaren, Norman 246

Merleau-Ponty, Maurice 80, 81–82, 93–94
Michaux, Henri 22
Michelstaedter, Carlo 95, 96–97, 164–165, 202
Moholy-Nagy, Lázló 246
Moles, Abraham 315
Montherlant, Henri de 126
Müller, Johannes 217

N

Nancy, Jean-Luc 65, 66, 73, 76, 77, 112, 229, 253, 292, 319
Niblock, Phill 294
Nietzsche, Friedrich 71

O

Olalquiaga, Céleste 311
Oswald, John 313
Oury, Jean 101, 176
Ovid 25–26, 66

P

Palestine, Charlemagne 294
Paulhan, Jean 176
Peignot, Jérôme 106
Pelé, Gérard 190, 228
Pfenninger, Rudolf 246
Plato 9–10, 190
Pliny the Elder 190, 205
Plotinus 282
Poe, Edgar Allan 170–172
Proust, Marcel 46
Pythagoras 10, 106, 184, 189–190

R

Rabelais, Akira 314–315
Rancière, Jacques 193, 226
Raudive, Konstantin xi, 20–23, 135, 173, 211
Ribettes, Michel 152
Rigaut, Jacques 292

Rilke, Rainer Maria 306–307
Rouget, Gilbert 17
Roussel, Raymond 239
Russolo, Luigi 187, 315

S

Satie, Erik 186–187, 278
Saussure, Ferdinand de 112–115
Scelsi, Giacinto 294–297
Schaeffer, Pierre 73–75, 103–110,
    124, 148, 157–158, 185, 231, 307
Schafer, Raymond Murray 57–59,
    178–183, 221, 240, 245, 268
Schmidt, Peter 277–278
Schopenhauer, Arthur 165
Segalen, Victor 8
Sey, James 48–49, 63
Simondon, Gilbert 120
Starobinski, Jean 290
Steiner, Rudolf 304
Sterling, Isaac 245
Sterne, Jonathan 36, 38, 44, 66, 216
Stockhausen, Karlheinz 300
Stommel, Henri 263–264
Strabo 205
Sun Tzu 213, 214
Szendy, Peter 79, 213–214, 319

T

Tacitus 205
Takis 236–237
Tesla, Nikola x, 49, 63, 64, 270
Thévoz, Michel 80, 189
Tomatis, Alfred 222
Toop, David 27, 59–60, 267, 270,
    284, 303–304
Tygar, J.D. 213

U

Uzanne, Victor 320–321

V

Vaché, Jacques 292
Valéry, Paul ix
Villiers de L'Isle-Adam, Auguste
    40–42, 158
Viola, Bill 235
Virgil 4
von Kempelen, Wolfgang 43

W

Waller, Stephen J. 27
Walser, Robert 60–61, 141–142
Weininger, Otto 130, 202, 280–281
Whitehead, Gregory 50
Winnicott, Donald 157
Wittgenstein, Ludwig 289

Y

Yau, Randy H.Y. 318
Young, La Monte 190–191

Z

Zbikowski, Dörte 213, 215
Zhou, F. 213
Zhuang, L. 213